THE ONE YEAR®
HEARING HIS VOICE
DEVOTIONAL

THE ONE YEAR®

HEARING HIS VOICE

DEVOTIONAL

365 DAYS OF INTIMATE COMMUNICATION WITH GOD

CHRIS TIEGREEN

TYNDALE
MOMENTUM®

The nonfiction imprint of
Tyndale House Publishers, Inc.

Visit Tyndale online at www.tyndale.com.

Visit Tyndale Momentum online at www.tyndalemomentum.com.

TYNDALE, *Tyndale Momentum*, Tyndale's quill logo, *The One Year*, and *One Year* are registered trademarks of Tyndale House Publishers, Inc. The Tyndale Momentum logo and *The One Year* logo are trademarks of Tyndale House Publishers, Inc. Tyndale Momentum is the nonfiction imprint of Tyndale House Publishers, Inc., Carol Stream, Illinois.

The One Year Hearing His Voice Devotional: 365 Days of Intimate Communication with God

Designed by Beth Sparkman

Published in association with the literary agency of Mark Sweeney and Associates, 28540 Altessa Way, Suite 201, Bonita Springs, FL 34135.

For information about special discounts for bulk purchases, please contact Tyndale House Publishers at csresponse@tyndale.com, or call 1-800-323-9400.

ISBN 978-1-4143-6685-2

Printed in the United States of America

24	23	22	21	20	19	18
8	7	6	5	4	3	2

INTRODUCTION

"GOD IS NOT SILENT. It is the nature of God to speak," writes A. W. Tozer, and it's true. God's relationship with human beings in the pages of Scripture and throughout history, as well as the very existence of the Bible, gives ample evidence that God guides, instructs, corrects, inspires, encourages, reveals, and more. Inspired writers even call Him "the Word." He has always been vocal, and He always will be.

Not everyone believes this. I recently heard a very prominent pastor scoffing at Christians who "think they can actually hear God directly." Of course, this pastor's perspective is nothing new. We hear it all the time from skeptics and cynics. A comedian once quipped that it doesn't bother him at all when people say they talk to God; it's when they claim God talks to them that he gets worried. Or, in the more direct words of Lily Tomlin, "Why is it when we talk to God, we're said to be praying, but when God talks to us, we're schizophrenic?" That's a good question, especially for Christians, whose entire faith is based on the truth that God wants a personal relationship with His people. We have to ask ourselves what kind of relationship He wants. One without conversation? Surely not. That would hardly be a relationship. No, God speaks, and His people listen. That's what following Him is all about.

Though many in the Western church insist that God doesn't speak to us today—because our hearing is too subjective, or because He has already said everything He has to say in the Bible, or because of any other objection not found in the Bible itself—Christians in less rigidly analytical and skeptical cultures are hearing Him daily and doing mighty works in the power of His Spirit, simply by following what they hear. We can find plenty of abuses and stories of people who misheard God, but there are far more testimonies of people hearing Him clearly and bearing much fruit from what they have heard. Anyone can learn to recognize God's voice—adults and children, the highly educated and the illiterate, leaders and followers, and any other category of hearer we can think of. God doesn't mind the skeptics. He simply speaks to people who will listen and believe.

What does He say? How does He say it? How can we know when we've heard Him? What can we do to hear Him better? These are some of the questions this devotional will explore. We could spend the rest of our lives learning how to recognize God's voice, and most of us likely will. But we can be confident that if we seek Him, He will make Himself available to us. If we listen, He will speak. And if we believe what we have heard, He will show us more. The God who speaks is always seeking to take us deeper into His will and draw us closer to Himself.

This book won't give you a step-by-step system for hearing God's voice. There's no such thing, although there are patterns and practices you can adopt to position yourself to hear Him better. But even if you don't learn any surefire "how to" principles here, simply turning your attention to hearing will stir up God's voice within you. Over the course of a year, you'll start knowing what He's saying intuitively, even if you don't know how you know. Those who hunger for Him will be satisfied.

There are 365 devotional readings in this book, and they cover many issues related to hearing God. One devotion each week is based on a story or a post-biblical example, some from Christian history and some from my own experience and acquaintances. Another is a "first person" devotional from the heart of God—things I have heard Him say and that I believe He wants to share with others who are listening.

Each devotion ends with a brief prayer. Some people (like me) tend to skip over guided prayers in books, but I would encourage you not to do that here. Some of the prayers may seem simple or superfluous, but there is a point to them. When we ask, we receive. God responds when we express our desires to Him. If your desire is to hear God's voice—and if you're using this devotional, it most likely is—then asking Him daily to hear Him better, no matter how basic the request, is an invaluable practice. If some of the prayers seem repetitive, that's okay. We're told in Scripture to keep asking, to persist until God answers. Over the course of a year, He will answer—often in surprising ways.

Listening to God is a process, a journey, and an adventure. This can take time, but it's worth the effort. He promises that those who seek Him will be rewarded with His presence and His voice. The words of the living God are powerful and life-changing. May He bless our desire to hear Him.

JANUARY 1

In the beginning the Word already existed. The Word was with God, and the Word was God.
JOHN 1:1

From the first pages of Scripture, God speaks. Every time He utters a word, things happen. He says, "Let there be light," and light comes into being—and He keeps talking until our entire universe is filled with order and life. He calls out a people from among the nations and reveals His purposes through them. He chooses prophets to deliver His messages when those people are in danger and need to return to Him. And when He sends His own Son to live among us, the Son is called "the Word." Clearly, we do not serve a silent God.

Many people can't say with any certainty that God still speaks today, much less to them personally. They can accept His written Word as His voice—generalized for all who read it, of course—but for personal conversations and direction, they strive and strain to hear. Our theology tells us that God is quite vocal, even if our experience tells us He isn't. The result of this paradox is a lot of theory, little practice, and a considerable amount of frustration.

Step one in hearing God is acknowledging that He still speaks. We have to be convinced of that in order to press through the frustrations on the way to hearing Him. Low expectations will undermine our efforts. If we know He's the Word who always has something to say, we won't give up easily in our attempts to hear Him. Most of all, we'll *believe*—a prerequisite to receiving anything from God. Faith opens our ears.

Believe not only that God still speaks, but that He's speaking *to you*. He calls you into a relationship, and relationships are based on communication. Conversations with God are normal—you were designed for them. Believe and listen—and know that you will hear.

Living Word, I invite You to speak to me. I know You have been; please open my ears to hear. I want to learn the sound of Your voice and know Your thoughts. In faith, I'm listening.

JANUARY 2

[Jesus said,] "My sheep listen to my voice; I know them, and they follow me."
JOHN 10:27

There are lots of voices in the world. Some are easily recognizable; others blend into the background noise. Some come from a distance; others from within our own heads. Some are tender and sympathetic; others strident and critical. And all compete for our attention.

Jesus knows how confused we can be. That's one of the reasons He gave His followers an illustration about shepherds and sheep. Sheep learn to recognize the voice of their shepherd so that when he calls to them, even in the midst of a multitude of other voices, they follow his distinctive sound. The other voices are just noise to the sheep of the Good Shepherd; they are uniquely tuned to His voice alone. When they hear it, they follow.

Our goal is to be tuned in to one voice only—to be so sensitive to the one true voice that we can hear it above the din of a multitude of rivals. To be so accustomed to the signature sound that called us into existence that it becomes our constant homing signal for every decision. In the depths of our spirit, we can learn to recognize that voice and distinguish it from all others. According to the desire and promise of Jesus Himself, we can hear His voice.

Don't make assumptions about what Christ's voice should sound like. Be willing to step into a learning process. But know that it's not only possible to hear His voice, it's assured. Somewhere within your soul, you will hear His heart-to-heart words and know they are His.

Jesus, my Shepherd, tune my heart to hear Your words. Let them sink into my soul and become a part of who I am. Help me ignore false voices and listen to Yours alone.

Let love be your highest goal! But you should also desire the special abilities the Spirit gives—especially the ability to prophesy.

1 CORINTHIANS 14:1

It is one of the most neglected instructions in the New Testament. Paul tells the Corinthians—not apostles, not church leaders, but regular people who haven't done a great job of handling spiritual gifts—to seek the gift of prophecy. And not only are they to seek it, they are told to seek it *zealously*—literally to *covet* it, be *jealous* for it, and *eagerly pursue* it. In other words, Paul wants us to listen to him and heed his teachings, but also to be able to hear God's voice on our own and express it to one another.

Clearly, this isn't an Old Testament–style warning: "If you say you speak God's words and get it wrong, the penalty is death by stoning." It's an open invitation, not a narrowing of the boundaries to limit impostors. It's an encouragement for all believers to listen, to tune in to the divine heartbeat and become vessels of revelation for others, to try to pursue and cultivate the gift of prophecy. And considering Paul's audience, the implications are surprising: Anyone can do this. It isn't just for Isaiahs and Jeremiahs and Ezekiels, with staggering words of warning and enormous burdens of responsibility. It's for average folks, anyone with a heart to hear. And, as Paul indicates in 1 Corinthians 14:3, it is for strengthening, encouraging, and comforting others.

God is a communicator looking for people who will learn the keys to hearing Him; who will listen for His insight and direction for specific situations and then express it to others. Too many people disqualify themselves from God's invitation, either by false perceptions of their own gifts or false perceptions of God. Still, He calls us to come deeper into His presence with listening ears—and with the rock-solid conviction that He will make His voice known.

Holy Spirit, teach me to prophesy. I choose to eagerly pursue all of your gifts, but especially the gift of hearing You and declaring Your words to others—to encourage them, comfort them, and build them up.

JANUARY 4

Surely the Sovereign LORD does nothing without revealing his plan to his servants the prophets.
AMOS 3:7, NIV

Ask the average person what a prophet does, and most will boil it down to predicting the future. A prophet is often perceived as the Judeo-Christian version of a clairvoyant, a seer who peers into the plan of God and perfectly describes how it will unfold. Somehow we got the impression that prophecy—hearing God's voice and declaring it—is entirely future oriented.

Prophecy can be about the future, of course, but the point of hearing God's voice is not simply to figure out what's going to happen down the road. It's to get God's perspective—whether on the past, the present, or the future. He reveals His thoughts about us, His interpretation of events and circumstances, the purposes He is working out, and His greatest desires for our lives. He portrays life in its true light—a vital point of view when we get stuck in dark places. When He speaks to His servants the prophets, He reveals not only His plans but also His heart. And His prophets, according to the New Testament, are any believers who will listen to Him.

In any situation we go through, we can know that God's perspective is available to us. He may not unveil every detail—we still have to walk by faith, not by sight—but He lets us know how He sees things. He imparts His truth and His wisdom whenever we need it and are patient enough to seek it.

Hearing God's voice begins with absolute trust in Him as a communicator—understanding that He doesn't arbitrarily carry out His will for humanity without making us participants in His plans. He reveals what He's doing, invites us into it, and involves us every step of the way.

Lord, involve me in what You're doing. Reveal Your purposes to me. Help me to see from Your perspective, think Your thoughts, and walk in Your ways.

Whether you turn to the right or to the left, your ears will hear a voice behind you, saying, "This is the way; walk in it."
ISAIAH 30:21, NIV

We long to hear God's voice. We come to a fork in the road, a moment of crisis, a point of decision that requires us to take a step in one direction or another because standing still is no longer an option. We tell God that if He just lets us know one way or another—this way or that way, heads or tails—we'll do it. Yet we're still not sure. Right or left? We just don't know.

What's the problem? Maybe the Spirit within us has already let us know, but our heads keep rationalizing the possibilities. Maybe we only *think* we're willing to do what God says, but really we're approaching His voice as good advice to consider, rather than a command to follow. Or—and this is often the case—we're merely seeking *information*, while God is calling us into deeper *relationship*. The promise of His voice isn't simply for the purpose of communication; it's for communion.

That's the mistake many of us make in our approach to hearing God. We want information, and He wants a relationship. Our approach reduces our hearing to in-and-out transactions—we come, we hear, and we leave with more knowledge than we had before. But God's desire—and the reason for His delays and silences—is to draw us closer and deeper. He withholds Himself enough to keep us seeking *Him*, as opposed to seeking His words alone. It takes more effort that way, but that's the nature of relationships. In order to grow close, we must invest time, energy, and interest. And God will withhold a right-or-left answer if it provokes us to make that investment. Seek Him above all else—and His voice will eventually become clearer.

Lord, forgive me for seeking You as a giver of information rather than seeking You as a person. Draw me close, not just so I can hear Your words, but so I can hear Your heart.

JANUARY 6

You go before me and follow me. You place your hand of blessing on my head.
PSALM 139:5

He heard it in his spirit during his morning quiet time: "The evil one cannot touch you." That fit with some of the verses he had been reading, and the phrase stuck with him most of the day. But it was only after the attack on his ministry—a legal threat from a religious extremist that would probably be backed by the country's hostile government—that the phrase made sense. He realized that God had known ahead of time the challenges he would face that day and had given him the assurance he needed to remain calm and trust God. This attack was not a surprise to God, and He would keep it from being effective.

When we commune with God regularly, reading His Word and listening for His voice, we often find that He prepares us for what we'll face. The messages we receive from Him don't make sense at first because we have no context for them. But in retrospect, they are very reassuring. If we had heard Him afterward, we would wonder if we heard only what we wanted to hear. But when He tells us ahead of time, we know it isn't a figment of our imagination. That may not change the situation, but it can certainly change our response to it. Only God can give us assurance before we need it because only He knows what's going to happen.

Make it a habit to listen in the morning for whatever verses God gives you and whatever impressions He whispers into your spirit. Write them down. They may seem random at the time, but if you review them at the end of the day, you may find a correlation between what He said and what you experienced. Not only will this encourage you in times of need, but it will also confirm that you are hearing God's voice—and that He goes before you to bless you.

Holy Spirit, speak to me in the morning about the journey ahead. Prepare me for each day. Let me experience the comfort of knowing that You are already watching over my future.

This is what the Sovereign LORD, the Holy One of Israel, says: "Only in returning to me and resting in me will you be saved. In quietness and confidence is your strength."

ISAIAH 30:15

FROM THE HEART OF GOD

"This is the normal, natural posture for My children. I want you to rest in Me. When I first spoke these words to Israel, they were desperately trying to arrange their own rescue. They looked around at the threats to their security and didn't believe I would come through for them. Their restlessness became their downfall. But this is My desire for you: to place your full confidence in Me to lead you, speak to you, deliver you, protect you, provide for you, and come through for you—even when for a moment it doesn't look like I will.

"If you will let this be your posture when you listen for My voice, you will hear Me. I want you to listen carefully, but I do not want you to strive and to strain. A restless spirit has a hard time hearing the pure, clear sound of My voice. A trusting, calm spirit will hear the echoes deep within. I rarely shout. You must be quiet to hear Me.

"Do you really want to hear Me? Then quiet yourself and be still. Be confident. Lay your doubts and skepticism aside. Rebuke your restlessness and your fears. Set aside your own agenda so you'll be able to recognize Mine. But bring your enthusiasm. I love your deep desire to know Me better. I long to connect with you and build our relationship. Long for Me without striving for Me. Seek Me without straining. Rest and trust, and be very patient. I will train your spirit to hear."

Sovereign Lord, Holy One of Israel, who am I that You would want to talk to me? But You do, and I have set my heart to listen. Sensitize my spirit to Your voice. I set aside my fears, plans, manipulations, anxieties, impatience—everything— to hear You. In my quietness and confidence, be my strength.

[Jesus said,] "There is so much more I want to tell you, but you can't bear it now."

JOHN 16:12

We know this is not simply a promise to future writers of the New Testament. Jesus is speaking to the entire inner circle of His disciples (minus Judas). Only three of these men would later pen portions of Scripture, and at least six other followers of Christ who did not hear these words would write more than half of the New Testament. Nor is this a prediction that Jesus would spend some time with them between His resurrection and ascension. The statement implies much more than a few days of conversation. No, this is a promise to speak to all believers, after the Resurrection, on an ongoing basis. We know that early believers expected to hear Christ's voice—people such as Agabus, Philip's daughters, members of the Corinthian church, and many more are said to have exercised prophetic gifts. They heard Jesus speak and confidently shared His message with others.

Jesus continues to speak to His people today. He draws us into a relationship with Him; He leads us in ways we need to go; He calls people into ministry; He teaches us the deeper ways of His Spirit; and He speaks through us to others. Long ago, God promised that we would hear a voice telling us which way to go (Isaiah 30:21), and Jesus was very clear that His sheep would know His voice (John 10:3-4, 16, 27). This is normal for our relationship with God.

But in order to hear God's voice, we must be absolutely convinced that Jesus has plenty to say to us—that "there is so much more" He will share as we grow closer to Him. Without knowing this, we question everything we hear, grow weaker in faith, and consequently hear less. But faith in His desire to communicate will open our ears to all He has to say.

Jesus, strengthen my faith to believe. As I search for the sound of Your voice, help me not to question whether You want to speak. You do—You have made that clear. Help me to hear all that You have to say.

JANUARY 9

When he, the Spirit of truth, comes, he will guide you into all the truth.
John 16:13, NIV

We wish we could sit down with Jesus face to face and start firing questions at Him. Audible words, no ambiguity, just straightforward answers. But when Jesus spoke with His disciples on the night before His crucifixion, He assured them it would be better for Him to leave and for His Spirit to come dwell in them (John 16:7). Somehow the mystical relationship between His followers and His Spirit would be better than the manifest relationship they already had with Him. They would be better equipped to hear and handle truth.

It's hard for us to imagine that an inaudible voice would be a better guide for us than audible words straight from the Savior's mouth, but that's what Jesus said. The Spirit is a teacher, a counselor, a communicator. He doesn't just share information with us; He guides us into truth—the reality on which we can base our entire lives. When we know His truth—whether we understand it or not—making the right decisions becomes a lot less complicated. And when we don't know His truth for a specific situation, we can trust that He will lead us into it.

Our primary experience with the Godhead in this age is with the Holy Spirit. That's the relationship we need to cultivate. Any direct experience of God, whether of sensing His presence or hearing His voice, comes through the Spirit. The more we build that relationship, being sensitive to the ways He moves and the thoughts He fills us with, the more we will be able to hear God's words in any given situation. It's a long-term process, not a short-term transaction. When being continually filled with the Spirit becomes our highest pursuit, hearing God's voice becomes a regular experience.

Holy Spirit, fill me with Your thoughts, acquaint me with Your ways, saturate me in Your presence. Help me to hear Your voice as You breathe into me moment by moment.

*When the Spirit of truth comes, he will . . . not speak on his own but will
tell you what he has heard.*
JOHN 16:13

We don't understand the mysteries of the relationship between Father, Son, and
Spirit, but we do know each has a distinct role in our lives. When Jesus tells His
disciples about the work of the Spirit, He explains that the Spirit will hear from
Jesus Himself, who in turn has heard from the Father. They share all things, but
the Spirit isn't the initiator; He's the connection between the will of the Father
and the souls of His followers. At times, Scripture refers to Him as God's Spirit,
and at other times as the Spirit of Jesus. Either way, He knows the heartbeat of
the Trinity.

Why is it important to understand the distinction of the Spirit? Because He's
the one to whom we relate. We often strain to hear God's voice externally, but
the Spirit resides within us. That's why His voice in our lives is rarely *audible*, as
it was with Moses or Samuel, at Jesus' baptism, or at Paul's conversion. Far more
often—in fact, almost always—it's that river of living water flowing out of us,
like a well bubbling up from the deep source of life in our human spirit. When
God speaks, it usually comes from within.

Many Christians fear this dynamic because it's so subjective. They forget,
of course, that all relationships are subjective. All relationships require time and
wisdom to translate the heart of the speaker through the filters of the hearer,
and even then we sometimes hear only what we want to hear. Nevertheless, this
is the dynamic God has chosen: personal, subjective, and highly relational. We
don't need to be afraid of it. We can learn to recognize the voice that takes the
will of the Father and the Son from outside of us and echoes it inside of us. The
Spirit really will tell us what He has heard.

✧ ✧ ✧

Holy Spirit, speak to me the things of the Father and the Son. You showed Jesus
what the Father was doing and what He said; do so with me, too. Present the
ideas of heaven within my spirit.

JANUARY 11

When the Spirit of truth comes, he will . . . tell you about the future.
JOHN 16:13

Everyone wants to know their future—or at least the positive parts of it. That's why many people read horoscopes and call psychic hotlines. It's also why many of us who shun these counterfeits will ask God for guidance and insight into His plans for us. Not only do we need to make decisions that are contingent on future events, we want to be reassured that our hopes are not in vain. When the Spirit speaks to us, He gives us such assurance. His voice is not one to fear or dread, even on those occasions when He must discipline us. His plans for His children are always ultimately good.

Jesus was clear that the Spirit would tell us about the future. That doesn't mean He tells us *everything* about the future, but He does give us glimpses of His plan. He gives us information we need for today's decisions, promises we need for tomorrow's fulfillments, and big-picture purposes we need in order to join Him in His work. He showed John a lot about the future in Revelation and gave Paul some glimpses of it regarding the Second Coming. He also gave His followers specific directions and warnings, as when He called Paul as a suffering apostle to Gentiles or warned him through Agabus about the coming imprisonment in Jerusalem. But it was never a complete picture—Paul writes in Philippians that he didn't know whether he would live or die. Still, there are times when God forewarns us or gives us inside information that we need to know. He sees the future, and it isn't entirely a secret.

Mostly, the Spirit instills hope. He sometimes gives us specific, personal details about what's ahead, but sometimes He simply fills us with expectation of God's goodness—that "future and a hope" from Jeremiah 29:11. Either way, He is leading us onward and upward in His Kingdom.

Holy Spirit, tell me things about the future. Lead me in the ways I need to go. Give me pictures of my purpose and Your plans. Open up Your secrets for me to treasure.

11

JANUARY 12

God said, "Let there be light," and there was light.
GENESIS 1:3

From the earliest pages of Scripture, God's voice plays a prominent role. This is how He created the world. He spoke. He didn't just think the world into being. Neither did He silently put it together in some divine workshop. He spoke, and it was.

All throughout Scripture, we see the power of the spoken word—especially the word declared by God. He breathed Scripture itself into being, and we are told that the Word cannot be altered or broken (see John 10:35). He declared prophecies to His messengers, who then declared them to others, and His words came to pass. We are told in Isaiah 55:11 that God's word will accomplish its purpose. It will not return to Him empty and unfulfilled but will cultivate the fruit He desires, just as the rain waters the land. Unlike us, He does not scatter His words randomly or carelessly. They are intentional, effectual agents of His will.

That may seem obvious, but the authority of His spoken word has huge implications for us. It means that when we hear from God, we cannot treat His voice as an item on the buffet line—available if we're interested but easily passed over if we're not. When He reveals something to us, no matter how difficult or unrealistic it may seem, we're obligated to believe it and receive it. We don't have the option of saying, "Maybe it's true, maybe it isn't." We don't have a right to say, "Maybe I'll accept it, maybe I won't." It is binding.

That may sound stifling, but it's actually liberating. We have turned our lives over to God, and managing them—orchestrating circumstances, making self-crafted decisions, forcing opportunities—isn't our responsibility. Our job is to listen, integrate what we've heard into the fabric of our being, and live from the certainty of those words. When we do that, our lives are backed by the power of the same voice that spoke worlds into being.

Lord, please speak specifically, powerfully, and purposefully into my life—with words that cannot and will not return to You empty.

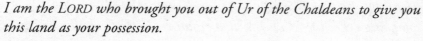

I am the LORD who brought you out of Ur of the Chaldeans to give you this land as your possession.

GENESIS 15:7

The man's business was going well, even growing, and the future seemed bright. But one day he heard God tell him to hold a going-out-of-business sale and close his doors. On the surface, it seemed like bad advice, and his wife thought so too. Surely this couldn't be God's will. Maybe the man had misheard. But God doesn't give bad advice, and sometimes His voice can't be so easily dismissed as a misunderstanding. This word was clear. So the man went out of business and, in the painful aftermath, remained unemployed for a year.

What went wrong? Had God misled him? No, after a year of second-guessing God, he saw how the Lord began to provide new opportunities. The career change ended up being one of the best things that ever happened to this couple. They have prospered ever since. But it wasn't easy at first. Following God rarely is. It takes time to see the fruits of obedience.

This is a common theme in Scripture. God called Abraham to leave home and go to a land He would show him later. Abraham had plenty of opportunities to second-guess his decision to follow—his wife was even captured at one point—but God eventually vindicated his faith. Plenty of other people in the Bible were led in seemingly absurd directions, yet following always proved to be the right thing to do. That's what life is like when you believe God speaks. He leads in ways that, on the surface, don't always make sense.

But His ways do make sense, and eventually we are able to see how. Hearing and responding to His voice is a real possibility. Others may question our hearing, but their voices aren't the ones we follow. We follow God into whatever land He shows us.

Lord, if You will speak to me clearly, I'll go in any direction You tell me, regardless of what other people think about it or how much sense it makes to me at the time. My steps belong to You.

13

JANUARY 14

The LORD longs to be gracious to you; therefore he will rise up to show you compassion. For the LORD is a God of justice. Blessed are all who wait for him!
Isaiah 30:18, NIV

FROM THE HEART OF GOD

"You may think it strange that I long to be gracious to My people, as if I have to wait to express My feelings toward you, to be merciful, or to act on your behalf. But sometimes if I acted on My compassion in the way you would like, you would receive it as an endorsement of your current direction or be overwhelmed by the weight of it. I want to do some wonderful things in your life, but My love for you demands that I wait until you can handle them well. So the expression of My compassion lingers.

"So does My voice. I long to speak to you with the same kind of longing that stirs My compassion. Why don't I, you ask? Because I have chosen to respect your willingness. I can do anything I want, but I don't often intrude on people's lives and force a relationship on them. I've startled a few choice servants throughout history by surprising them with My voice, but generally I wait for people to come to Me. The relationship is much more satisfying for both of us that way. I much prefer that you realize you have this longing deep in your heart than for Me to tell you that you do.

"So you are blessed if you turn toward Me—and blessed if you wait for Me. Many cry out to Me, but not many wait. If you do both, you will be one of the few. You must understand that My heart of compassion is instantaneous, but My acts of compassion are not. Sometimes I wait for you, and sometimes I expect you to wait for Me. You will always be glad when you do."

Father, I need to know Your compassion even before I see it, and I need to know You will speak even before I hear. Give me the resolve and the tenacity to wait for You. You reward those who diligently seek You; I commit to being one of those who do.

JANUARY 15

Man shall not live on bread alone, but on every word that comes from the mouth of God.
MATTHEW 4:4, NIV

The New Testament uses two words for "word"—*logos* and *rhema*. Some Greek authors use the two as practical equivalents; others treat them as subtly but significantly distinct. Where there's a difference, *logos* refers to the Word of God, or to Jesus as "the Word," while *rhema* seems to imply more immediacy—a spoken word for a particular moment. In Matthew 4:4 when Jesus talks about our feeding on every word from God's mouth, *rhema* is used. In other words, listening to God's voice moment by moment is necessary for our spiritual lives and growth. If we don't hear Him, we don't thrive.

Whether or not there's a huge difference between *logos* and *rhema*, most of us have experienced a difference between the written Word of God and verses or passages from that Word that struck our hearts in a powerful, immediate way. All of God's words are true, obviously—He cannot speak lies or deception—but some are true for a given moment, particularly suited for a present need. For example, is it biblical to stand still and see the salvation of the Lord or to move forward boldly in faith? The answer is yes, absolutely, on both counts. But which one for which moment? Those listening for God's voice will hear Him highlighting one or the other of those directions at a critical time, and they will know which one to do. Those who rely on only the written Word as an instruction manual, uniform in its seasons of application, will be left confused by two equally biblical options.

Get to know God's Word thoroughly, but listen at all times for His specific word for your specific situation. Notice when words jump off the pages of your Bible or when God seems to highlight the same truth in several ways during a particular season. Your life is sustained by feeding on *every* word that comes from His mouth. Learn to recognize them.

Lord, I hunger for and feed on Your truth. Let my spirit jump when I hear Your voice.

JANUARY 16

The voice of the LORD splits the mighty cedars.
PSALM 29:5

We thought the voice of God was much more subtle than that. We thought it was almost imperceptible, the kind of voice you have to strain to hear when the breeze is blowing in exactly the right direction and all else is quiet. But Psalm 29:4-9 tells us otherwise: "The voice of the LORD is powerful . . . majestic . . . splits the mighty cedars . . . strikes with bolts of lightning . . . makes the barren wilderness quake . . . twists mighty oaks and strips the forests bare." The same voice that created entire universes with just a word is still active today. When He speaks, things happen.

So why the discrepancy? Why is this powerful, majestic, forest-stripping, lightning-bolt voice so hard for us to hear? How does it radically transform the environment, yet fall ever-so-subtly on our ears? Perhaps we're listening with the wrong ears. God's voice is an intense and immensely powerful force, rather than a series of sound waves. Perhaps He issues loud commands to nature's obedient instruments but whispers His love and guidance to those whose spirits can choose and must relate to Him by faith. Perhaps if He dictated everything to us clearly and decisively, it would be the end of a relationship and the beginning of rote servitude—a condition for which He did not design us.

Regardless, we need to understand that the voice we strain to hear isn't weak. Just one word from God can change any situation at any moment. He may whisper to us, gently guide us, tell us about His plans for us, and counsel us in the midst of our circumstances, but when He issues a command, it's done. We must never mistake His quietness for reluctance or weakness. We can depend on the power of His voice—even when we aren't hearing it clearly.

Lord, I invite You to speak powerfully into my circumstances and into my heart. I trust Your timing and Your ways. Change whatever You want to change.

Come to me with your ears wide open. Listen, and you will find life.
ISAIAH 55:3

Christians are fond of quoting the Bible as God's Word. We believe it is the collection of writings in which the God of the universe has revealed Himself. It tells of people's encounters with God, quotes prophets who heard Him, relates the story of His Son coming into this world and dying on our behalf, and testifies to the miracles of God's intervention in human lives. This book is a supernaturally inspired unveiling of ultimate reality.

This is an honorable belief; but when we admit that we haven't actually read the whole thing, it's also a hollow belief. Do we really value knowing God through His Word? Getting a glimpse behind the veil of the physical world? Hearing the divine voice and feeling the divine heartbeat? Walking in the wisdom rooted in eternity? Apparently not as much as we say we do. Surveys indicate that most Christians spend precious little time in the life-giving Scriptures or even asking God what He wants to say to us.

Why do we keep our distance from His voice? Perhaps we don't expect to hear Him or understand what He says, or we don't trust that what we heard was actually Him. Or maybe we're afraid He will say things we don't want to hear—words of correction or rebuke or demands that will require time and energy on our part. But if we come with ears wide open, we won't be discouraged or humiliated by what we hear; we'll find life. His words will breathe energy into us. They will give us hope, not obligations; constructive advice, not destructive rebuke; opportunities and promises, not limitations and denials. Our days tend to suck the life out of us, but coming to God with open ears infuses life back into us. If we listen, we will find the supernatural support we need.

Father, Your Word is more than truth; it is life. Why would I ever neglect it or, worse yet, hide from it? I have nothing to fear in what You say and everything to gain. My ears are open; speak life to me.

Seek the LORD while you can find him. Call on him now while he is near.
ISAIAH 55:6

Now. While God is near. That's when we are told to call to Him; because, apparently, there are times when He can be found more readily than at other times. We generally assume that God makes Himself available to all who call on Him, and Scripture seems to indicate as much. Yet, throughout history, there have been long, dark ages of relative distance in the divine/human relationship. God *can* be found anytime, but He is more readily encountered when His Spirit is doing a widespread work.

In post-Pentecost Scriptures, God does not hide. The book of Acts, the New Testament letters, and Revelation all speak of God's will being made known, of mysteries being revealed, of formerly hidden things being made manifest in the new age of the Spirit's work. Some seeking may be required, to be sure, as when Paul tried to venture into northern Asia Minor but was forbidden by the Spirit, or when the church leaders gathered in Jerusalem to seek God's will for Gentile believers. And some messages may be encrypted, as in the book of Revelation, which we still struggle to decipher. But, in general, God makes Himself known. He may not explain *everything* to us, but He directs and speaks nonetheless.

God is not silent. We are children of a very vocal Father. In this era in which the Holy Spirit inhabits all who believe, we are not left to figure things out on our own or wonder what to do next. We may need to seek diligently and persist tenaciously, but God will make His will known to us in every situation. We don't have to speculate about whether He is near. He is. He has made Himself "findable." The time of His presence is at hand.

Lord, Your Word tells me to "seek" and to "call." That's it. But I have a hard time believing the simplicity of it all. Please reward my seeking and calling quickly and decisively enough to establish this posture as a pattern in my life. Captivate me for life with the sound of Your voice.

JANUARY 19

Jesus traveled through all the towns and villages of that area, teaching in the synagogues and announcing the Good News about the Kingdom. And he healed every kind of disease and illness.
MATTHEW 9:35

When we're listening for God's voice, we're often seeking specific direction for a particular issue in our lives. There's nothing wrong with that; God is intimately aware of and deeply concerned about every aspect of our existence. His conversations with us can get very personal. But we also face the danger of becoming so inwardly focused, so self-absorbed in our talks with Him, that we forget His overall purposes. We're so busy talking about the things at the forefront of our minds that we neglect what's on the forefront of *His* mind.

When Jesus walked among us, He spent His time teaching about the Kingdom of God—not the Kingdom as we often define it (a spiritual-only approach or an evangelism-only emphasis), but the Kingdom as *He* defines it: God's rule and reign in every area of life. Jesus demonstrated the Kingdom by healing people of every kind of disease because disease is not a characteristic of the Kingdom. He taught us how to relate to God, because knowing Him is what the Kingdom is all about. In thought, word, and works, the Kingdom was among us.

It only makes sense, then, that as we listen for God's voice, we can expect to hear Kingdom values and purposes. The King is still among us, teaching us and healing us and leading us into the blessings of His realm. Yes, this applies to the details of our day and the personal crises we face, but it's also bigger than that. When we hear God's voice, we should assume that whatever He says is part of a greater picture. He is leading us through the day, but He is also leading us into a significant destiny—probably more significant than we realize. We have to tune our ears to the big vision and let His words draw us forward into all that a Kingdom citizen is meant to experience.

Jesus, tell me great and glorious things I do not know. Give me a vision that's bigger than my own life. Lead me into the fullness of Your Kingdom.

JANUARY 20

Today when you hear [the Spirit's] voice, don't harden your hearts.
HEBREWS 3:7-8

Jim had survived epic battles with his past addictions, and he had lived the last few years in relative freedom. Well, mostly. There were occasional, low-level lapses, but nothing like before. He was on a steady path toward victory.

But when he found himself in a tempting situation—traveling alone, far enough from home that no one would ever know—the old triggers were almost irresistible. The voice in his heart told him to step back, but he didn't listen. That voice seemed like nothing more than an overworked conscience, and it was easy enough to tell it to be quiet. "I'm okay. It won't spiral out of control like it used to. This time it will be different." But the next morning, Jim was overwhelmed with guilt, feeling as if he were being sucked back into old habits, and wishing he had listened to the voice of caution the night before.

The writer of Hebrews urges his readers not to harden their hearts to God's voice. He writes about faith in Jesus and the salvation He offers, but the dynamic of hardening our hearts when God speaks applies to much more than our big-picture calling. God is constantly calling us toward a Promised Land, the place of fruitfulness and fulfillment that He intends for our lives; yet, we find it easy to ignore Him at critical moments when He warns us of danger. We think we're in control of ourselves, able to navigate the minefield of habits, relational patterns, and emotional and behavioral triggers that "used to" trip us up. We suppress the voice of caution, not realizing that it belongs to the God of the universe, who loves us and is looking out for us.

What's the solution? *Listen.* Live with a soft heart, avoiding any hint of rebellion. Understand that God always urges us toward wholeness. His voice is telling us the truth.

Lord, why is it so easy to push Your voice to the back of my mind when I want to? It seems almost accidental, but it's really negligence or even rebellion. Soften my heart and make me sensitive to everything You say.

JANUARY 21

I hold you by your right hand—I, the LORD your God. And I say to you, "Don't be afraid. I am here to help you."
ISAIAH 41:13

FROM THE HEART OF GOD

"There have been times when you don't believe I'm here to help you. I've seemed inactive toward you, or I've disciplined you, or I've let you experience the needs and challenges that cause you to cry out for Me. You've even wondered if I'm opposing you or ignoring your pleas. But you need to understand that whatever situation you're facing, whatever hardship you endure, it isn't because I'm not on your side. Even when I allow difficulties, I'm working on your behalf. You need to grow in faith, wisdom, and love, and you can't do that when you aren't being stretched by situations that require faith, wisdom, and love.

"Notice in My Word how every crisis is an opportunity for people to experience Me and learn more of who I am. Your difficult situations set the stage for moments of revelation. I reveal who I am in the midst of your need for Me. You would never know Me as Healer, Deliverer, or Provider if you never needed healing, deliverance, or provision. And because your need to know Me is greater than your need to be immune from these challenges, I will allow you to be put in challenging situations.

"Still, My words to you are, 'Don't be afraid. I am here to help you.' Time and circumstances will attempt to mock your belief in those words, but you must not let them. Cling to what you know to be true. Deep down, you know My heart—that My desire is for you, and My purposes always favor those who love Me. Never let go of those truths. However things appear, I am on your side. I want the very best for you, and I'm in the process of working it out."

Lord, is this true? I can easily believe this for other people, but I wonder if it's true for me. Let Your love for me—and Your presence and Your help—sink into my heart as unshakable realities. I choose to trust that You are holding me by Your powerful hand.

I will climb up to my watchtower and stand at my guardpost.
HABAKKUK 2:1

Sometimes people are startled by God's voice. They haven't really been listening for Him, but He steps into their lives anyway with some vital information or direction. That's what He did with Moses, who was hardly looking for a new direction from God when he encountered the burning bush. That's what God did with Samuel, who thought that Eli the priest was calling to him in the middle of the night; he had to be told it was God. And that's what God did with Mary, who may have sought God's will diligently but would never have expected a visit from an angel and an announcement about her beautiful, scandalous pregnancy. God will surprise us when He is about to do something major in His overall plan and wants to use us as part of it. But that isn't the usual way of hearing Him.

No, we will rarely be aware of His voice if we go through life thinking, *If God wants to speak to me, He has my number.* He much more readily speaks to those who are actively listening—who, like Habakkuk, have stationed themselves on the wall and are waiting to hear what God says. This kind of attentiveness requires faith and patience, but eventually it will be rewarded. The more we listen, the more we hear. The more we practice hearing, the more we learn to recognize which voice is God's. Sure, practice involves failure—we will misunderstand some things as we learn—and there will be times when our attentiveness tunes us in to all kinds of voices, not just God's. But over time, we learn to recognize His voice out of all the others.

Whatever it takes, we need to position ourselves like satellite receivers waiting for a signal from the spiritual realm. We need to ask God to speak, and then we need to listen for His voice. He will develop our ears to hear.

Lord, I'm listening. Please speak, and please help me to recognize Your voice. Speak to the questions I've put before You. Give me the pleasure of hearing Your voice clearly.

I will wait to see what the LORD says.

HABAKKUK 2:1

Habakkuk positioned himself to receive communication from God, but he uses very visual terms. He has climbed his watchtower, and he is waiting to see what God says. Surely he is speaking figuratively, isn't he? Obviously, we can't *see* a voice. He must mean he is opening his ears to hear, right?

Not necessarily. God often communicates in the pictures of our lives. We see in Scripture that His preferred language is visual. He has given us a book full of sensory experiences and manifest encounters, He instructs Ezekiel and other prophets to act out many of their prophecies, and He incarnated Himself into flesh so He could be fully realized right before our eyes. He is constantly painting pictures, whether with the symbolism of the Passover, the demonstrative details of the Tabernacle and the Temple, or the life stories of our heroes of faith. It only makes sense that if God has communicated with stories and symbols and visions, we might want to open our eyes to "hear" His voice. Again and again, throughout the Bible and history, God is a God of graphic parables.

What does it mean to "see what the LORD says"? At the very least, it means watching for demonstrations of His goodness through His people and our circumstances. The events of our lives aren't random. "Coincidences" may be God's effort to draw our attention to what He is doing, or they may be illustrations of greater truths. In the words of Malcolm Muggeridge, "Every happening, great and small . . . is a parable whereby God speaks to us; and the art of life is to get the message." In a multitude of ways, God portrays His plans, His thoughts, and His desires to us. And we might begin to notice if we open our eyes to see what He is saying.

Lord, thank You for speaking in ways I can understand. Open my eyes to see the pictures Your voice creates around me. Fill my senses with parables of Your nature and invitations into Your ways.

> *[Jeremiah said,] "Just as the LORD had said he would, my cousin Hanamel came and visited me in the prison. . . . Then I knew that the message I had heard was from the LORD."*
>
> JEREMIAH 32:8

Jeremiah was accused of only posing as a prophet, but he was entirely genuine, one of God's finest. Scripture and history have vindicated his words as truly coming from God. So it's a little surprising when Jeremiah gives us a glimpse of the hearing process—and, as it turns out, it isn't quite as neat and clean as we might think. He receives a message from God that a relative will come and offer to sell him a piece of the family property. When the relative comes and makes the offer, just as God had said, Jeremiah admits, "Then I knew that the message I had heard was from the LORD."

We imagine God's prophets hearing so clearly and decisively that there's no question of whose voice they heard. But Jeremiah apparently wasn't sure until circumstances confirmed it. Yes, he had heard a message, but was it truly from God? He thought so, just as we think God is speaking to us sometimes. But the origin of those whispers, impressions, and messages we receive isn't always clear. Sometimes we need confirmation. Sometimes—almost always, in fact—hearing God is a process.

There's nothing wrong with being uncertain. When we think we might have heard God's voice but need confirmation to make sure, that's normal. If a prophet like Jeremiah didn't always know for certain until events confirmed what he had heard, we can be comfortable with the same dynamic. This is what it's like to hear God when He isn't booming like thunder from heaven—which is most of the time. God is patient with the process and will refine our hearing and draw us closer to Him in the midst of it.

Father, teach me how to discern whether the things I hear are from You or not. Give me confirmation when I'm not sure. Train my ears to recognize Your voice.

Until the time that his word came to pass, the word of the LORD tested [Joseph].
PSALM 105:19, NKJV

Often when God speaks, circumstances begin to move in the opposite direction of what He says. That was certainly the case with Joseph; he had two dreams that depicted him in a position of power, and he saw his family members bowing down to him. Very quickly, some of those family members betrayed him and sold him into slavery, and he found himself at the bottom of Egypt's social order for the next few years, spending much of that time in prison. This was the antithesis of what God had spoken, and surely Joseph must have wondered what had gone wrong. Did he mishear God? Did God change His mind? Had Joseph blown it by telling everyone the dreams? God clearly wasn't doing what He had said—*if* He had even said it in the first place. According to the psalmist, the word of the Lord tested Joseph until what he had been told came to pass.

That's a common dynamic when God has given a promise or direction. The visible world seems to stretch us in uncomfortable directions while we wait for God to do His part. In the meantime, we ask questions: Did He really speak? Did we hear Him correctly? Did He change His mind? Did we mess it up somehow? The wait can be painfully long, and many are tempted to give up before the fulfillment. But when God has really spoken and we have really heard, waiting in faith is the right response. Even if the wait is excruciating.

We need to understand that God often gives us a view of the *end* of a matter, not a view of the *process*. Our choices in the meantime say a lot about what we believe about God's goodness. As we cling to hope, maintain faith, and learn patience, He works His nature into us. In the process, we eventually receive not only the fulfillment but also a changed nature.

✧ ✧ ✧

Lord, give me strength to persevere through the process, hope to see from Your perspective, and faith to endure.

We all, who with unveiled faces contemplate the Lord's glory, are being transformed into his image with ever-increasing glory, which comes from the Lord, who is the Spirit.

2 Corinthians 3:18, niv

Am I in tune with God's Spirit? Am I exercising His gifts appropriately? Are my desires in line with His? Am I praying according to His will? Am I hearing His voice? If we can't answer these questions with a high degree of certainty, we will walk out our relationship with God tentatively. We will make decisions, offer prayers, and listen for His guidance without much conviction, and our uncertain faith will waver. There's a lot of humility in this walk, but not a lot of holy boldness. And we can't accomplish much in God's Kingdom without both.

The most significant variable in answering these questions is whether or not we are gazing at Jesus. When He is front and center in our minds and hearts—when He is bigger and better than our deepest desires, getting our prayers answered, and discovering God's will—He will align us with His heartbeat. When we contemplate His glory and pursue Him above all else, we are transformed into His image without even being aware of it. We become like whatever we love, so if Christ is our greatest love—not just in theory, but in daily consciousness—we become like Him. And as we do, we hear, pray, walk, and talk like He does. Just as He is the radiance of the Father, we reflect God's radiance too. We don't have to worry about being misguided when our greatest passion is knowing Jesus.

When Jesus becomes and remains the focus of our attention, a lot of other things in life fall into place and a lot of spiritual questions get resolved. We may not know exactly how that happens, but it does. Our perspective changes. Even our questions change. And uncertainties about our relationship with God begin to vanish.

Jesus, may my gaze never depart from You. Show me Your glory. Impart Your nature to me. Implant Your heartbeat within me. Be my truest and deepest passion.

O LORD, you have examined my heart and know everything about me.
PSALM 139:1

She saw the guy in the back row and heard something in her spirit: "Caleb." Was that actually his name? Did he remind her of someone she used to know named Caleb? No. She was sensitive enough to God's ways to know that seeing the man as a "Caleb" was a word from God, a timely illustration of something going on in this man's life. So she walked up to him later and said, "I'm sensing from God that you are like Caleb in the Bible. You see the giants in your life, but you have no reason to be afraid of them. God is calling you into a promise, and you have enough faith to go, no matter how intimidating the path seems. You are called to ignore those who say it can't be done and to take your mountain by faith."

The man was moved to tears. As it turns out, he had been sensing God's call into a new endeavor and yet had encountered obstacles. He had been reminding himself that God was with him. But, as most of us do, he wondered if he was on the right track. He needed confirmation. The woman who saw him as a Caleb gave it to him.

That's one way to hear from God and speak His encouragement into other people's lives. The woman didn't say, "God told me," and then prescribe direction for his life. She simply sensed a message from the Holy Spirit and shared what she had heard. If it didn't apply to the man's life, no harm done. But it did, and the man was greatly encouraged and strengthened to pursue what he had been hearing from God.

Don't be afraid to share what you are sensing from God. Do it in humility and in a way that doesn't try to dictate God's will. Let your Spirit-inspired insights encourage and strengthen others. This is how He often speaks to His body.

Holy Spirit, give me insights that build up Your people, and give me the courage and humility to share them well. Use me to speak Your words and to represent Your heart.

JANUARY 28

I am the LORD your God, who rescued you from the land of Egypt,
the place of your slavery.
EXODUS 20:2

FROM THE HEART OF GOD

"Sometimes when I speak to you, I need to remind you of what I've done for you. This isn't because I'm holding it over your head. I just want you to remember the relationship we have. If you remember where we have been together, you'll be much better prepared to trust Me for where we are going together. I want you to understand that I have created you, loved you, been patient with you, redeemed you from your captivity, listened to your prayers and answered them, provided for you, healed you, restored you, and so much more.

"Why do you need to remember these things? Because if you forget the context of our relationship, you will often hear Me through the wrong perceptions. When I give you instructions you don't want to follow, you will feel as if I'm unfairly imposing My will on you. When I give you extravagant promises, you will question whether I'm going to carry them out. When I correct you, you will take it personally and assume that I'm angry with you rather than lovingly drawing you into freedom. When I tell you that I love you or that I'm with you, you will take My words as empty encouragement, without realizing how emphatically I've proven them to you. Do you see why I come to you with a reminder of who I am? You need to know, because the way you perceive Me shapes everything you hear from Me.

"I want you to hear Me without distortions from your own insecurities and wounds. Listen carefully when I remind you of who I am and what I've done for you. Your hurts and struggles will fade into the background as you embrace My goodness toward you. Then I can speak words of love, instruction, encouragement, correction, and guidance that will transform your life."

Lord, let me hear You with a pure and whole heart. Cut through my distorted perceptions to help me hear the truth in Your words. Let my heart be shaped by the history of our relationship.

[The Lord said,] "I will give you a new heart, and I will put a new spirit in you. I will take out your stony, stubborn heart and give you a tender, responsive heart. And I will put my Spirit in you so that you will follow my decrees and be careful to obey my regulations."
EZEKIEL 36:26-27

If a cat wanted to become a dog, it would take a lot more than learning how to bark, dig, and slobber. It would require having the heart and mind of a dog, taking on the entire canine lifestyle, being doglike—not just because that's how dogs behave, but because it's who the cat has become. It would take a new set of instincts, a genuinely transformed nature that results in new behavior.

A cat can't become a dog, of course; it's impossible. But so is the transformation from a person who does the right things because they are right to a person who does the right things because that's his or her nature. It's one thing to do good because we're told it's good and therefore we obey. It's quite another to do good because we're good deep down inside and goodness is what naturally flows out. That's the new heart we're promised and the new nature we're given by God's Spirit. That's what it means to partake of the "divine nature" (2 Peter 1:4).

That's also the process for hearing God's voice. We often look to Him for information, when really He is transforming our inner nature so that the direction and motivation we seek comes out of who we are deep inside. He is after a deep, inward relationship, not just a conversation about facts. And as He transforms us, we find more and more that His voice comes from within us, because that's where He resides. This is our goal—not merely a voice from beyond, but a voice from within that springs from our new nature. This is where God reveals His heart.

Lord, I want to hear Your heart and share Your heartbeat. I want to carry Your voice within me, not just hear words. Please plant Your will deep within me.

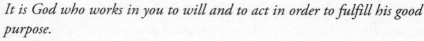

JANUARY 30

It is God who works in you to will and to act in order to fulfill his good purpose.
PHILIPPIANS 2:13, NIV

We talk a lot about our own sinfulness and depravity—how there's nothing good in us, how we want "all of Him and none of me" in our relationship with God. This is a very humble attitude, of course, but it isn't very scriptural. Yes, in and of ourselves, we have no righteousness, but God hasn't left us in that condition, has He? According to His Word, He has filled us with His Spirit and given us a new heart. He has transformed us, not replaced us. We were created for a reason—to partner with Him, not fade out of the picture. And Paul assures us that it is God who works in us both to will and to act in order to fulfill His purposes. In other words, there are many desires inside us that are from Him and many actions we want to do that are exactly what He wants for us. He has implanted His will and His voice within us.

It's true that we have other desires and voices within us at times; not everything we think or do is godly. But we are moving in the direction of godliness if we're growing in Christ and allowing Him to be the source of our life, and He is rearranging our internal environment so that we become one with Him.

This is the context for hearing God's voice. There will be times when we don't know whether it's our own voice or His because our minds and hearts are being shaped by Him. It is God who is working within us to desire and to do His will. As long as we have any vestige of fallen nature, we can't make that truth absolute and say that it's *only* God at work within us. But neither can we downplay this truth. This is God's preferred method for speaking to us: *being within us.*

Lord, work powerfully within me to desire and to do Your will. Let Your thoughts and dreams become my thoughts and dreams.

[Jesus said,] "I have given them the glory you gave me, so they may be one as we are one. I am in them and you are in me. May they experience such perfect unity that the world will know that you sent me."
JOHN 17:22-23

Normally, Jesus' prayer for oneness is seen as a call for Christian unity. When He says, "so they may be one," we instinctively add the words "with each other." It certainly includes that, but it's more. We can just as easily add the words "with Me" and understand this as a prayer for oneness with God Himself. After all, the rest of the sentence implies something far more supernatural and mystical than we're accustomed to. Jesus is praying that we may be one with Him in the very same way that He is one with the Father.

How is Jesus *one* with the Father? In motives, in desires, in mission and purpose, in character and attributes, and even in substance. He has already made that clear in His teachings: "The Father and I are one," He said to an infuriated crowd (John 10:30). Now He prays for that kind of oneness with *us*. It's an invitation into the fellowship of the Trinity. We are united at our very core with the life of God Himself.

So when Ezekiel and Jeremiah prophesy a new heart, and Acts describes the coming of the Spirit, and Paul says that it's God working within us, the picture we get is far more than a new set of motives and desires. It's an inner union between us and the substance of God. The practical aspects of this union aren't inevitable—many Christians live in rebellion or apathy—but they are certainly available. We can truly know that He is powerfully dwelling in us and that His life within us has very practical implications. One of those implications is that the Word Himself speaks. Within. Almost constantly. And we can hear because this is why He came.

Jesus, fulfill this union in every way possible. Let me have Your heartbeat and breathe Your breath. And may Your voice flow through me and out of me constantly.

Against all hope, Abraham in hope believed.
ROMANS 4:18, NIV

One of the key lessons for us to learn in God's school of faith-building is the fine art of staring at seeming contradictions to what He has said while maintaining our hope in His promises. After Abraham was given a promise—that he would be a father of nations—he waited a quarter of a century for it to come to pass. God didn't tell him *how* or *when*, so Abraham tried several times to fill in the blanks for himself. But the promise got more specific over time: It would be fulfilled from Abraham's own body, not through an adopted servant; through the body of his wife, Sarah, not through her maid. And there was nothing for Abraham to do but wait. When the time finally came, both he and Sarah laughed. The promise seemed long overdue. But God had spoken, and they had believed. So even when circumstances seemed hopeless, Abraham trusted what God had said.

That is to be our posture as well when we've heard God's voice. We may encounter enormous contradictions, but faith holds on and hopes. Sometimes we'll misunderstand, and our faith will need to be redirected. Sometimes we'll expect results in a certain time frame, and we'll be disappointed. But one way or another, God will fulfill what He has spoken. His word does not return to Him empty. Sometimes we have to contend with our own hearts and circumstances to remember that.

Our training isn't complete until we can stare contradictions in the face and still have peaceful hearts that hope against all hope. We might prefer that God would cultivate our faith by rewarding it immediately, like a dog trainer who rewards a good trick with a treat. But God doesn't normally work that way; He cultivates our faith by hiding Himself and encouraging us to seek Him. This now-you-see-Him-now-you-don't process can be frustrating, but it's essential. And when we learn to hope against hope in what God has promised, our hope receives its rewards.

Lord, fill me with hope, the kind that does not disappoint. Keep me rooted not just in what You've said but in who You are. Help me to trust Your heart no matter what I see.

FEBRUARY 2

*Now our knowledge is partial and incomplete, and even the gift
of prophecy reveals only part of the whole picture!*
1 CORINTHIANS 13:9

We see only in part. Many mistakenly believe that anyone who claims to hear God's voice is also claiming omniscience. But God reveals only what He wants us to know, and that's almost always a very incomplete picture that still requires faith. He unveils the next step, or the encouragement we need at the moment, or the information necessary for the next decision; but He graces none of us with the ability to know His will at all times for all purposes. Everyone, even the greatest of Scripture's prophets, has to wrestle with partial glimpses and meager explanations.

Why does God speak to us only in part? Doesn't He want us to know the fullness of His plan? Certainly He wants us to appreciate what He has done, but why doesn't He give us that appreciation on the front end of the journey rather than afterward? Perhaps it's because the journey is designed to build faith, a vital key in our relationship with Him. Or maybe He knows that if we see the full picture, we will attempt to accomplish it with our own limited wisdom and resources. We *don't* and *can't* have the perspective needed to oversee the whole plan, so God gives us only one piece at a time. We have to cling to Him—and tune our ears to the sound of His voice—moment by moment. Otherwise, we risk serving our own ends in our own wisdom and developing a dangerous sense of independence.

Get used to hints and whispers and brief glimpses of His purposes. We can hear His voice clearly and confidently, but never comprehensively. That's why we need the rest of the body of Christ; together we can discern God's will. He reserves the fullness of revelation for a day when we can look back and give Him glory for the beauty of all He has done.

Lord, partial pictures are so frustrating, yet I know You don't offer more to any one person. Help me to discern the parts I see and to trust in the parts You reveal to others.

FEBRUARY 3

As [Saul] was approaching Damascus on this mission, a light from heaven suddenly shone down around him. He fell to the ground and heard a voice.
Acts 9:3-4

The young man had been a devout, lifelong Muslim, but he was beginning to search for something more. In fact, he had prayed that if there were more—if he had been missing the truth all these years—God would lead him into the light. Not many days later, a bright light in the shape of a man came to him in his room. He couldn't move, but he didn't want to. The light spoke to him, identified Himself as Jesus, and called this man into the truth. It changed his life forever.

This is not an unusual occurrence in the Middle East, or even in other parts of the world. Jesus doesn't seem to be bothered that many Christians in the West question the authenticity of spiritual experiences; He manifests Himself to people anyway. Sometimes He comes in a dream, sometimes in a vision during prayer, and sometimes in a tangible form in the middle of the day's normal activities. He doesn't appear this way to everyone who seeks Him, but He has radically changed many lives, even of those who formerly opposed Him. There is no limit to the ways He will encounter those He has chosen. He finds a way into the hearts of His people.

Saul had a dramatic encounter with Jesus on the road to Damascus. He wrote later that more than five hundred people had seen the resurrected Jesus before the Ascension. Many people throughout history have told of similar experiences, and the fruit of their lives has validated their testimonies. An encounter with Jesus can turn anyone into a radical, passionate believer who will go to any lengths to give Him glory. He is more than willing to step into our experience in powerful, life-altering ways.

Jesus, show Yourself to even more people. Captivate the hearts of seekers everywhere—Muslims, Hindus, Buddhists, cult members, and even me. Step into this world whenever and however You choose. Let us see Your glory.

I am the LORD who heals you.
EXODUS 15:26

FROM THE HEART OF GOD

"Sometimes when I speak to you, I tell you the side of My nature you will soon need to experience. I'm not trying to alarm you when I do this; there is an important spiritual truth at work. You need to know who I am going to be for you, so you can appeal to Me in faith when the need comes.

"Do you understand? I respond to you based on your prayers of faith. But you will not pray those prayers—or you will pray them in desperation rather than in confident faith—if I haven't assured you of who I am. You may be surprised when I tell you I'm your Healer, Provider, Comforter, Deliverer, Promise-keeper, Guide, or anything else, especially if you hear those assurances in times when you aren't in need of them. But a time will come when you will need to appeal to Me based on what you already know of My character. And you will need to know who I am on your behalf, and you will be glad for the words of promise.

"Don't be afraid when I tell you that I'm your Healer. I am simply strengthening your faith before you need to exercise it in that area. Don't be afraid when I tell you I'm your Provider, your Deliverer, or your Comforter. It doesn't mean that lack, captivity, or grief are just around the corner. But you already know what life in this world is like. You know you will find yourself in times of deep need. And when you do, I don't want you to call to Me tentatively or in hopeless desperation. I want you to anchor your hope and faith in who I am. That's why I tell you who I am now. Embrace My nature and learn to depend on every side of Me that I choose to reveal to you."

Lord, I do need You—often. I need to be able to call to You without wondering if You'll come through for me. Please develop my confidence in Your nature. Fill me now with the certain knowledge of who You are.

FEBRUARY 5

His father and mother didn't realize the LORD was at work in this, creating an opportunity to work against the Philistines, who ruled over Israel at that time.

JUDGES 14:4

We've heard it said again and again: "God will never lead you in any way that contradicts what He has revealed in His Word." So it's a real conundrum for us when we encounter places in Scripture where God leads someone in ways that seem contrary to revelation He had already given. We see Samson defying God's orders not to marry the women of the land (Deuteronomy 7:3; Joshua 23:12-13), yet when his parents protest, Scripture tells us they didn't know God was in it. We see in Proverbs some extremely strong prohibitions about going near a prostitute, yet God leads Hosea to marry one (Hosea 1:2). And though the revelation of law hadn't been given yet, we know God in His very nature loathes child sacrifice and says so quite often. Yet He commands Abraham to take his child up on a mountain and sacrifice him—not to an idol but to God Himself. In the moment, we would have argued with all of these people emphatically that they were *not* hearing God's voice. Yet they were.

God does not contradict Himself, but He also has specific guidance that may not be uniform for everyone. He doesn't defy His own nature, but we sometimes define His nature too narrowly and reduce it to rules He Himself has given. Does that mean anything goes? Of course not. But God will never call us into a relationship with principles alone. We can't just read His Word, decipher it with our minds, and say that we've heard Him. We are in a relationship with Him, and we have to hear His voice as a living, dynamic reality. That stretches us, and even frustrates us at times, but it leads to a heart connection that goes well beyond words on a page. It brings us face to face with God.

Father, I want that—to be face to face with You, really hearing Your voice and not just reasoning on my own. Please lead me in Your ways.

I will meet with you there and talk to you from above the atonement cover between the gold cherubim that hover over the Ark of the Covenant.
EXODUS 25:22

God gave Israel a picture of His presence—a chest containing specimens of His Word, His provision, and His authority. This Ark had an atonement cover, a "mercy seat" on which the priest would sprinkle sacrificial blood as a sacred symbol of the price paid for our forgiveness. And this, God said, is where He would meet and talk with Moses.

That's because our conversations with Him are based on a completely clean relationship. We don't live in the Tabernacle era anymore, of course, but the symbolism is the same. Our defiance of the divine order—and we're all guilty of it, whether we realize it or not—has been thoroughly covered and removed. God no longer meets us in the place where sacrificial blood was sprinkled on an ark; He meets us in our relationship with Jesus, whose sacrificial blood was sprinkled in the depths of our souls. We may think there are obstacles between us and God, but not if we've confessed our sins and received His forgiveness.

Outside of this place of covering, we can't know Him. We can know *of* Him, and we may be able to hear His voice sometimes, but we can't know Him in the experiential, face-to-face interaction that defines relationships and makes them rich. Only at the covering can we draw close. That's why God seems so distant—and silent—when we try to relate to Him out of a strong sense of guilt and shame. We assume a rift where there is no rift or a grudge where there is no grudge. God has chosen to be blind to that which separates us. And when we fully believe that, He interacts with us in deeply meaningful ways.

Lord, I choose to fully believe that I am covered—that my offenses no longer exist. Thank You that I can freely meet with You and hear from You. In this freedom, please let me hear Your voice.

> *Put the Urim and the Thummim in the breastpiece, so they may be over Aaron's heart whenever he enters the presence of the LORD. Thus Aaron will always bear the means of making decisions for the Israelites over his heart before the LORD.*
>
> EXODUS 28:30, NIV

After God gave them the law, a very specific set of principles to live by and commands to heed, the people of Israel knew God's will for them—it unfolded at Sinai in a very dramatic encounter. They had all the information they needed for living the kind of lives God wanted.

But they didn't have specific direction. They still needed to be led by the cloud and the fire that directed them through the wilderness toward the Promised Land. They still needed to know when and where to go into battle, whom to accept help from, which prophets to believe, which kings to anoint, and so on. These were specific choices not covered in the law but vital to following God's will. The people needed more than general guidance and rules for living. So God gave them a means to hear Him—in this case, two mysterious stones carried by the priest—with instructions to use them in God's presence to discover His will.

Many people argue that God has already said in Scripture everything He is going to say, and therefore we can't expect Him to speak to us individually. Aside from being entirely unscriptural, this argument also fails to make a distinction between God's general revelation for all of us and His specific will for us personally and corporately. Clearly He isn't going to reveal new doctrine or lead us to add anything to Scripture, but that doesn't preclude Him from speaking to us in the context of a personal relationship with Him. He wants us to follow Him in His big-picture plan and in the minute details of life. If we'll listen, He will lead.

Father, thank You for being vocal—for being willing to make Your intentions known at times when we need to understand them. Guide me daily in the ways I should go.

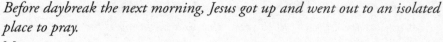
Before daybreak the next morning, Jesus got up and went out to an isolated place to pray.
MARK 1:35

Silence is a rare commodity. That's partly the fault of our increasingly noisy, sound bite–saturated world. But we can take a good bit of the blame too; we fill many open moments checking status updates, tweets, headlines, scores, and other bits of communication. We live in a generation with significant attention-deficit issues, and we rarely take time for long periods of quiet. That makes hearing God's voice extremely difficult.

One of the necessary conditions for hearing His voice is quieting all the others. There's no way to do that when we keep filling our eyes and ears with the innumerable messages swirling around us. God's voice is in the mix, but we can hardly distinguish it if we are tuned in to all the rest. What are we to do? Like Jesus, we need to find solitary time—to get away from the chaos and commotion of the world and tune in to the Spirit. Quiet hearts can hear Him; distracted hearts can't. It's that simple.

Whatever it takes, find times to withdraw from your normal environment and get alone with God. Quiet your spirit and listen to His. Make it a regular practice. That isn't easy when you have a demanding schedule, but easy isn't the point. Hearing the voice of God is worth any sacrifice, isn't it? Scripture repeatedly urges us to be still, to rest, or to quiet our hearts, and those who wrote such words were people who heard Him well. Deep in our redeemed spirits is the voice of the one who birthed us into new life. Only when we calm the storm of thoughts and words around us will we be able to discern His voice.

Lord, I don't know when I can get alone to be with You. My schedule is packed; and even when I'm alone, I'm constantly thinking of things I have to do and problems I need to deal with. I'll set aside time if You will meet me there and help me focus. Please reward my solitude with Your company.

Nathan replied to the king, "Go ahead and do whatever you have in mind, for the LORD is with you." But that same night the LORD said to Nathan, "Go and tell my servant David, 'This is what the LORD has declared: Are you the one to build a house for me to live in?'"
2 SAMUEL 7:3-5

Nathan was a genuine prophet who knew when to speak boldly into David's life. But when David inquired about building a temple, Nathan told him that the Lord would be with him—and then had to backtrack when God corrected him. Something similar happened to Isaiah when he told King Hezekiah that he would not recover from his sickness. Isaiah's absolute statement had to be retracted (see 2 Kings 20:1-6). And after Jonah flatly declared that Nineveh would be overthrown in forty days, he had to be somewhat embarrassed when God saw Nineveh's repentance and relented (see Jonah 3:4, 10). All three men were true prophets who gave unequivocal statements about God's plans. And all were redirected.

We often assume that the biblical prophets heard perfectly and never had to modify their prophecies, but Scripture tells us otherwise. Sometimes they were mistaken and had to revise their statements, and sometimes they were right but had to retract their absolute declarations when God seemed to change His plans. The communication process between God and prophet wasn't always simple or smooth. And God seemed to have no problem with that at all.

When we listen for God's voice, we must realize that we will inevitably misunderstand some things, sometimes even falling flat on our faces. But God is okay with that. Even the greatest prophets had to sort things out sometimes. We may correctly hear God say one thing and then seem to lead us in another direction. Or we may be convinced we've heard Him accurately and be mistaken about it. Just as a parent is patient with a toddler's attempts at language, God is patient as we learn His voice. And we will eventually understand Him well.

Lord, thank You for Your grace and patience as I learn Your voice. Help me learn to recognize it immediately, and guide me clearly when I don't.

As the Scriptures say, "The facts of every case must be established by the testimony of two or three witnesses."
2 CORINTHIANS 13:1

I was struggling, wondering if God had changed His mind about the calling He had given me. Numbers 23:19 rose up from my memory—it declares that because God is not a man, He neither lies nor has any need to change His mind. So I printed the verse and taped it above my desk, perhaps trying to convince myself that it must be true in my situation. Every day—no, numerous times a day—I stared at the verse and repeated it emphatically to myself and to God, in case He needed any reminding about it. As the verse implies, He has never made a promise and not carried it through.

Yet, I had to keep reminding myself that God is faithful even when visible circumstances seem to indicate otherwise. A few days later, when I was struggling again, I asked some friends to pray and see if God was saying anything to them for me. They offered some encouraging words, and then one said, "I feel as if God wants you to know that He is not a man that He should lie, nor a son of man that He should change His mind." I was floored. Not surprised, just blown away by the confirmation. God spoke directly to my heart through a friend who knew absolutely nothing about the struggle within my heart.

God is not reluctant to confirm His words to us, nor is He put off by our asking. A multitude of requests may indicate a lack of faith, but a sincere appeal for confirmation does not. His Word requires that accusations be confirmed by two or three witnesses; the same principle can apply to our hearing and our insecurities about it. Has He really spoken? Ask Him. He'll say it again.

Lord, thank You for Your patience, not only to speak to dull ears like mine but to repeat Yourself when I'm not sure about what You said. I'm so grateful that You aren't focused on my imperfect hearing; You're focused on helping me understand.

FEBRUARY 11

You must worship no other gods, for the LORD, whose very name is Jealous, is a God who is jealous about his relationship with you.
EXODUS 34:14

FROM THE HEART OF GOD

"Jealousy is a painful emotion, and you may be surprised that I feel it. But I do. I have told My people repeatedly that I am jealous for their love. I even spoke through the prophets, saying that I burn with jealousy for My people. How could I not? I've told you that I am love; I have a love for you that is beyond your comprehension, a love that can't be quenched. This explains all My other emotions: My anger (at anything that interferes with or distracts from My love), My joy (which celebrates those whom I love), My grief (which laments those who don't receive My love or who miss its blessings), My hatred (which opposes everything that attempts to thwart My love), and yes, My jealousy (which is an expression of My desire for the exclusive affection of your heart). When I speak to you, you will hear My emotions for you in My words. They will come from a heart that wants your love.

"You need to know how I feel about you. You need to understand this jealous love I hold in My heart for you. If you don't, you will receive My words of correction as a rebuke rather than as an invitation to come closer. You will receive My words of anger as a statement against you personally rather than as a statement against the things in your life that interfere with our relationship. You will think I'm driving you away when I'm actually removing from your life all that hinders and hurts you. My words need to come to you through true perceptions. You need to cling to the fact that everything I say to you comes from a heart of deep, intense love. Then you will hear without being offended or hurt. And you will see how everything I say draws you closer to Me."

Lord, soften my heart to hear the love and jealousy behind Your words. Everything You say to me is for my good. Help me to receive Your words as an expression of limitless love.

[Anna] never left the Temple but stayed there day and night, worshiping God with fasting and prayer. She came along just as Simeon was talking with Mary and Joseph, and she began praising God. She talked about [Jesus] to everyone who had been waiting expectantly for God to rescue Jerusalem.

LUKE 2:37-38

Anna was a fixture at the Temple—an eighty-four-year-old widow who had spent most of her time there since her husband died in their youth. She worshiped God day and night, praying and fasting in wholehearted devotion. So when Joseph and Mary brought the infant Jesus to the Temple for His dedication, Anna knew. She sensed His uniqueness. She perhaps overheard the prophecy of Simeon about this child's destiny, and it resonated with her. This worshiper had ears to hear.

That's because worship draws us close to God and opens our ears to His voice. We may think of adoration and worship as separate issues from receiving God's guidance, but they go hand in hand. When we spend our time adoring Him in gratitude and praise, our hearts synchronize with His. As we cultivate the relationship, we begin to hear and know things we didn't expect to hear and know. When our focus is on God, we perceive the things of His Spirit. That's just how it works.

Perhaps that's why many who strain to hear God's voice as an end in itself often find nothing but frustration, while those who focus on God and their relationship with Him often hear His voice without even trying. When we can relax and do what we were created to do—enjoy God and adore Him for all His goodness—we sense His heartbeat. We tend to prioritize hearing His voice, and as a result, we miss out on both the voice and the relationship; but prioritizing the relationship gets us everything that comes along with it, including His voice. Our love and worship are vital in opening our ears.

Father, I pour out my love for You—not because I want things from You, but because You are my priority. Let me enjoy Your goodness and seek Your heart above all else.

I tried to understand. . . . Then I went into your sanctuary.
PSALM 73:16-17

Asaph was full of questions about the apparent injustices he saw. Why did the wicked prosper? Why were many of God's most faithful servants suffering? Asaph was focused on the visible and the immediate and needed a bigger, longer view. When he stepped into God's presence, he got it. He understood what he had not understood before.

Like Anna the prophetess and many others, Asaph discovered the dynamic of worship and how it leads us into new perspectives and opens our ears to God. Those whose hearts align with God's soon find that their thoughts align with His as well. They begin to hear—perhaps not audibly, but in the depths of their souls. Their points of view get rearranged. Worship prepares the heart to hear.

If our ultimate goal is to hear God's voice—to get answers and information from Him—we won't hear very much. But if our ultimate goal is to know Him—not His information, but *Him*—then the answers eventually flow. Solomon was very wise, but when his heart turned apathetic and even unfaithful toward God, his wisdom was powerless to keep him on track. He lost his understanding because he lost his passion. The king who was blessed in all ways was careless about his worship, and he ended up skeptical and disillusioned.

Do you want to hear God? Then forget about hearing for a while. Focus instead on Him. Stir up your passion. Get into His sanctuary—His presence. Cultivate the relationship simply for the sake of the relationship. Tell Him that's more important to you than hearing His secrets. Let Him tell you He loves you without pressing Him for details about your future. Enjoy His embrace.

When you desire God more than His answers, He can give both to you freely. You're past the stage of seeking His voice, hearing it, and then leaving because you got what you wanted. You'll seek to be satisfied only in Him.

Lord, it's more important to me to know You than to get information from You. Help me to love You completely.

[John], leaning back against Jesus, said to him, "Lord, who is it?" Jesus answered, "It is he to whom I will give this morsel of bread when I have dipped it."

JOHN 13:25-26, ESV

Acquaintances share pleasantries. Close friends share personal information. We would be surprised and somewhat offended if an acquaintance tried to pry personal information out of us before getting to know us and establishing a relationship of trust. Yet this is what many of us do with God; we come with frequent prayer requests and ask Him to speak about things concerning our own small spheres of interest. Few of us take time to ask Him what's on His heart, to be good listeners, and to show real interest in the aspects of His will that don't pertain to us. We can assume God doesn't *need* to be surrounded with good listeners, as if He would want to get something off His chest or seek counsel. But God created us for relationship—deep, personal interaction—and though He doesn't need our counsel, He seeks our interest. He wants to connect with those who share His heart.

There's a reason why John was leaning back against Jesus at the Last Supper and was thus privy to inside information about the betrayer. John was "the disciple whom Jesus loved," one of the men who had developed a real friendship with the Messiah. This was no mere acquaintance probing Jesus for personal secrets. This was a follower who was truly interested in the heart of his friend and who interacted with Him on multiple levels—not just when he needed something, but at any time and for any reason. John did not relate to Jesus as a servant under orders. He related as a friend with quite a few interests in common. And that put him in a position to hear.

That's how it is with us, too. When we relate to Jesus as a friend, truly interested in what's on His heart, He shares His heart with us. And we connect at a very personal level.

Jesus, what's on Your heart today? I really want to know. Please share it with me.

One who prophesies strengthens others, encourages them, and comforts them.
1 CORINTHIANS 14:3

Paul tells us to eagerly pursue the gift of prophecy (see 1 Corinthians 14:1). In response, many believers have spoken judgmental words of correction or demanding words of guidance to the people around them. Perhaps they imagine God as angry and harsh, or as someone entirely interested in obedience and works, so the only words they can conjure up about His will are commands that require compliance. But Paul is clear what prophecy should accomplish in the life of the receiver. It should strengthen, encourage, and comfort. It should find hope in the recipient's future or treasure in his or her calling. It should build up rather than tear down, heal wounds rather than create them, pull us forward rather than harping on the past. God's voice is a balm, not a battering ram. He embraces His children with warmth.

It's true that God corrects us sometimes, but only as a loving father corrects a child. His discipline always comes with heavy doses of encouragement and comfort, and rarely through the mouth of another. Prophetic words don't provoke guilt, fuel fear, or expose our sins to others. God much prefers to cover them in privacy.

So we can expect His voice—especially His voice as it comes to us through other believers—to strengthen, encourage, and comfort. And when we speak His heart to those around us, our words will be seasoned with these gentle and affirming tones. If we hear or speak words that don't have this flavor, they are not from God. Those condemning or fearful words we hear inside of us sometimes—about how we could have done better, or didn't do enough, or are disqualified from God's blessings, and so on—are also not from Him. Why? Because God speaks life to us, not death. Whatever He says to us will be strengthening, encouraging, and comforting.

Lord, open my heart to accept the blessings of Your voice, and close my heart to false, condemning words. Help me to recognize the warmth of Your love when it is spoken to me.

FEBRUARY 16

The LORD said to me, "Write my answer plainly on tablets."
HABAKKUK 2:2

Write it down. That's what God told Habakkuk, Isaiah, Moses, and John—and probably quite a few other prophets—when He spoke to them. His words were important enough not to be forgotten or unintentionally edited when told to others. He wanted them inscribed for the sake of clarity and permanence. Many people, even from future generations, would be able to read what He had said.

That's good advice. Journaling what God has told us will help us remember it and share it with others. Unlike the biblical prophets, we aren't writing words that will become Scripture, so the imperative isn't quite the same as it was when God instructed them to do it. But it's helpful to keep track of what God has said over time. When we look back at this journal, we can determine whether we are following the instructions He gave us and remembering the lessons He taught us. Casual hearers don't record what they have heard, and a week later they may not even remember it. Attentive hearers, however, are diligent about following God's words and applying them. Just as a couple may keep old love letters or chronicle their love in a diary, we celebrate our relationship with God when we preserve what He has said.

We can't afford to risk letting God's words fall to the ground without applying them. He speaks in order for lives to change. The best way to honor His voice is to respond and change according to what He says. And the best way to respond and change is to write down what He has told us and cling to it over time. When we do, we will be able to appreciate how the relationship has grown, how He has invested in us, how He has led us step by step, and how His direction today builds on what He has told us in the past.

Lord, journaling may never have been my forte, but Your words are too valuable for me to forget them. Help me to write them down accurately, and remind me to review them frequently. Teach me to treasure Your voice.

Such things were written in the Scriptures long ago to teach us.
ROMANS 15:4

Augustine's soul was in deep distress. He had spent years dabbling in spiritual counterfeits and living an immoral lifestyle, yet now God's Spirit was convincing him of truth and calling him away from sin. In his heart, a battle raged between his passions and his conscience. One day, as he was seeking a moment of peace in a garden, he heard a voice repeating the phrase, "Take up and read." So he picked up a volume of Paul's letters and read the first words he saw: "Let us walk properly, as in the day, not in revelry and drunkenness. . . . But put on the Lord Jesus Christ, and make no provision for the flesh, to fulfill its lusts" (Romans 13:13-14, NKJV). At that moment, Augustine's heart was flooded with the light of faith, and darkness was dispelled. He became a Christian.

God speaks generally through His Word, but sometimes the words of Scripture come alive in an unusually personal way. We are not only taught by the truths of the Bible; they seem to be directed at the deep places of our hearts for the need of the day. Augustine had certainly read those words before, but they had not pierced him as they did in that moment when the war in his soul was at its height. He was divinely guided to the exact phrases that would address his urgent questions and struggles.

Read God's Word every day, and learn at every level of your heart and mind. When a verse or phrase jumps off the page and into your question or crisis, pay special attention. It is the Spirit enlivening and illuminating His thoughts and applying them to your situation. It is the voice of God, the living Word, the *rhema* for the moment. God is speaking again through the Word He has already spoken.

❖ ❖ ❖

Holy Spirit, I want You to speak to me like that. I love Your Word, but I need it personalized. Pour it directly into my heart like a spiritual injection of truth. Highlight what I need to hear.

Do not be afraid, for I have ransomed you. I have called you by name; you are mine.

Isaiah 43:1

FROM THE HEART OF GOD

"No matter how often I tell you not to be afraid, you approach crisis moments of life in fear. That's natural; I understand. But I want you to grow beyond that. I want your heart to trust in Me so easily that your first reaction in a troubling situation is not to wonder *if* I'm going to work it out, but to look to see *how* I will. Your spiritual reflex needs to bring you to a place of rest, not of worry. I have never let go of you, and I never will.

"Do you understand why? I've invested a lot in this relationship. I've ransomed you at no small cost to Myself. It was painful to do so, but I willingly accepted that pain. I have called you by name, completely aware from the beginning of who you were, are, and will be. I saw the end of your story before it even began, and I chose you in that light. I did not begin a relationship with you only to be disappointed. I did not cultivate your love only to give up on it later. I did not lead you down this path without knowing where it's headed. That's why I can tell you not to be afraid. I know the end. It's going to work out well for you, no matter how things appear right now.

"When I calm your nerves and remind you that I'm with you, you have a choice. You can remain stressed and worried, or you can believe Me and relax. These are your options. Far too many people choose to continue in worry and stress, but they are wasting their energy. They have forgotten the nature of our relationship. You, however, must remember that I don't speak empty words. When I say, 'Do not be afraid,' it's because I know you have nothing to fear."

Lord, stress is a natural instinct for me, but I want my heart to intuitively rest in You. Fill me with trust in You and peace in Your purposes at the sound of Your voice.

All Scripture is inspired by God and is useful to teach us what is true and to make us realize what is wrong in our lives. It corrects us when we are wrong and teaches us to do what is right.

2 TIMOTHY 3:16

We serve a very vocal God. The world cannot contain all the words He has spoken, but we do have a record of many of them. The Bible is the written account of His words, the only authoritative source of doctrine and expression of His overall will. In it, God tells us what He is like, what His purposes are, and how we can relate to Him. He has uttered many words that weren't written in Scripture—references to prophets who spoke for Him but never wrote anything are enough to convince us of that—but what is written is reliable. In our search for His voice, the Bible is our primary source.

We have to learn how to interpret God's Word, however. At times, He is quoted directly. At other times, writers describe Him or tell stories about encounters people had with Him. The Bible is always true in reporting what people said or believed, but not everything they said or believed is true. For example, Job's friends had a lot to say about God and His ways, and the book of Job records their arguments accurately. Some of what they said was true, but much of it wasn't or was wrongly applied. The reader is left to discern when the person being quoted is reliable and when he or she isn't. It isn't always clear. We have to ask the Spirit to help us with the interpretation.

That means that even when we're reading the inspired Word of God, we still have to listen for God's voice. Many are attracted to the "objectivity" of reading the written Word, but centuries of differing opinions and misguided interpretations should be enough to convince us that our objectivity isn't very objective. We need God's help to hear His voice in His Word. When we read, we must open our ears to hear.

❖ ❖ ❖

Lord, give me understanding. Enliven Your Word and let it sink deeply into my heart.

FEBRUARY 20

Your word is a lamp to guide my feet and a light for my path.
PSALM 119:105

Many of us have experienced an interesting phenomenon. While we are reading God's Word, a certain verse—or maybe even just a word or a phrase—will suddenly come alive, as if it were printed in neon lights. Or a verse or passage quoted audibly will suddenly sound much louder than all the other words before and after. It rings in the depths of our spirits, as if highlighted for a specific purpose. It speaks directly and powerfully.

All of Scripture speaks to us, of course, but sometimes God has specific guidance or encouragement for a particular situation or season. When we read or listen with an open spirit—a heart that is ready to hear—He will magnify portions of His written Word and apply them directly to our lives. Psalm 119 extols the benefits of Scripture—its teachings revive us, keep us from sin, encourage us, show us His ways, and so on—but it also tells us that we can receive specific light for our next step. As we read the Bible, the Holy Spirit will often illumine His thoughts and engage us in a specific conversation. When we listen to the written Word, we may hear it as an inner voice.

It is futile to think of hearing God on a regular basis outside of Scripture, without also listening for Him within it. This is where He has already spoken perfectly, revealing His general, eternal purposes and His ways with His people. Words that were inspired long ago still resound as we read or listen to them now. And, if we ask—and sometimes even when we don't—they will jump off the page and into our hearts. In those moments, we will know we have heard the voice of the living God.

Father, as I come to Your Word, speak to me. Make Your words—specific, applicable, direct words—a lamp to guide my feet and a light for my path. Shine Your light very specifically on exactly what You want me to hear.

You must commit yourselves wholeheartedly to these commands that I am giving you today.
DEUTERONOMY 6:6

The Bible has often been described as an instruction manual for life, as if we are simply to read the Word and follow the directions. And for many, this approach is the beginning and end of God's voice to them. God has given His commands, and we are to follow them. We read, and then we do. It's like assembling a piece of furniture; the instructions are printed on a page, and we follow them step by step. That's how it's supposed to work—*if* the Bible is only an instruction manual.

The problem with that perspective is that God is intensely relational, and instruction manuals aren't. God never intended for His voice to be reduced to a reading list or a long-distance letter or a business plan. Though we certainly receive His instructions through His Word, we also receive them through our hearts during the night (see Psalm 16:7), through a voice speaking into our ears (see Isaiah 30:21), and many other ways. And though part of our relationship with God is instructional, most of it goes much deeper. It isn't enough to merely follow instructions; our hearts have to be engaged (see Deuteronomy 28:47-48; Matthew 15:8). Jesus made it very clear that it's possible to know the Word thoroughly yet not know God. (In John 5:37-39, He tells the religious leaders, who knew Scripture quite well, that they had never heard God's voice.) Reading His Word and hearing His voice are not necessarily the same thing.

Let Scripture be your entryway into a conversation with God, not the sum total of your communication. Hear His instructions, but let your relationship with Him go much deeper than that. Never let the Bible be reduced to a spiritual to-do list. Let it launch you into God's presence.

✧ ✧ ✧

Lord, I understand that reading the Word and hearing Your voice are not the same thing. Please help me to hear Your voice in the Word and to use Scripture as the beginning of a conversation with You, rather than as the conversation itself.

[God said,] "The LORD will be your delight. I will give you great honor."
ISAIAH 58:14

FROM THE HEART OF GOD

"When you stop trying to figure Me out, when you stop trying to relate to Me as a set of principles, when you stop trying be religious or 'spiritual,' and instead seek to know Me and show concern for the desires of My heart, you will experience a new delight and favor in your life. When you truly turn toward Me, you will find Me turning toward you in unusual ways. I respond to those who come to Me with the assumption that I want to share My passions with them. When you lean against Me to listen to My heartbeat—and let the heartbeat of your life align with it—I will give you great honor.

"Do not mistake this invitation for a step to fulfill or a hoop to jump through in order to please Me. Many people come to Me saying they want to know Me, but what they really want is for Me to do something for them. They want to see themselves or be seen by others as a person who 'knows God,' but they aren't actually interested in My deep desires. I know your motives, and I know when you're really after something else. I want a heart connection. I delight in you already, and I want you to delight in Me.

"You can never earn My favor, but you can step into the favor I've already offered and given. Many will tell you that life with Me doesn't decrease the number of struggles in your life, but they are wrong if they assume that My presence doesn't increase your ability to overcome obstacles. My favor isn't theoretical; it's real. It's tangible. You can experience it. When I choose to honor you, you will overcome difficulties and win victories, even if the battle is difficult. Delight in Me, and I will satisfy your heart with good things."

Lord, I really do want to know You, and not simply because I want Your blessings. Of course I want Your blessings, but more than that, I need to connect with You—to experience Your closeness. Please give me Your heartbeat.

Jesus took them through the writings of Moses and all the prophets, explaining from all the Scriptures the things concerning himself.
LUKE 24:27

Hebrew Scripture had been scrutinized for centuries. Some parts of it were older than others, but it had all been the subject of intense study among Jews long before the time of Jesus. Yet Jesus was somehow able to unveil meanings in Scripture that applied to Him and that no one had yet understood. The Messiah had been hinted at, symbolized, foreshadowed, and foretold for hundreds of years, but no one had seen Him clearly in God's Word. The plain meaning of the text had not been all that plain.

Many today argue that the meaning of Scripture is clear, and in many respects it is. God's plan of salvation and His general will for our lives are spelled out in simple terms. But when people argue that all the meaning is on the surface and urge others to quit looking for deeper truths, they are denying the layers in which God speaks. Rabbinic interpreters have long seen at least four approaches to the Word: (1) a literal, surface meaning; (2) a deeper meaning often found in hints and nuances of words; (3) a metaphorical or allegorical meaning taken from symbolism in a passage; and (4) a hidden, subjective, mystical interpretation. Whether every passage is subject to all four approaches is open to discussion, but God has shown Himself capable of embedding truth at multiple levels in Scripture, which is why commentators are still uncovering the meaning of certain symbolic expressions in ancient texts. God's voice is able to express infinite truths in a finite number of words. He can creatively apply His words to a variety of situations at one time.

Always embrace the plain meaning of Scripture, but also hear God's voice between the lines, underneath the stories, through the symbols and images, and behind the printed words. He is communicating more than meets the eye.

Lord, heighten my senses to hear deeper truths, see bigger visions, and feel the weight of Your voice. Let Your Spirit explain the Scriptures to me personally and specifically.

FEBRUARY 24

You know my thoughts even when I'm far away.
PSALM 139:2

She was in an intense battle with depression after a series of personal and professional setbacks. Nothing seemed to be working out for her, even though she was faithfully following God. In trying to encourage her, her brother reminded her of scriptural promises and stories of biblical characters who persevered through the worst of times. That helped, but it came across as general wisdom that could have applied to anyone, anywhere. So her brother asked several of his friends, none of whom knew his sister, to listen for God's voice on her behalf. He told them no details and explained no issues. He didn't even tell them that the person was his sister or that she was going through a hard time. He simply gave them a first name and asked them, independent of one another, to listen to God.

The friends prayed, sensed what the Spirit was saying, and wrote out what they had heard. None heard exactly the same thing, but there was a common theme throughout: "God sees what you are going through, and He wants to encourage you that this season will end. You are an overcomer, and as you grow stronger, your trials will grow weaker. Nothing that has happened will harm you. He has measured your difficulties carefully, and a day is coming when you will dance on top of them rather than struggle beneath them. You will not be overwhelmed."

Those words are all biblical truths, and they could apply to anyone. But since they had come from people who did not know her situation—who could have given her random messages about career direction or ministry callings or anything else she was not struggling with at the time—she knew the words had come from God's heart. When we learn to listen to God on behalf of others, He speaks powerful, personalized words directly into their circumstances.

Holy Spirit, inspire in me the words You want to speak to others. Use me as a mouthpiece, an ambassador of encouragement through whom You can touch people's hearts in their moments of need.

FEBRUARY 25

> [The Lord said,] *"When you go through deep waters, I will be with you. When you go through rivers of difficulty, you will not drown. When you walk through the fire of oppression, . . . the flames will not consume you."*
> ISAIAH 43:2

FROM THE HEART OF GOD

"I never promised that you wouldn't go through deep waters, rivers of difficulty, or fires of oppression. I have promised, however, that I will be with you and bring you through. You need to understand the difference. When you encounter trials, even painful or difficult ones, don't think that I've let you down. I'm with you even in the midst of them.

"Many people think I've broken My promises when they encounter unexpected or traumatic crises. Then they let those disappointments color everything I say to them in the future. They don't trust My words because, after all, I seem to have let them down last time. But I never let anyone down who trusts Me. Yes, you experienced pain. No, it didn't overcome you. You made it through because of Me.

"Many people believe that My voice will make their lives easier. It does make your life stronger and deeper, but it will rarely make things simpler for you. You will be led into battles and intense situations that need My touch. You will always be given the best instructions, but seldom the easiest ones. I will lead you into the places of greatest need in this world because you heard and responded to Me, qualifying yourself to be My instrument in those places. I speak strength and encouragement into your heart because you will need them.

"Don't lower your expectations for what you might hear from Me. Raise them higher. You will go on great but challenging adventures. And I will be with you in all of them."

Honestly, Lord, Your ways scare me a little. But they also excite me. I am willing to go anywhere and do anything as long as I know You are with me.

The instructions of the LORD are perfect, reviving the soul. The decrees of the LORD are trustworthy, making wise the simple. The commandments of the LORD are right, bringing joy to the heart. The commands of the LORD are clear, giving insight for living.
PSALM 19:7-8

God inspired Scripture, and Scripture gives us instruction, encouragement, insight, correction, and all sorts of spiritual benefits. So it may seem rather obvious to insist that if we want to hear God's voice, we can find it by opening the pages of our Bibles. This is where we start and how we measure whether or not something is God's voice in the first place. The words of Scripture are His words, spoken through His servants. Whatever we think we hear outside of Scripture must line up with the revelation of God's nature and will *within* Scripture. The Bible is the truth that frames all other communication from Him.

That said, we can't develop a relationship with the words of Scripture and think that equates to a relationship with God. The religious scholars of Jesus' day—and many throughout history ever since—were experts on Scripture, able to quote and expound on huge sections of it from memory. Yet, in spite of their knowledge of the Word, they missed the God who inspired it. They had read about the Messiah with great interest, but they were still blind to Him when He stood right in front of them. They confused mental knowledge with spiritual knowledge, and it was a fatal mistake.

Many Christians do the same today. Some of us act as if the Trinity is the Father, the Son, and the Holy Bible, not the Father, the Son, and the Holy Spirit. But without God's Spirit, the Scriptures are useless to us. We must be inspired when we read and hear, not simply know that the Word was inspired when it was written. It's a living breath, and we must inhale it deeply.

Holy Spirit, make the Word alive to me as I read it. Every time I hear the words of Scripture, let Your voice come through clearly. Let it breathe life into me.

FEBRUARY 27

[Rebekah] went to ask the LORD about it. "Why is this happening to me?"
she asked. And the LORD told her.
GENESIS 25:22-23

Rebekah had questions for God. So did Job, who didn't understand what God was doing in his life. So did Habakkuk, whose prophecy starts with a series of questions that sound a bit accusatory regarding God's fairness. Many others in Scripture and throughout history have been bold enough to bring their most pointed questions to God, expecting a response. Sometimes they got answers, sometimes they didn't, and sometimes their attitudes were corrected. But God never rebuked them simply for asking.

If we want to hear God, we need to ask Him questions. Most of us do that indirectly—sometimes tentatively, hoping for guidance and direction, and sometimes with hints of complaint, wondering why He isn't doing what we want Him to do. But asking God specific questions with the expectation that He will respond to us is an act of faith. We can ask Him what His desires are, how He sees us, how He sees others, how He feels about this situation or that problem, how He wants our relationship to develop, how He wants us to see things differently, what He wants to teach us, and much, much more. These questions may include guidance and specific requests, but they go well beyond those concerns and delve into the heart of the relationship. And God invites us into that kind of conversation. He wants to be known. Questions that open our hearts for Him to share Himself are always welcome.

When we do this in an attitude of faith and expectation, we begin to see and hear things we didn't notice before. Divine moments of instruction—"aha" moments that unveil His nature—come much more frequently. We begin to feel God's heartbeat and synchronize with it. We become not just hearers of God's voice but conversationalists with God Himself.

Lord, what is on Your heart today? What do You want to teach me? My eyes and ears are open—please share Your heart with me.

I listen carefully to what God the LORD is saying, for he speaks peace to his faithful people.
PSALM 85:8

When we ask God questions in faith that He will answer, it's like plowing a field in our hearts and inviting Him to sow seeds in it. He loves that kind of expectancy—and that kind of conversation. His answers may not come immediately, or in the ways we thought they would, but they almost always come eventually. He responds to those who long for His words.

One way to hear God is to ask a question and then watch for a living parable to play out in front of our eyes. Several people in Scripture "looked to see" what God would say, knowing that His preferred language seems to be pictures. He spoke to most of the prophets in visual pictures—Jeremiah learned deep spiritual lessons from a potter's wheel and a basket of figs, for example, and Ezekiel saw a valley of bones and acted out most of his prophecies visually. When we ask God a question, we shouldn't be surprised when we're hit with a metaphor or parable in real life—some relationship dynamic or turn of events that gives us a glimpse into God's heart and addresses our concern. If we ask God how He feels about us or someone else, He may point us to a father doting on a child or a husband showering affection on his wife. If we ask Him why He seems to be so slow in keeping a promise, He may show us the fruit of patience in the life of someone who didn't rush into a major decision. Regardless of the question, there's likely something in our world that portrays it. And the Spirit has a remarkable ability to steer our attention to divine illustrations. He knows how to dramatize His truth.

Listen to God by opening your eyes. Expect Him to share His heart. He loves to speak to His people.

Holy Spirit, please direct my attention to parables of truth. Teach me Your ways in everything I see.

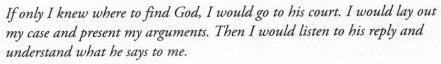

MARCH 1

If only I knew where to find God, I would go to his court. I would lay out my case and present my arguments. Then I would listen to his reply and understand what he says to me.

Job 23:3-5

Even though God loves to speak to His people, He sometimes maintains long silences and lets us search for Him. That can be an uncomfortable process, especially during life's painful seasons, but it has profound results. Somehow in the search, His distance draws us closer. Some people may give up and lose the benefit of the silence, but those who keep pressing in will reap rewards for their persistence. They will learn to depend on the God they cannot hear, cannot see, and cannot sense in any other way. His most recent words will continue to echo in their souls, forcing their hearts to choose between faith and fear, between assurance and uncertainty, between hope and despair.

Were those words real? Another voice will whisper to us that they weren't— that our imagination was misleading us. But the heart of the believer will actually believe. God has spoken before, and yes, He will speak again.

God's silences are as much an aspect of His communication as His voice is. They test our mettle and teach us to listen more attentively. We refine our hearing and our faith when He doesn't speak as He once did. When we ask Him questions and hear nothing but silence, as Job did, the appropriate response isn't to walk away. It's to draw nearer. We can be encouraged by moments of distance; it means He wants us to come closer.

When you don't hear God, don't get impatient or give up. Know that He is drawing you nearer, tuning your ears to His voice and teaching you the fine art of waiting for Him. The silence won't last forever. The rewards of persistence will.

Lord, when I can't sense Your presence or hear Your voice, please keep drawing me toward You. Give me the patience and persistence to keep seeking Your face.

If you need wisdom, ask our generous God, and he will give it to you.
JAMES 1:5

Many Christians approach God with the assumption that it will be difficult to hear Him and that only the superspiritual are close enough to God to know His thoughts. Scripture tells us just the opposite: If we need wisdom, we're to ask for it. That's it. No hoops to jump through, no requirement of long hours of monastic solitude and self-discipline, no prerequisite of a master's degree in biblical interpretation. Just ask and receive.

That's what James told his readers, and many of them were new believers without much experience in the ways of God's Spirit. Somehow James expected them to be able to hear and discern God's voice, to sense His direction, and to know His nature by direct revelation. In other words, receiving wisdom from above is meant to be a natural experience. The divine heartbeat is meant to flow into our own souls simply for the asking. The Father's thoughts can be implanted into our minds.

The problem for us modern Christians is that we are masters at second-guessing the voice of wisdom. In some ways, we are overly fastidious, asking far more questions than we need to. *Was that Him or just me? Are these my desires or His will? Are those thoughts from His Spirit or from my psychological makeup, my past issues, or my emotional biases? Am I being deceived?* There are legitimate concerns in all of these questions, but we have to remember that God's ability to guide us is greater than our own ability to be deceived. If we are not willfully fooling ourselves—if we are humbly seeking God's wisdom with an open mind—He will make it clear. We can trust the Holy Spirit within us, the desires He births in our hearts, and the thoughts that He brings to mind. If we ask, we will receive.

Lord, I know You speak to me, but I question which voice is Yours. Please help me to trust You and follow with an open heart. Give me Your wisdom as You promised.

MARCH 3

This is the sign from the LORD to prove that he will do as he promised:
I will cause the sun's shadow to move ten steps backward on the sundial
of Ahaz!
ISAIAH 38:7-8

"Lord, if I'm believing in the wrong thing and heading in the wrong direction—
I'll walk away. Just speak to me clearly. But if you want me to press ahead, show
me the sign I'm looking for." I prayed that prayer on a discouraging day when I
was headed out the door for a walk. The sign I was looking for—cardinals—was
a common symbol to me. God had spoken to me this way before, the cardinal
representing hope and promise. The more I saw, the greater the affirmation.
Where I live, seeing one cardinal isn't unusual, but the timing in my conversations with God has been uncanny. In desperate times, they've flown over my
head, landed in branches in front of me, and seemingly stared at me as if God
were delivering a personal message. I believed He had spoken this way many
times, and on this day I desperately needed another bit of confirmation.

By the end of my walk, I had seen nine cardinals (and nine happened to be
a symbolic number in the situation I was praying about). The most I had ever
seen on that route was four, and usually it was one or two at the most. Very
often I would see none. But on this day, right after I said, "Lord, I'll take any
cardinals as affirmation to continue in the direction I've been going," I saw them
flying across my path, landing in the bushes next to the path, darting over my
head, and perched on branches above, chirping emphatically. Just as Hezekiah
asked for and received a sign with the sun, I asked for a sign with one particular
bird. And the God who orchestrates His creation gave it to me.

Lord, I know You often choose not to speak this way, and I can't assume that
the absence of a sign means "no." It may simply mean You want to speak
another way. But when You do speak this way, it is so very encouraging. Thank
You for designing well-orchestrated "coincidences."

[The Lord said,] "Others were given in exchange for you. I traded their lives for yours because you are precious to me. You are honored, and I love you."
ISAIAH 43:4

FROM THE HEART OF GOD

"Many people like to believe that I'm impartial. I'm not. It's true that My gifts and blessings are available to anyone who chooses to enter into a relationship with Me and live by faith; I offer My love to all. In that sense, I am no respecter of persons. But I don't treat everyone the same, because not everyone responds to Me the same way. I favor those who love Me and trust Me.

"You've realized this even as you've sought to hear My voice. You've understood that people who do not listen will also not be able to hear; but people who do listen will learn how to recognize what I'm saying to them. You've acknowledged that I reward those who diligently seek Me and that My sheep—not all people, but My sheep—hear My voice. You instinctively understand that some blessings come only to those who position themselves to receive them. I draw close in love to those who draw close to Me in love.

"I want you to know this so you won't take My voice for granted. When you hear Me speak, know that you hear because you are favored. You are honored as one whom I've chosen. Though much of the world refuses to believe that I exist, or that I speak, or that human beings have the ability to hear Me, you have come with an open heart and a desire to tune in to My desires. I've loved you always, but your pursuit of Me—which is actually your response to My pursuit of you—causes Me to delight in you. You are precious to Me. And I speak often to those I delight in."

Lord, I know You don't love me any less when I don't hear Your voice, but I'm so glad for the favor You show me by speaking to me. Thank You for choosing me, for giving me ears to hear, for pursuing my heart. May I always respond in ways that delight You.

I pray for you constantly, asking God, the glorious Father of our Lord Jesus Christ, to give you spiritual wisdom and insight so that you might grow in your knowledge of God.

Ephesians 1:16-17

God's voice always comes to us in some context. Are we in turmoil or anxiety when we listen for Him? Do we perceive Him as a demanding or hard Master? What does He want from us when He speaks? Is He on our side? Perceptions about God, dreams and desires for our own lives, thoughts about our current circumstances, and many more ideas condition the environment in which we hear. And that environment colors the lenses through which we see God and clutters the filters through which we hear Him.

But Paul's prayer in Ephesians 1 aims at breaking through the clutter of our thought life and giving us a clear picture of God. Some translations say "a spirit of wisdom and revelation," emphasizing the divine help we need in order to know God. We have to grasp who He is—the goodness of His heart toward us, His desire to lavish His gifts on us, the mission He holds close to Him at all times, and more. And though we can mentally understand His nature by reading His Word, that understanding doesn't really sink in unless His Spirit comes with the key that unlocks our hearts. Truth has to be imparted to us. Knowing who God is can happen only when He unveils Himself to us. We need a revelation.

So Paul prays for wisdom and insight—a spirit of revelation—and we should too. Constantly. If we don't have a revelation of His true nature, we may interpret all the information we get about Him through the wrong filter. We'll know something of God, but we won't know *Him*. But if He removes the veil from our hearts, we will see with spiritual vision. And His voice can flourish in that environment.

Lord, open my eyes to see You—to really know in the depths of my soul who You are. May Your voice come to me from the purity of that place: uncorrupted, unbiased, and straight from Your heart to mine.

*I pray that your hearts will be flooded with light so that you can
understand the confident hope he has given to those he called.*
EPHESIANS 1:18

By nature, our hearts are darkened with discouragement and despair. Some
people may be cheerier than others, but most go through some phase in which
they ask whether life has any meaning, and many never arrive at a satisfying
answer. We may hope for the best, but we frequently fear the worst. We search
for purpose and fulfillment, often in desperate ways, filling ourselves with all
kinds of substitutes for true joy. Anxieties about big, eternal questions nag at our
souls, and unless we're careful, cruelly leave us in the dark.

But God doesn't leave us in the dark. He has sent His Spirit to shine into
every corner of our souls and give us understanding about Him. He enlightens
us in every way, even when we are carrying heavy burdens or going through
painful times. If He turns on His light within us, the nagging questions and
darkened thoughts dissipate. He doesn't do battle with the darkness; He simply
shines. And when He shines inside us, we can see clearly.

In God's Kingdom, clear vision always gives hope. God is always optimis-
tic, always heading somewhere good, always intent on working out the best
for those who love Him. That's why despair in the life of a Christian is always
a misperception. It isn't based in the reality of a God who shines. Our hope—
confident, unwavering expectation of His goodness—can flourish when He
floods our hearts with light.

Pray daily that God would shine into every corner of your life. Refuse to live
in discouragement. Know that His voice will always inspire hope because it is
always based in reality. And the reality is that He is building something beautiful
in you.

Father of light, I need You to shine in me. I need to hear Your encouragement.
Let my heart be flooded with Your brightness, and lift me higher to live in
confident, life-giving hope.

I also pray that you will understand the incredible greatness of God's power for us who believe him.

EPHESIANS 1:19

When we listen for God's voice, we generally listen to Him with limited expectations. We don't mean to; we just don't know how to open ourselves to anything and everything. We need context, so we create one. But it's often a narrower context than it ought to be. Like a radio receiver tuned to one station, we rule out all other signals. We place limits on what we think we might hear. And if God speaks outside of those limits, we may miss His message.

Paul's prayer in Ephesians 1 is meant to raise our expectations. It pleads for wisdom and revelation to enlighten us and convince us of hope. In verse 19, it expands our vision to know a God who can do the impossible through those who believe Him. In effect, it asks God to build a greenhouse in our souls where His word is cultivated and blossoms. When we are convinced that God's power is available to us through faith, our faith is able to grasp greater possibilities. When we listen for His voice, we pray with more boldness. We look forward to miraculous answers. And we learn to expect the unexpected.

If we would pray Paul's prayer for ourselves daily, we would not only grow dramatically in our knowledge of God and in our relationship with Him, but we would also hear Him more clearly. The soil of our hearts would be better prepared for the seeds He wants to plant there. Our capacity for envisioning God's will would expand to accommodate the great things He wants to do. And we would begin to step more fully into the plans He has for us.

God, help me to understand the incredible greatness of Your power—not just in theory but in every way it applies to my life. I want to walk in Your strength. I want my heart to be big enough for Your purposes. Please let me hear all You want to say.

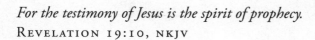

For the testimony of Jesus is the spirit of prophecy.
REVELATION 19:10, NKJV

We may have a hard time discerning some voices in our lives, but there's one we can always know is God's: a testimony of what Jesus has done. The enemy isn't interested in highlighting Christ's works, though he may try to distort them at times. And our human nature would rather give credit to ourselves. But when we hear a testimony of Jesus, we know God is speaking. There is power in the declaration of what Jesus has done, and it's a power that isn't directed only at commemorating the event. The goal is for the work to be reenacted or reapplied to our lives.

The testimony of Jesus is a prophetic message. The voice isn't only saying, "Look at what I did!" He's also saying, "I want to do this again!" The message is an invitation to believe in His power, His compassion, and His desire to miraculously intervene. Spiritual passivity may cause us to think, "I *wish* He would do that in my life," but His invitation is greater than that. The response He encourages is, "I *believe* You will do this in my life." When we hear a testimony of Christ's restoration, we can have faith that He wants to restore something for us. When we hear a testimony of healing or provision, we can have faith that He wants to heal or provide. The testimony stirs up our faith, and it expresses His desire. When we hear what Jesus has done, we hear His longing to do more.

The testimony of Jesus, whether coming out of your mouth or someone else's, is never just a memorial. It's a living word. When you embrace it as such, it will be accompanied by God's power in your life and the lives of others. His works will come alive in a new way. And His voice and His presence will become self-evident.

Jesus, help me to recognize the Holy Spirit in testimonies of Your work. Stir up my faith to accept Your testimonies as my invitations. Let me receive Your power and love every time I hear of what You have done.

These are the words of Jeremiah. . . . The LORD gave me this message.
JEREMIAH 1:1, 4

God has spoken many times to many people, including the prophets and messengers of Scripture. And if we're observant, we'll notice an interesting phenomenon when we read the words of these messengers: They wrote with distinctive styles and personalities. They heard God's voice and expressed it through their own individuality. Ezekiel's prophecies sound like Ezekiel; Jeremiah's sound like Jeremiah; Paul's letters sound like Paul; and so on. It was God's voice through their voices—an intersection of the human and the divine.

That's how God's voice comes to us, too. We often expect Him to sound like a deep-voiced narrator with a Shakespearean accent, but that's not His style. And when His voice comes bubbling up through our own inner thoughts, we discount it as our own self-talk. It sounds so much like our imagination or the wandering of our reckless ideas. Rarely do we remember that the Spirit flows from within us. He is not coming from the outside as an objective experience to be measured; He has infiltrated our minds and hearts and transformed them, and He speaks subjectively through them. As with the prophets of old, He sounds a lot like the person through whom He is speaking.

Our rationalist minds, steeped in Greek linear logic, may have trouble with this experience. We're apt to say that the voice sounds like us because it *is* us. But apart from burning bushes and open visions, this is how God normally speaks. Our job is to discern which impulses within us are Spirit-inspired and which are not. Is that subjective? Of course. But all relationships are. We all communicate through filters of perceptions and feelings and past experiences. If we are to relate to God at all, it will have to be through a subjective conversation and intuitive perception of His Spirit. And we will have to trust the God who lives deep within us to speak to us there.

Lord, speak to my thoughts. Let me know which ones are Yours. Help me to discern the deep impulses of my heart that come from You—and to believe them.

> *[A slave girl] followed Paul and the rest of us, shouting, "These men are servants of the Most High God, and they have come to tell you how to be saved."*
> ACTS 16:17

A student at a Bible college was scheduled to deliver a chapel message, and a truth was burning inside her. She was bothered by a false teaching that kept many from experiencing God's best, and her chapel message seemed to be the right occasion to refute it. She prepared powerful points with plenty of scriptural evidence. But the night before her presentation, she couldn't sleep. God spoke to her spirit: "Don't preach that message. Your beliefs are right, but you are arguing your points from the wrong spirit. You aren't speaking in love." Disappointed, she gave an entirely different message about love—and realized later how abrasive and alienating her planned message would have been.

It's possible for someone to say the right things with the wrong attitude. The slave girl who followed Paul and Silas in Philippi is one example; she spoke the truth (generally) about these men, but she was filled with an agitating demonic spirit. Contentiousness, strife, pride, bitterness, and an obsession with proving a point can cause us to speak the right words while not representing God's heart. Just as important as what we say to others or hear from God are the emotional and spiritual filters through which we say or hear it. The spirit behind a truth is as significant as the truth itself.

This student's sensitivity to God's voice spared her from an argument she might have won even while losing her audience. She was able to avoid alienating those who disagreed with her and to discuss her beliefs more winsomely later. In a sleepless night, God spoke to her clearly enough to redirect her, and she sensed His message clearly. When we bring our "right" perspectives to God, He shapes them to reflect not only His truth but also His heart.

Holy Spirit, give me that kind of sensitivity to Your voice—not only to know Your truth but to know the heart behind it. Help me to believe and discuss what is right and to saturate my words with the right spirit.

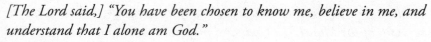

[The Lord said,] "You have been chosen to know me, believe in me, and understand that I alone am God."
Isaiah 43:10

FROM THE HEART OF GOD

"You have gone through times in your life when you thought My greatest desire for you was to behave. Or to fulfill the great commission. Or to accomplish great spiritual feats. Or to teach, to serve, or to love one another. And it's true that all of these things are good. But My greatest desire for you is simply to know Me, believe Me, and worship Me alone as God. Your life isn't nearly as complicated as you've made it. I have called you to relate to Me.

"You call this 'the greatest commandment' because that's how My Word expresses it, but what you've done with the word *commandment* isn't what I originally had in mind. I'm not giving you orders to love Me; love under compulsion isn't love at all. I'm simply telling you that loving Me is your highest goal and the one purpose that will lead to your fulfillment. This is your purpose, your design, the reason I made you. Your primary responsibility in life is to look to Me. If you don't do that, nothing else you do will be enough.

"You need to be aware of this when you listen for My voice. If you're seeking guidance, correction, wisdom, revelation about the future, insight into your problems, or anything else, but are seeking it without this understanding of My highest goal for you, you will hear with the wrong ears. My voice will turn into a harsh command or a never-ending instruction manual or an impossible assignment. You will dread hearing Me and hope that I remain silent. Your perception of Me will become more and more skewed until you lose sight of My true nature. But if you are thoroughly convinced of My highest purpose for your life—to know and love Me—My words will take on a different sound. You will crave Me every day and be satisfied in what you hear."

Father, there's freedom in choosing simply to know and love You. That takes the pressure off my spiritual agendas. May I hear everything You say through that perspective.

MARCH 12

His Spirit searches out everything and shows us God's deep secrets.
1 CORINTHIANS 2:10

God knows all things. As creator of the universe, He knows even the deepest mysteries it contains. He knows every "why" and "how" of existence, the answers to all those questions that nag us about our purpose and destiny. His Spirit knows every motive of the Father's heart and every nuance of His relationship with us. He is a guardian of deep secrets.

In Christ, many of those deep secrets are unveiled—Paul wrote often of the "mystery" of the gospel that was being revealed in his generation. Yet Scripture implies that there are more secrets to be known, and logic confirms it. An infinite God must always know more than He has revealed and always harbor thoughts that finite minds cannot fathom. We don't know exactly how history will unfold, for example, though God has revealed its general direction and ultimate goal. We don't know exactly how our lives will unfold either, though God has given us a purpose and continues to call us forward. There are Scripture passages that we have not yet fully grasped, reasons behind evil and suffering that we can't even remotely understand, dynamics of human relationships that we haven't sorted out yet. Although God has unveiled many secrets, the details are often still hidden.

But God's Spirit shows us His deep secrets. The wisdom of the world can never grasp the heart and mind of God, but He shares His counsel with those who love Him. He wants to reveal His nature and His plans to those whose hearts belong to Him. He doesn't tell us to figure things out or to rely on our own wisdom; He invites us into His private counsel. When we are immersed in His Spirit, we begin to understand things we never understood before. We have sudden ideas that we know are not our own. And we begin to walk in directions we had never planned on. Why? Because the deep secrets of God are unfolding in our hearts.

Holy Spirit, work Your secrets into my heart. Every day, show me more of You.

Only those who are spiritual can understand what the Spirit means.
1 CORINTHIANS 2:14

We're trained from a very early age how to acquire knowledge. We try out words and behaviors and learn when we are corrected by our parents. We go to school and try to remember what we are taught before we are tested on it. At each stage of growth, we experiment with relationships and experiences to expand our horizons. We explore, gather information, and go through many trials and many errors to grab the information and skills that are out there and get them into our hearts.

But in matters of the Spirit, learning is a different process. Sure, we still gather external information and internalize it, and becoming disciples involves a lot of observation and a lot of trial and error. But our primary source of understanding is through revelation. In the Spirit, we don't weigh pros and cons; we discern truth. We don't develop theories and prove them; we follow God and experience reality as He defines it. We don't understand in order to believe; we believe in order to understand. Acquiring knowledge in the Spirit is different than acquiring knowledge with our mental faculties.

How do we do that? We have to learn how to "know" through prayer and revelation, not through analysis and deduction. God will say things to us that do not make sense to the human brain—Paul's discussion of the Cross in 1 Corinthians is a good example. This is why Paul came to Corinth not with persuasive words of wisdom but with a demonstration of the Spirit's power (see 1 Corinthians 2:4). God doesn't follow human logic. He is above it. We can get above it too if we will ask for revelation from Him and accept the spiritual wisdom He imparts. There is no step-by-step process for this, though human wisdom craves one. We have to trust that if we ask, He will teach us. And if we are depending on the Spirit, we will hear.

Lord, I want to be one who is spiritual—to understand the things of Your Spirit, all that You choose to reveal. Please teach me how.

MARCH 14

We understand these things, for we have the mind of Christ.
1 CORINTHIANS 2:16

Many a Christian has searched for knowledge that he or she has already had. Many of us have cried out to receive guidance and wisdom from God, not realizing that the mind of Christ is already operating in us and filling us with the wisdom we need. We often know the right decision to make, but we have talked ourselves out of it by our own biases and logic. We do not trust the mind within us because we seem to have several minds.

Nevertheless, we have the mind of Christ. Yes, there may be other voices speaking to us, but we already have His wisdom. We are not told that we can have it if we believe, that we will have it when we have become holy, or that we might have it if we have read God's Word. No, we have been joined together with Christ by faith and are one with Him. We already have the Spirit of God and the mind of Jesus living and breathing within us. He is there. We only need to access Him.

We don't access the mind of Christ by study. There's a place for study, but it isn't the means of revelation. Neither do we access it by asking for advice, though God can speak through the counsel of others. We access His mind by faith—by believing that His wisdom is given to us and by praying until we have an internal "knowing" that can't be swayed. "I just know" won't satisfy many skeptics, but we aren't listening to God in order to satisfy skeptics. We're listening in order to hear. And according to New Testament truth, the mind of the one who speaks is already within us.

Trust the wisdom you have been given. Listen to the deep knowledge at the core of your spirit. Rely on Jesus, who inhabits your heart.

Jesus, thank You for Your mind—for sharing Your thoughts with me. Let my mind be filled with Your nature, and give me understanding of Your ways.

The LORD has sought out a man after his own heart.
1 SAMUEL 13:14

David was a man after God's own heart, we are told. Later in the writings of the prophets, God reiterates His desire and tells Israel that He will establish shepherds after His own heart (Jeremiah 3:15). Eventually, God would wrap up His own nature in human flesh and demonstrate the kind of heart He has. From beginning to end, His relationship with human beings has been aimed at showing us who He really is and drawing us into fellowship with Him.

But that's often not the context of our desire to hear God's voice. When we're at a fork in the road, we want information. We want Him to point one way or the other and tell us what to do. If God were seeking people after His own *business*, we would qualify easily. But He isn't just interested in people who want information; He is interested in people who share His heart. That's different. That goes well beyond a transaction of information. It's highly relational.

This is why those who desperately seek guidance from God often don't find it. We are after His information, not His essence. We have not immersed ourselves in His nature and sought to be like Him. We have not been zealous about hearing His joys or sorrows or interests. So when the time comes to hear from Him—when we have a keen desire to communicate with Him—we find ourselves out of practice. We try to listen for His counsel without having spent much time listening for His heartbeat.

One of the most effective ways to hear God's voice is to want to, even when getting information from Him isn't urgent. If we ask Him to talk to us about His desires, He will impart them to us. If we ask Him to whisper His joys, we will begin to notice them. Our conversations with Him now lay the groundwork for deeper conversations with Him later when we need guidance. As we seek His heart, He will share His nature—and His guidance—with us.

Lord, I want to hear You well—on all things, even Your sorrows and joys today. Impart Your thoughts to me. Let me feel Your heartbeat.

MARCH 16

If anyone speaks, they should do it as one who speaks the very words of God.

1 PETER 4:11, NIV

Scripture tells us that we who believe have the mind of Christ (see 1 Corinthians 2:16). It also tells us we can do the works of Christ and that we can be filled with the fullness of God (see John 14:12 and Ephesians 3:19). So why would we be surprised when Scripture tells us that we can speak the very words of God? It only makes sense that the God who loves to communicate—the God who inspired a Bible full of truth and incarnated His Son as "the Word"—would continue to speak through His people.

We often wonder why God is so silent, even while He has been speaking to us through the voices of Spirit-inspired people around us. We hardly recognize His voice because it sounds like the voice of fellow believers, and because they would deny any awareness that God was speaking through them. But God speaks nevertheless, filling human beings with His Spirit, giving them His mind, and letting His desires and His truths spill out through their voices. We have to be discerning, of course; not everything that comes out of the mouths of other Christians is God's voice. In fact, most is just human communication. But if we're listening, we'll hear Him. And when we speak, we can pray that He will speak through us.

In fact, this is what Peter urges us to do. Some see this verse in the context of a preaching ministry, and it certainly applies to that. But we can assume it applies more broadly, simply because it was written to Christians in general, not just to preachers. Those who speak—whether in front of a church assembly or in smaller, more personal settings—have the capacity to utter God's words. And we should speak and listen with that awareness, knowing the sacred possibilities before us. We can declare divine insights.

God, let me declare Your words, and let me recognize them in others. We ask You to speak, and it only makes sense that You would use people to do so. Help me to hear and speak Your sacred thoughts.

[The Lord said,] "In those days when you pray, I will listen. If you look for me wholeheartedly, you will find me."

JEREMIAH 29:12-13

Charles Finney was in a wrestling match with his own soul to give his heart to God. He resolved one Sunday in 1821 to settle the question of his salvation once and for all, before all other concerns in his life, and he spent days trying to pray and grasp the truth of the gospel. The next Wednesday, on his way to the office, he heard an inward voice: *What are you waiting for? Are you endeavoring to earn a righteousness of your own?* Immediately, he saw the fullness of the atonement of Christ. And later, while on his knees before God, yet worried that someone might see him, a passage of Scripture "seemed to drop" into his mind—the promise of Jeremiah 29:13 that those who seek God wholeheartedly will find Him. Finney had vowed to give his heart to God, and the verse assured him that his vow could be fulfilled and his gift would be accepted. He suddenly saw his faith as a matter of the will and not of the intellect. Over the next few days, he experienced the presence of Jesus and the love of God in profoundly personal ways.

God has promised that He will speak to us, especially to our searching hearts. Once Finney determined to settle the question of his salvation, he heard an inward voice, sensed God's leading, and experienced relevant verses coming to mind in the moment he needed them. There was no need to question whether he was hearing God; God was leading him into salvation and a life of fruitful ministry. Finney simply followed what the Spirit was doing in him, acutely aware of the burdens of sin, and yet also aware of the freedom in Christ that was offered to him. He heard God because he desperately sought Him. God makes the same promise to every soul who wrestles with the questions of His truth and is willing to follow the sound of His voice.

Lord, may my heart follow the burdens, the convictions, the joys, the freedoms, and the insights You give me—in full confidence that You are speaking to me.

From eternity to eternity I am God. No one can snatch anyone out of my hand. No one can undo what I have done.
ISAIAH 43:13

FROM THE HEART OF GOD

"I want you to understand all that 'from eternity to eternity' includes. It means that not only can no one can undo anything I have done, but that no one can undo what I have *said*, either. It's true that I often interact with My people with a softness in My will; like Moses, you can change My direction with your prayers and pleas. And, also like Moses, you can forfeit promises that might have applied to you if you had been careful to believe and follow Me closely. But when I have spoken My promises and purposes to you, and you have believed them and been careful to align your life with them, you never need to worry about losing what was promised. No matter how things look, My words will come to pass. Whatever circumstances or arguments come up against them, no matter how unlikely My words may seem, they cannot be quenched or deferred by outside interference. The things I have spoken to you are a sacred trust, and you can hang on to them relentlessly and without fear.

"This may be hard for you to grasp, because you don't know anyone else whose words are unfailing. In the world, you can never be certain that people are able or willing to keep their word. But I am always able, and I would not have spoken My words if I had not been willing. I see the end from the beginning, and I would know if I were giving you false hope. When I speak hope into your life, that hope is real. It is certain. Hang on to it as the voice of an infinite, all-powerful God who cannot fail. You can listen well only when you remember this about Me and cling to who I am."

Eternal God, I'm so used to human wisdom that I forget how eternal and invincible Your words are. Help my spirit to get a true sense of their weight, and forgive me whenever my heart questions Your faithfulness. Nothing and no one can alter what You've spoken.

MARCH 19

I cry to you, O God, but you don't answer. I stand before you, but you don't even look.

JOB 30:20

Job begged for some kind of explanation, some answer, even just a hint. He cried out to God and longed for a response. He wanted truth from God, not platitudes from friends. But for a long, excruciating time, he heard nothing. The God who desires a relationship with His people, who has promised that His people will hear His voice, didn't say a word. And Job was left to wonder.

We go through seasons of wondering too. We listen for God, and for painfully long times we don't hear what He is saying. Sometimes we draw false conclusions about whether He really speaks or whether we are equipped to hear. We believe He wants a relationship with us, but we are missing the communication necessary to have one. Like Job, we cry out for more.

Sometimes God remains silent—not forever, but for seasons—and gives us no explanations, directions, or affirmations. Very often, the reason for His silence is a matter of trust. His silences reveal the condition of our hearts. Do we trust Him? When we feel as if we have to understand the details in order to believe a promise, or that we have to understand the reasons in order to follow an instruction, we are implying mistrust. We are saying that there might be details we don't accept or reasons that would make obedience an option. If we trust God implicitly, the details and the reasons don't matter. We assume they are valid because they're of Him. And His silence reveals where we stand.

Even when God doesn't give us explanations or details, He has accounted for them. We can accept them without knowing them. Why? Because we trust Him. Even when He is silent.

 ✧ ✧ ✧

Lord, I refuse to let Your silences shake my faith. I don't need to understand Your will in order to trust Your heart. I don't need to know the details of how You will fulfill a promise in order to believe the promise. I trust You even when I don't hear You.

MARCH 20

The Spirit of God came powerfully upon Saul, and he, too, began to prophesy. When those who knew Saul heard about it, they exclaimed, "What? Is even Saul a prophet?"

1 SAMUEL 10:10-11

Saul was chosen as the first king of Israel, and God had just given him a new heart (see 1 Samuel 10:9). Yet from what we know of Saul's life story, he wasn't a particularly godly king, he didn't have very pure motives, and he was eventually stripped of his kingdom, which drove him to extreme jealousy and an unstable mind. Even so, there was a time when God's Spirit enabled him to prophesy. We don't know what Saul said, but we do know he was hearing God accurately. A very imperfect man was enabled to hear God's voice clearly.

Many people mistakenly believe that we have to achieve an extreme level of holiness in order to hear God. But hearing Him is more about His sovereign work than it is about our ability to become superspiritual. Of course, those who pursue God and spend significant amounts of time in His presence are likely to hear Him more often and more clearly, but that doesn't mean we must wait for a certain level of maturity in order to hear. God never demands that we earn our spiritual stripes in order to receive His benefits. The gospel of grace is just that— good news based on grace. If we think we're disqualified from God's blessings, we're probably in exactly the right frame of mind to receive them.

Don't wait for perfection—or anything remotely resembling it—to listen expectantly for God. And when you sin, don't assume you've prevented Him from speaking anytime soon. He comes to anyone who listens and whose heart is ready to receive and respond. Seek God wherever you are.

Father, thank You for basing Your Kingdom on grace. I earn nothing, yet Jesus qualifies me to receive everything. I need to hear You regardless of my condition, and You know that. Thank You for leading all of Your sheep, including me, by the sound of Your voice.

The sons of the prophets said to Elisha, "See now, the place where we dwell with you is too small for us."
2 KINGS 6:1, NKJV

There are times in Israel's history, particularly during the ministries of Elijah and Elisha, when the "sons of the prophets" lived in groups under a well-known prophetic master. Elijah had his followers, and so did Elisha. Apparently, these disciples were in a learning mode—living with their teacher in order to grow in the practice of their prophetic gifts. This defies many of our assumptions, namely that in biblical times, someone was either a prophet or he wasn't. But as with any spiritual gift, there is room for practice, learning, and growth. The path to hearing God's voice and declaring it isn't traveled in an instant. It's a process.

If Old Testament prophets had to go to school to learn how to hear God's voice, we can too. If we aren't hearing clearly, we have no reason to assume that it's because we aren't equipped. Or that we just aren't gifted. Or that God doesn't speak to us today. Or any other disclaimer that causes us to stop trying. We can position ourselves to hear God better, both in our inward attitudes and our outward actions. We can fine-tune our spiritual receptors to recognize His wavelengths and ignore others. We can become sensitive to His inner prompts and His external signals, looking for His will like explorers on a treasure hunt. We can grow in our confidence in what He is saying.

Most Christians get discouraged early in the process, long before learning how to recognize God's voice. When our prophetic instincts don't mature immediately, we think they aren't there at all. But Jesus made it clear that all of His sheep can hear His voice, and He never implied that our hearing is an instant skill. We have a lot to learn. If we press on, we will learn it.

Father, I want to enroll in Your school of prophecy. No matter how long the learning curve lasts, I will persist under Your training. Teach me to hear and to speak.

An angel of the Lord said to [Philip], "Go south down the desert road. . . ."
So he started out, and he met the treasurer of Ethiopia. . . . The Holy Spirit
said to Philip, "Go over and walk along beside the carriage." Philip ran over
and heard the man reading from the prophet Isaiah. . . . Beginning with this
same Scripture, Philip told him the Good News about Jesus.
ACTS 8:26-27, 29-30, 35

Philip was carrying out a fruitful ministry in Samaria when an angel gave him
instructions to go to a remote desert road along the Mediterranean in Gaza.
While Philip was there, the Holy Spirit spoke to him about an Ethiopian traveler he encountered. The Ethiopian was reading Scripture. And then Philip
spoke God's message to him. Here in the space of a few short verses, we can
observe several modes of God's voice, and we might wonder why.

Why did God send an angel to Philip, rather than simply speak to him
through the Spirit or the Word? On the desert road, why did God speak to him
through the Holy Spirit, rather than through the angel again? Why didn't God
send an angel directly to the Ethiopian or speak to him through the Spirit? If
the man was already reading a Christ-centered portion of the Bible, why was
Philip needed at all? Clearly God was speaking at many levels, not just one, for
a reason.

Perhaps for such an unexpected command, Philip needed a startling encounter, not just a subtle, internal voice, so God sent an angel. Once the situation
was clear, the Spirit could prompt Philip quietly. In either case, Scripture alone
wasn't specific enough to send Philip to Gaza, and he needed detailed revelation about what to do there. Yet the Scripture was the perfect vehicle of revelation for the Ethiopian—although he still needed a human messenger to explain
it to him. Clearly God's voice is varied, and the appropriate messenger in one
moment might not be the appropriate messenger in another. Philip tuned in at
all levels, and the Good News was carried to the continent of Africa.

Lord, forgive me for the ways I've limited my hearing to one or two expressions
of Your voice. Speak from all angles. I'm broadening my reception to hear You
everywhere.

The Holy Spirit said to Philip, "Go over and walk along beside the carriage."
ACTS 8:29

What did it sound like when the Spirit spoke to Philip? Apparently, the voice was very clear and specific; Philip knew exactly what to do. But it seems the voice wasn't audible or visual; somehow it was different from the words of the angel who had just spoken to Philip. So he heard tangibly from the Spirit, yet the words were likely inaudible. God quietly let him know exactly what to do when the time was right.

We have the same Spirit, so why do we not hear from the Spirit with the same clarity? Perhaps it's because we haven't been as attentive or as steeped in the Spirit's ways as Philip was. He was one of seven well-respected men, "full of the Spirit and wisdom," who were selected by the apostles to run a food program for Greek-speaking widowed believers in Jerusalem (Acts 6:1-3). Or perhaps it's because we hear the same kind of prompts that Philip heard but second-guess them until they are mere wisps of unheeded revelation. Regardless, there is a solidity to Philip's relationship with the Spirit that we long for. We want to be able to say, "Then the Spirit told me . . ."

Ask God for concreteness and clarity. Place some faith in the Spirit's ministry of conversation with you. Take some risks in stepping out on the words you think He is speaking. Let Him use you as an instrument of hearing and speaking His truth. And perhaps He will change a life—or even a city or nation—through your words.

Holy Spirit, I want to hear You as clearly as Philip did. I want to be able to follow Your specific instructions. Give me the faith to do so and the ears to hear You. And speak powerfully through me as I respond to what You are speaking to me.

After the wise men were gone, an angel of the Lord appeared to Joseph in a dream.
MATTHEW 2:13

A friend had dreams in which a man she knew was introduced to her as her husband. That alone would never be the basis of a decision, but it certainly opened her eyes. Later, that man confided to her that he had been having unusually clear dreams about her. Again, that would not be enough on which to base a decision, but it was quite enough to begin a conversation. That conversation, along with other divine pointers, led to the growing realization that God was bringing these two lives together in marriage.

Scripture is the record of God's revelation to His people, but it doesn't tell us where to move, whom to marry, when to change careers, or any other direction for specific situations. For those individual decisions, we need to hear His voice—in the context of Scripture, of course, but more personalized than the Word can give us. And one of the ways He speaks is through dreams.

God spoke to Joseph several times in dreams to guide him through the traumatic events surrounding the birth and infancy of Jesus. He also spoke to the patriarchs, the prophets, and even pagan kings through their dreams, and He gave prophets like Daniel the ability to interpret all kinds of visions and dreams (Daniel 1:17). Even in the New Testament, dreams guided significant movements and decisions of the people of God.

There is nothing wrong with asking the Spirit to inspire your dreams. He may not often give specific direction through dreams, but sometimes He does. And He frequently gives insights into the situations we are going through, or alerts us to spiritual or emotional dynamics we haven't noticed during our waking moments. The heart is open to His voice, even at night.

Holy Spirit, I believe You speak to me in my dreams; please give me the discernment to recognize which ones are from You, and the insight to grasp what they mean. Plant Your pictures, Your desires, and Your attitudes in me as I sleep.

[The Lord said,] "But forget all that—it is nothing compared to what I am going to do."
ISAIAH 43:18

FROM THE HEART OF GOD

"Sometimes I've spoken to you, and you have not heard. Sometimes you've heard but did not recognize the voice as Mine. And sometimes you've heard and known, deep in your heart, that I was speaking, pouring out My love and giving you My thoughts. Like Israel, you have received My discipline at times, and it hasn't been easy. You've had questions. You've wondered if My love for you is as deep and true as I say it is. And you've let those questions linger.

"I understand. I'm perfectly content knowing that no matter how much you wrestle with false perceptions of Me, you will eventually know who I am and rest in My love. But as you listen for My voice now, try not to let our conversations be colored by assumptions you've made before. If you thought My will for you in the past was difficult, don't assume it will be so today. If you thought My guidance was obscure then, don't expect it to be the same now. The ways I dealt with you in the past were appropriate for the situations and attitudes you had then. Today, you are not the same. I know you've grown. I understand what you're dealing with. And My words for you are new.

"Every day with Me is fresh. My nature doesn't change, but the tone of our conversation does. Your natural parents related to you differently according to the stages of your life. So do I. If there's any bitterness toward Me from your past, forget it. Set old assumptions aside. What you've seen from Me in the past is nothing compared to what I'm going to do."

Lord, help me not to bring the baggage of yesterday's misunderstandings, questions, struggles, and false perceptions into the conversation of today. I know I haven't always seen You rightly. Break my old ways of thinking and breathe fresh air into our relationship. Let me hear with new ears.

MARCH 26

This is what the LORD, the God of Israel, says: I have heard your prayer about King Sennacherib of Assyria. And the LORD has spoken . . . against him.

2 KINGS 19:20-21

The Assyrians had surrounded Jerusalem and were about to take over the city, enslaving its citizens, and probably killing King Hezekiah and his family. Judah's army was no match for the invaders. Defeat seemed imminent, and the Assyrian king, Sennacherib, was not reluctant to taunt, intimidate, and remind everyone of his invincibility. Hezekiah could surrender, saving the city by potentially sacrificing his own and his family's lives and submitting Judah to slavery, or he could pray and ask God to deliver His people, hoping against all hope that God would answer and avert a massacre.

Hezekiah prayed, spreading out his need before the Lord, and God heard. Isaiah prophesied Sennacherib's demise: The king would have to leave to face another enemy, and before he would be able to return and carry out his threats, he would be killed. The prophecy was fulfilled, and Assyria's army was wiped out during the night by the angel of the Lord. Sennacherib was later murdered by his own sons. Judah was saved.

Hezekiah's dilemma was resolved by the voice of God through Isaiah. Before deliverance came, deliverance was spoken. God did not leave the king in a desperate situation without any direction. He didn't prevent the desperate situation in the first place, but He did guide Hezekiah through it. Another of Judah's kings, many of whom were ungodly, might have made a catastrophic decision in that moment. But Hezekiah, stuck between choices A and B, was given a choice C—to expect miraculous deliverance. God's voice allowed him to cooperate with the divinely ordained outcome.

That's why we need to pray, wait, and listen. God has solutions, but we can experience them only if we know to cooperate with them. And we can know them only if we present our need, listen closely, and believe.

I have impossible situations too, Lord. Please speak into them. Turn back the threats, reverse the momentum, and open doors of opportunity. Let me see the miracles that come from Your mouth.

A time to be quiet and a time to speak.
ECCLESIASTES 3:7

Parents wait for the right time to correct their children. Children wait for the right time to pop a big request on their parents. Friends and spouses wait for the right time to give hard advice or share exciting news. Public relations experts wait for the right time to leak bad news or make big announcements. And businesspeople wait for the right time to announce everything from layoffs to mergers to bold new directions. As human beings, we have a keen sense of critical moments.

Unless we're talking to God, of course. Then we expect Him to answer our prayers right away or reveal His will soon after we ask. We lose all sense of timing in our relationship with Him, forgetting that subtleties and patience are a part of any communication. Our spirits far too easily accuse God of holding out on us, or assume that a few days of silence must mean the answer is *no*. But God has a better sense of timing than we do. He knows the right timing to tell us things, and sometimes it isn't now.

Conversations with God require patience. Sometimes they follow a pattern of asking a question and waiting a few days for the answer, then asking the next question and waiting a few days for that one to be answered, and so on. These conversations can take months, even years. Though God sometimes gives us a glimpse of the big picture—a vision or a calling to be fulfilled over time—the process of stepping into that big picture usually involves stops and starts, twists and turns, and some excruciating growing pains in the interim. It's rarely a fast-paced conversation.

Hang on. Don't rush the process. If God hasn't answered your question yet, it means only that the moment isn't right. But it will be. He not only understands when it's time to speak. He knows when it's time to be quiet.

Lord, the waiting is the hardest part. I don't always know how to interpret the rhythm of our conversations. Give me patience to wait and watch for Your words.

Go now, Daniel, for what I have said is kept secret and sealed until the time of the end.
DANIEL 12:9

God had given Daniel a sweeping vision of the world's unfolding drama, and Daniel didn't understand it. But he was told that the words were to be kept secret, only to be unsealed at the end. Given the purpose of communication—to transmit information in an understandable way—the revelation seems odd. A secret told but still secret? A message sent more than 2,500 years ago to be unveiled at some future point? What's the purpose of a message delivered but not understood? Regardless of God's reasoning, we know this: He sometimes speaks cryptically and lets the true meaning come to the surface over time.

God not only did this in Scripture, He does it in our personal conversations with Him. Paul writes of mysteries now revealed, implying that God's nature is to deliver a truth without the full explanation and then wait a painfully long time for the true meaning to be known. And sometimes it isn't known until after the fact, when hindsight makes all things clear. He gives us enough to hang on to and look forward to, but not enough to eliminate the need for faith or an ongoing conversation with Him. Like an artist who explains the true meaning of his semi-abstract work after all speculation has been offered, He shows us the picture and then gives us the details much later.

Remember that the next time you're holding on to a promise from God or a calling yet to be fulfilled. The essence of the picture He gave you was true; the path to its realization was probably never stated. Our tendency to accurately see the destination but to falsely assume the path will frustrate us. With God, the shortest distance between two points is rarely a straight line. It's a winding road that He reveals along the way until, in the end, we finally understand.

Lord, Your secrets are still mysteries to me even after You tell them. Show me enough to keep me going. Help me keep the destination in view, regardless of how the path turns. Give me the faith to get there.

He is the one who mediates for us a far better covenant with God, based on better promises.
HEBREWS 8:6

Twice we are reminded that Jesus offers us a "better covenant"—here and in Hebrews 7:22. But better than what? Better than the covenant instituted in a dramatic encounter with God at Sinai. Better than a legal system that allows a priest to enter the holiest place and encounter God directly. Better than the relationship God had with Abraham, Moses, David, and the prophets. In fact, better than what has been recorded in the pages of Scripture with ink on paper.

Many tell us that God no longer speaks because everything He has to say to us has been included in the Bible. Yet if God met Moses face to face and merely gave us a book, we do not have a better covenant. If He performed signs and wonders in nearly every book of the Old Testament yet remains silent in our day, we do not have a better covenant. If He spoke directly to prophets of old but never speaks to us personally, we do not have a better covenant. If the written word were better than face-to-face communication, couples would always converse by e-mail and never in person. No, God speaks because we live in the days of the new covenant and the indwelling Spirit. We are redeemed in order to relate to Him. Personally.

Never fall for the deception that God's general revelation to everyone precludes His personal conversation with us as individuals. Yes, He speaks through His Word and anchors His conversations with us there. But He still speaks specifically into our particular circumstances and in response to our unique needs. He has not fallen silent. He has not sent us love letters from a distant land. He is here, with us and in us, always expressing His heart.

Lord, I embrace every word of Your revelation in Scripture, and I choose to take it personally. Yet I know You give specific direction, too, and I know You enjoy my company. Please keep our conversations lively and refreshing—and very unique to us.

It is God's privilege to conceal things and the king's privilege to discover them.

PROVERBS 25:2

God has a strange tendency to hide from those who are seeking Him and relentlessly pursue those who are not. Perhaps He enjoys the playful give-and-take of a spiritual hide-and-seek. Or maybe He simply insists on being found on His own terms. More likely, He is like a suitor who seeks out the object of His affection but won't overplay the intensity of His desire. There must be a genuine response from His beloved, not a forced one. Even so, He conceals Himself—His voice, His specific will, His reasons—in ways that are sometimes frustratingly obscure for us. He gives us a taste of His goodness, opens our ears to hear, and then steps back. He pursues us and then withdraws, provoking an intensity in our desire that drives us deeper into His heart. He conceals things and waits for us to seek them out.

The proverb above specifically mentions kings, but it reveals God's nature as it applies to all of us. He doesn't normally thunder His voice from the heavens; He hides it in secret places and waits to see who is really hungry for it. Who will persist in the search to hear Him? Who really wants to feel His heartbeat and understand His will? Who desires a relationship, rather than a set of principles to live by? These are questions that are answered only in the searching. Those who are content with religious practices will give up early in the quest. Those who can be satisfied only with God will persist until they really encounter Him. That's the way it works.

God conceals deep secrets and then subtly provokes us to discover them. Will we continue in that search without losing heart? At times, that's the very issue for the one who wants to hear Him speak. And the response must always drive us closer.

Lord, I'll never give up my desire for more of You—more closeness, better hearing, a deeper connection. Draw me closer and show me the secrets of Your heart.

Though an army besiege me, my heart will not fear; though war break out against me, even then I will be confident.
PSALM 27:3, NIV

Besieged. That was the word that kept coming to mind as I faced enormous crises on several fronts. At least three situations of major concern for me were turning drastically for the worse. I felt as if the whole world were against me, as if I had vicious enemies who had conspired to strike at my most vulnerable points all at the same time. As I drove down the road—on my way to deal with one of the crises—I cried out to God. "Lord, I feel besieged. I'm overwhelmed. I don't know what You're doing and why these disasters are happening. Please, please help."

Stopped at a traffic light to turn left, I noticed the cars passing in the right lane. The number on the license plate of one was 273. Then another passed with the same number on its license plate: 273. Coincidence? Possibly. But when I see "coincidental" repetition of numbers, I often look up the closest possible biblical reference, usually from the Psalms. As soon as I could, I pulled up the Bible app on my phone and looked up Psalm 27:3: "Though an army besiege me, my heart will not fear; though war break out against me, even then I will be confident."

Immediately I felt confident. The situations wouldn't change for some time—in fact, some of them still look bad—but I had heard from God. I knew He was with me. I could rest in the fact that I wasn't suffering from random events or experiencing God's discipline. He knew I was surrounded by hostile forces, or at least felt that way. And He reminded me, somehow, through divinely orchestrated passing traffic, that I had every reason to be confident in Him.

Lord, there is no limit to the ways You can speak. Help me notice "coincidences" that apply Your general Word to my specific situations. Point me to Your long-ago truths that address my right-now needs.

APRIL 1

I am about to do something new. See, I have already begun! Do you not see it? I will make a pathway through the wilderness.
ISAIAH 43:19

FROM THE HEART OF GOD

"A season of disciplining My people had passed. When the prophet heard these words of promise, he captured My sense of excitement. I love doing new things in life and taking you to new places—physically, spiritually, emotionally, relationally, and in all other ways. I am the God of adventure. My desires for you are not stagnant. In one area or another, I'm always leading you somewhere.

"You know you have a limited point of view. That's why you cry out to Me for guidance. Your perspective is low enough and small enough to see only a short distance. Many possibilities are hidden to you. You need revelation from a higher perspective. And I can give it to you. The shepherd sees and understands the terrain much better than the sheep do. Or to put it in your terms today, your GPS pictures the whole map. Even more than a human view from space, My vision accounts for everything. I see every path, every contingency, every potential obstacle, and every step before you take it. I know how to make a pathway through your wilderness.

"Your wilderness may seem vast and permanent, but I see the end of it. I'm leading you through it. If you search for your own way, you may wander longer than necessary, but if you listen carefully to Me, I will show you the right paths. You *will* get to the destination I have planned for you, and you will find it more satisfying and fulfilling than you thought possible. Don't get impatient; just listen, believe, and follow. I have already begun to do something new."

Lord, open my eyes to see at least the next step, if not the whole path. I grow weary and wonder if I'm stuck where I am. But You put adventure in my heart. Lead me into every place You've prepared for me. As I'm faithful with the old, open my eyes to something new.

APRIL 2

In these final days, he has spoken to us through his Son.
HEBREWS 1:2

The writer of Hebrews talks a lot about God's voice. The fathers and prophets of long ago are not depicted as crafting theology, but as hearing God—and in a way that is relevant to all times. And it is clear throughout the letter of Hebrews that all other encounters with God point to one ultimate expression of His voice: Jesus. The Son is the perfect picture of what the Father is saying.

We need an anchor for interpreting God's voice, a lens through which we choose to see all else. That anchor, that lens, must be Jesus. Hebrews calls Him "the exact representation" of God the Father (1:3, NIV), which means that if we want to know what God is like, we simply need to look at Jesus. That suggests different things to different people, of course. Some imagine a stern expression on His face as they read His words; others imagine Him smiling; and still others see that vapid look so often depicted in the movies. His words come across with radically different implications, depending on which face one sees. But we know how Jesus responded to people who came to Him and to those who opposed Him. We know what He said about prayer, what He promised to His disciples, how He told them to love and serve, what attitudes He wants us to have, and more. The exact representation of God is described to us in the pages of the Gospels. God has spoken in that description.

He still does. The Son still speaks. He is a living Lord who dwells with us and within us, so we have no need to search for His words as if He were ancient history. But His words are in those books, they are still alive and active, and they still speak loudly. If we want to hear God, we can surely hear Him there.

Jesus, speak to me through the pages of Scripture. Let me see the expression of Your face and hear the tone of Your voice as I read. Make those words come alive in my heart.

APRIL 3

We must listen very carefully to the truth we have heard, or we may drift away from it.
HEBREWS 2:1

The book of Hebrews begins with a discussion of what God has said—to prophets, to angels, to the Son, and, by implication, to all of us. It assumes that His voice has been persistent throughout history, that He is an active and vocal participant in human affairs. The author of the letter doesn't appeal to the witness of "it is written," but rather of "God has said." The difference may seem subtle, but it's significant. Written words can be seen as records of times gone by, not as current invitations to respond. Spoken words have more urgency; they can't be treated nearly so passively.

Our frame of mind when we read Scripture is hugely important. If we read its instructions as options—that God's messages from long ago may or may not apply to us now—we will scarcely be motivated to embrace them. But if His voice resonates in the divine Word—aligning our minds and hearts with His and calling us into His purposes—every thought in those pages becomes a powerful influence on us. Hearing His voice in Scripture requires careful listening by hearts that are eager to follow. Some people are eager to obey religiously and legalistically, but that doesn't lead to life. We, however, must be eager to know His thoughts and feelings and synchronize ourselves with them. And we will find many of them in the pages of the Word.

Watch your heart when you read Scripture. Are there "ears to hear" at your core? Are you interested only in getting instructions to follow, or are you eagerly seeking to understand the heart of God? Some attitudes will turn your reading into a religious exercise or a study program, while others will open your spirit to the living voice. It's important not only to listen carefully, but also to be careful about *how* you listen.

Spirit of God, I want to know Your thoughts and to hear Your heartbeat. Breathe the power of Your Word into me.

APRIL 4

Today when you hear his voice, don't harden your hearts.
HEBREWS 4:7

Borrowing a reference from Psalm 95, the writer of Hebrews urges his readers to enter into the place of rest given to us in our salvation. In a time of falling away, when many Jewish believers are facing opposition and losing heart, he appeals to the voice of God. It's calling us into a Promised Land that makes the original land of Canaan pale in comparison. This new Promised Land is the ultimate destination, and we can enter it only by listening to God and following what we hear.

Not only does salvation come through God's spoken invitation, so does everything else He has planned for us. Many believers wander aimlessly through life—or walk somewhat mindlessly through open and closed doors without much discretion. But for those who will take a more active role in listening, God speaks, guides, and directs.

That's when the critical moments of our lives occur. The hinges of God's doors of opportunity swing open when our hearts are soft and we respond to His whispers. But it's possible in those moments to harden our hearts too—to quiet an unsettled conscience or stuff an unwanted word of direction, telling ourselves "it's only my imagination" when really it is the voice of God. When we hear Him, our hearts cannot remain in neutral. Either we respond willingly or we become more hardened. His voice cannot be ignored. By nature, it compels a decision.

Our decisions are sometimes subtle, so subtle that we may not be aware of making them. An impulse to give generously, a conviction to get rid of a habit or start a new one, a prompt to move toward reconciliation—all can be easily ignored. But those who prove themselves sensitive to God's voice—not just someday but the very day it is heard—will hear it far more frequently.

Oh, Father, increase my sensitivity to Your promptings. May I never be content with an unsettled spirit. May Your slightest whispers sound like a megaphone to me. And may I have the wisdom and the courage to respond.

APRIL 5

Hold firmly to the word of life.
PHILIPPIANS 2:16

History books tell us stories and give us background information. Teaching material gives us instruction. Philosophical treatises give us lofty ideas and speculate about the meaning of life. Critiques and analyses give us reasons for the way things happen and try to shape and predict better outcomes. Sacred Scriptures from a variety of traditions throughout the world offer a synthesis of thought, and structure it with meaning. The Bible does all of these things, but none is its ultimate purpose. Scripture inspired by God gives us stories, backgrounds, lofty ideas, analysis, and meaning—but all toward a greater goal: to pierce our souls and fill us with living truth. Even more than that, the Bible opens the doors of our hearts for God Himself to come in.

That's why spending time in God's Word isn't just a learning activity. It's more than steeping ourselves in biblical history and thought. It isn't just an effort to know the truth. It can be reduced to all of these things, but it's meant to be more. When we spend time in the Word, we are supposed to be encountering the voice. We are experiencing a living reality that cuts to the core of our being. We are being enlivened by the same voice that spoke the world into being and that raised Jesus from the dead.

That's why we should never excuse absence from the Word with thoughts like, "I already know that passage," or, "I've got too much to do." That's like saying, "I've eaten that meal before," or, "I'm too busy wasting away to be revitalized." The Word—when we actually connect with it as "the Voice"— nourishes our spirits in a way that nothing else can, even when our minds and feelings have already had their fill. It breathes into us deeply and shapes us to be like God.

Holy Spirit, breathe Your Word into me at every level of my being. Feed me with the life and the power of Your voice.

APRIL 6

A voice from the cloud said, "This is my Son, my Chosen One. Listen to him."
LUKE 9:35

Jesus and three of His disciples went up to a mountaintop to pray. As Jesus was praying, His appearance changed, Moses and Elijah appeared, a cloud descended, and God spoke. He singled out Jesus as the one to listen to. The shining representatives of the law and the prophets withdrew from the scene. The Son stood alone.

Jesus is the clearest, most direct voice of God in Scripture. It isn't that Moses' law or the prophetic declarations weren't also from God, but they weren't the final revelation. They were not the words that would become the foundation of the Kingdom. They were directions, warnings, and glimpses of God's heart, but they weren't full expressions of the divine will. Jesus' words were somehow qualitatively different. They came not through the filter of a sinful human being's mouth or pen, but directly from the mouth of God incarnate. We have to follow the instructions of the voice from heaven: Listen to Him.

"Listen" in Scripture doesn't mean just to comprehend. It means to embrace or to heed. It implies not only that we hear what is said but that we also carry it out. As when an older adult admonishes a child to "listen to your parents," the goal isn't simply to hear. It's to take the message to heart and do something about it. Far too few Christians diligently *listen* to Jesus' words in Scripture. We admire them and honor them, but we often aren't zealous about following them. That has to change.

Never be on the lookout for God's voice of personal guidance if you aren't also on the lookout for God's voice in Jesus. When He says "love your neighbor as yourself," for example, He really means it. God doesn't expect you to become a legalistic Christian Pharisee, but He does expect you to embrace His heart as it is revealed in what Jesus said. In every way we can, we must listen to Him.

Jesus, I want Your words to carry full weight in my life. Please let them sink deep into my heart. Let them become a part of who I am.

APRIL 7

You are the salt of the earth.
MATTHEW 5:13

Like many others in her country, the young Egyptian woman wanted change. She supported the political protests, though not the Muslim influences behind some of them. And she knew the protesters in the square would be in danger. Should she get involved? Should the Christians of her generation voice their support for change? She asked God and heard Him say that the Christians would be the protection for the square.

In fact, that's what happened. When Muslim protesters were injured by the military, Christians gave them first aid. When Muslim protesters took time out for their daily prayers, Christians surrounded them to keep them from being shot at that vulnerable moment. And now, many who witnessed the Christian involvement are asking about God and visiting church. Muslim seekers are coming to Christian prayer services. God's word to this young woman and many of her friends has borne fruit.

God has plenty of creative ideas for using His people as salt of the earth and lights in the world. Many of those ideas go against our natural instincts to "make a statement" for the faith. But if we listen, we'll hear them. We will find God leading us into the world, not as those who criticize and condemn, but as those who bless. He will direct us to places where we can represent His goodness. He will take us out of our comfort zone and into a place of fruitfulness.

Ask God how He wants you to influence the situations around you. Notice impulses to get involved and don't dismiss them easily. Listen for any direction, whether conventional or not, that sounds like a divine idea. Be the salt of the earth wherever He takes you.

Lord, lead me into the middle of what You're doing, even if it's in unexpected places. Give me an ear for Your surprising and unconventional voice. Use me to bear fruit in Your world.

[The Lord said,] "I will pour out my Spirit on your descendants, and my blessing on your children."
ISAIAH 44:3

FROM THE HEART OF GOD

"Many cry out for an outpouring of My Spirit, but few are willing for Me to do that in whatever way I please. Do you understand what it means when you ask this? You are asking for an experience with Me, and then your theology treats experiences as insignificant. You ask Me for something that you are much too willing to push out of your life. I will pour out My Spirit on those who are open to receiving Me however I come. I am glad to respond to those who won't define how I should appear.

"Do you long for this? Many look back to the age of the apostles or look forward to a distant age to come. But why would I—the one who intensely desires to lavish My love and blessings on you and has infinite power with which to do it—make such a limited promise? Why would I be so sparing with My gifts? Why would I confine My plan to a brief moment of history or a distant era after your lifetime? I wouldn't. The offer stands—always. Your hunger and zeal will keep you pressing toward Me in faith, and I am a rewarder of those who diligently seek Me. If you choose—if you are persistent in faith and refuse to become discouraged—then the promise I gave ages ago will continue to be fulfilled to you and to anyone else in your generation who asks. You will experience My Spirit abundantly.

"Ask for this. I told you to seek first My Kingdom, and this is the highest priority in that search. The Kingdom must come *in* you before it comes *through* you. Don't look for the Kingdom around you without looking for it deep inside. I will pour out My Spirit—My perspectives, My thoughts, My power, My heart—within you. Only believe. And then be open to whatever I do."

Lord, pour out Your Spirit in me. Saturate me in the ways of Your Kingdom, the sound of Your voice, the beat of Your heart. Fill me as You promised.

[Philip] had four unmarried daughters who had the gift of prophecy.
ACTS 21:9

It's often argued that the gift of prophecy no longer applies to the church because the Bible is complete. Therefore, the gift isn't needed. But it's pretty clear from Scripture that God spoke many things that weren't included in the Word. They were "extra-biblical"—specific direction that didn't apply to the canon of Scripture and would never be added to it. Hebrew Scripture mentions the existence of groups of prophets—hundreds of them—whose names we will never know and whose prophetic utterances were not intended to be written down. In 1 Corinthians 14, Paul urges all of his readers to seek the gift of prophecy, not so they can add to Scripture, but so they can know God's specific voice in the moment. Here, Acts tells us that Philip had four daughters who spoke prophetically. Their words did not come from Scripture, nor would they ever be added to it. But they were words from God. Apparently, He likes to communicate messages beyond the realm of the written Word.

Throughout the Bible, we see the prophetic gift in and among people who needed specific direction for specific situations. They had Hebrew Scripture and intimately knew God's general will for His people, and they clung to that revelation tightly. But they needed more. They needed to know what to do in a certain set of circumstances. They needed God to speak. And He did—through normal, prophetic people who could hear Him.

Prophetic declarations were not unusual in the New Testament era, and there's no reason they should be today. God still has things to say. The Holy Spirit lives within us and helps us apply the Word specifically to our lives. He gives us relevant interpretations. The gift of hearing God can certainly be abused, and often has been; but that doesn't mean it isn't a legitimate gift. It's always appropriate to listen for God's voice.

Holy Spirit, let me hear You. I seek the gift of hearing and telling about what I've heard. This is Your promise to us; I accept it wholeheartedly.

APRIL 10

Trust in the LORD with all your heart; do not depend on your own understanding.
PROVERBS 3:5

Some people suggest that many Christians spend too much time trying to discern God's "perfect will" rather than simply following the heart and wisdom God gave them. The assumption behind this suggestion is that God doesn't have a single-minded purpose for us but allows us a range of choices. And if a big purchase or a geographic move or a marriage partner seems okay to us, why not feel the freedom to take a major step without hearing from God about it?

There's a kernel of truth in this argument—God does put desires and wisdom into our hearts—but not enough truth to make this the prevailing pattern for our lives. Especially in major decisions, God loves to speak to us and guide us. In fact, Proverbs urges us to forsake our own understanding as we seek God's direction. Why? Because God's will often runs contrary to our own thought processes. He led Abraham, Joseph, Moses, Joshua, the prophets, and many others in absolutely ludicrous directions, from a human point of view. Why, then, would we abandon our attempts to hear His voice and make His guidance a matter within our own minds? That's the solution of a generation that doesn't have the patience or yearning to press in and wait for God to speak, no matter how long it takes or how much deeper into His presence He calls us. That's the advice of an impatient spirit that doesn't believe God speaks very often. And it isn't very biblical.

Scripture is filled with specific guidance from the voice of God, and it presents the possibility of hearing Him not as a rare exception but as a normal lifestyle. We have a tremendous capacity for making wrong decisions, and when we look in the rearview mirror, we often wish we had gotten clearer guidance. If we will be patient and persistent in seeking God's direction, that guidance will come.

✧ ✧ ✧

Lord, I don't want to just do whatever *seems* right. My understanding is limited, but You know what's best. I want to hear You clearly and specifically.

Seek his will in all you do, and he will show you which path to take.
PROVERBS 3:6

When God seems distant, well-meaning Christians take God's guidance out of the context of a relationship with Him and put it in their own heads. "Sanctified reasoning" is all they have for making decisions. But if God wanted us to live entirely by sanctified reasoning, He wouldn't have given us a Bible full of the cloud and fire that guided His people, the fleeces of Gideon, the dreams and visions of priests and prophets and people like us, the signs and wonders of ordained circumstances, or the whispers of the Spirit that filled the early believers with a sense of direction. No, God clearly has multiple means of communicating with His people. Sanctified reasoning may be our only option when He hasn't spoken, but we aren't told to default to that. We are told to seek His will in everything and believe that He will direct our paths.

Living by Christian principles rather than by a personal relationship is lazy spirituality. This approach may reflect a desire to know God's Word, but it doesn't reflect a persistent pursuit of knowing God Himself. It doesn't come from long hours of prayer and fellowship with Him, or of asking Him specific questions and being patient for specific answers, or of a oneness with His Spirit that cultivates sensitivity to His voice. It interrupts the path toward intimacy with Him.

The listening process is long and intense by design. Why? Because in that uncomfortable, awkward, drawn-out silence between our asking and God's answering, He pulls us deeper into a relationship with Him. Living by principles requires knowledge, but no fellowship. Living by God's voice—that's much more personal. And that's God's desire for those who love Him.

Lord, I'm seeking Your will in everything, just as You instructed me to do. I want to live without regrets, which means living with clear vision and purpose. I'll wait as long as I have to in order to hear You. Please reward my persistence with direction and a deeper knowledge of You.

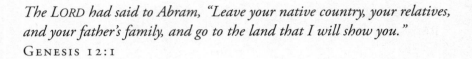

The LORD had said to Abram, "Leave your native country, your relatives, and your father's family, and go to the land that I will show you."
GENESIS 12:1

We long for more details. All we're told is that "the LORD had said to Abram." There's nothing about what the voice sounded like or how Abram heard it. Was it in a dream? Did it thunder from the sky? Was it the subtle impressions of a heart seeking God? We don't know. Why didn't God tell us more so we could listen for His words more specifically?

Perhaps He withheld the specifics because of what we usually do with them. Whenever we see details in Scripture, we tend to make templates out of them. We establish principles and then develop a relationship with the principles rather than with God. Then we fail to see anything outside "the norm" as genuine—even though God is almost always outside the norm. So the Bible describes a variety of modes of hearing God, and sometimes it simply tells us that He spoke and tantalizes us with the lack of specifics. We are left with nothing but our hunger to know what He is saying—which is likely exactly what He intends.

Those of us who want to hear God cannot afford to limit our attention to one mode of expression. Perhaps He will speak through the words of a friend, or draw our attention to specific scriptural passages with a divine magnifying glass, or align circumstances in a way that confirms the inclinations of our Spirit-led hearts. More likely, He will reach out to us in a combination of expressions that complement each other and serve to strengthen our faith in Him. Then we can move forward confidently, knowing that the God who governs every detail of our lives is speaking through them and leading us to the places He will show us as we go.

Lord, I'm listening for You in whatever ways You want to speak. Please draw my attention to the messages You want me to notice. Let me hear Your singular direction from multiple angles so I can believe it's Your will.

APRIL 13

So Abram departed as the LORD had instructed.
GENESIS 12:4

Abram did what God said. If God had looked into his heart ahead of time and seen a spirit of defiance, rebellion, or apathy, He probably would not have spoken. God's word accomplishes what He sends it to do (see Isaiah 55:11), so He must have seen in Abram a willingness to follow the voice before the voice ever spoke. Even so, His words must not have been inescapable. The rest of Scripture tells us that Abram demonstrated faith, which means that he heard God and had a choice of what to do about it. He could have stayed. He could have questioned whether the voice was really from God—or even from any god at all. He could have decided that other deities in his culture wouldn't give such irrational or incomplete directions. He could have heard and shrugged it off.

But he didn't. He heard clearly enough to follow, but not clearly enough to eliminate the need for faith. That's how the listening dynamic always works. If we want to hear God's voice, we need to understand that He will not speak so definitely that no faith is required to follow; yet He will speak definitely enough for faith to have some direction. The key for us is to move forward when we think we've heard Him.

Some of us don't do that. We wait until our hearts are absolutely certain—a waiting that never comes to an end because, underneath it, there is a fear of acting on faith. But God is looking not simply for our ability to hear. He wants a believing response. With very rare exceptions, His voice will give us enough room to talk ourselves out of it. He wants us to willingly follow His lead, not slavishly comply with His dictates. He always leaves room for the heart.

Lord, I don't want to be paralyzed with uncertainty. Help me to follow Your voice even when I have questions. Please direct me as I move forward, and keep me in the middle of Your will.

Encourage each other and build each other up, just as you are already doing.
1 Thessalonians 5:11

The couple came to us, hoping we would hear from God on their behalf. They had listened for His voice too, of course, but members of the body of Christ are to minister to one another. So three of us, none of whom had met this couple before, asked God what He wanted to say to them. On the screen of my imagination, I began to see a sailboat spinning around in a whirlwind. Then God settled the wind and blew it gently. The boat sailed on calm waters in the direction it was pointed.

I described what I was envisioning and said, "I think God wants you to know that in this season of your life, even though you've felt like you're spinning around, He is going to point you in the right direction. When things calm down and you are able to move forward, you'll find Him to be the wind in your sails and the waters to be calm. You will go in the direction He's blowing."

The couple had, in fact, been searching for direction, and they were having a difficult time. Their world did seem to be spinning, and they could not figure out which way to go. On top of that, the husband had been dealing with vertigo for more than a year. God gave me an image that spoke to their situation at multiple levels—one they could easily relate to. He wanted to encourage them that the season of spinning was coming to an end. They needed to know they were not off track. He would lead them well.

Don't be afraid to ask God to give you mental pictures that will encourage others. He knows how to speak *through* His people *to* His people, and He can do so in ways that powerfully address the concerns of their hearts. The Spirit knows our needs, and He inspires us to build each other up.

Holy Spirit, use the screen of my imagination to write Your will, impress Your thoughts, and draw Your pictures. Speak into the hearts of Your people through me.

[The Lord said,] "I have swept away your sins like a cloud. I have scattered your offenses like the morning mist. Oh, return to me, for I have paid the price to set you free."
ISAIAH 44:22

FROM THE HEART OF GOD

"You would be shocked if I told you how many people refuse to seek My voice because they feel disqualified. They assume they are not 'spiritual' enough. The vast majority of people who believe I speak to human beings have enough faith to believe I will speak to someone else. But they doubt that I will speak to them. They don't consider themselves worthy enough, devoted enough, tuned in enough, deep enough, prayerful enough—or anything else 'enough'—to be able to know Me well and sense My presence. They speak of My amazing grace and relentless love . . . for others. But their faith fails to accept My grace and love for them.

"When will you understand? I've taken away everything that interferes with your ability to hear Me and receive My love. I've cleared the path between Myself and you. All that remains is for you to ask, seek, and believe. You are already holy enough, spiritual enough, and worthy enough. You must position yourself to hear, but not by earning the right. The only things you must achieve are rest and trust. I give gifts, not merit badges. There's never a need to doubt My willingness to make Myself known to you.

"Don't keep your distance from Me. I've gone to great lengths to bridge that distance and unite us as one. When you run from Me, hide from Me, or even just grow cold toward Me—whether through your guilt, shame, fear, or apathy—you are wasting a gift I have paid an enormous price to give you. I'm intensely interested in your relationship with Me. That relationship will flourish if you are intensely interested too."

Lord, may I never let my own insecurities come between us. You have invited me freely into Your presence; any hindrances are my own doing. Help me to come to You freely.

> *The angel of the LORD appeared to him in a blazing fire from the middle of a bush.*
> EXODUS 3:2

There are times in Scripture when God speaks so clearly and unmistakably that the hearer has no questions about His will. Those times are rare and generally reserved for major events in salvation history and for people with critical prophetic roles. But in discerning the varying degrees of intensity of God's voice in Scripture—He subtly whispers at some times and announces emphatically at others—we notice an interesting dynamic: The more clearly He speaks, the greater the demand for obedience.

Moses had few options. He tried to dissuade God from His plan, but God left him with no alternatives. There was no mistaking the words, no confusion about the instructions, no wiggle room at all. If Moses had decided not to go back into Egypt, he would not be able to claim that he misunderstood or that the voice wasn't clear. He would have had to willfully rebel.

Many of us say we long to hear God more clearly, but do we really? The clearer the revelation, the greater the expectations that come along with it. We can't hope for a clear direction from God and then consider whether we will follow it. When He speaks emphatically and unmistakably, it's usually because He is putting us in situations in which the temptation to flee will be great. There's a reason Moses saw a burning bush and heard God's voice audibly; his calling was dreadfully dangerous and intimidating. There's a reason Mary was visited by an angel; carrying a child out of wedlock was treacherous business. If we want this degree of hearing, we are also asking for this degree of responsibility. And it isn't as delightful as we might think.

Yearn for God's voice, but make no mistake about what the yearning will lead to: greater hearing and, therefore, much greater responsibility. An exceptional encounter with God demands stepping into an exceptional destiny.

Lord, I know the costs of hearing You are high, but I still want to encounter You. I am willing to face the responsibility of knowing Your will.

APRIL 17

Now bring me someone who can play the harp.
2 KINGS 3:15

The kings of Israel, Judah, and Edom were leading their armies out to battle against Moab when they found themselves in a land without water or provision. The king of Judah—Jehoshaphat, the only one among them who had any faith—suggested that they inquire of the Lord. An officer recommended Elisha as one through whom the Lord would speak. So the kings sent for him and persuaded him to ask God for direction.

How did Elisha respond? He asked for a harpist. He had agreed to listen for God's voice, and he needed some background music to do it.

Most of us can't hear God through the turbulence of our own souls, so we need to be calmed. He rarely chooses to compete with the clutter in and around us; He prefers for us to still the storms so we can listen. The great prophet Elisha, a student of Elijah's and a master at hearing God, apparently calmed his spirit with music. This was no psychological trick or mood booster; it was a means to get on God's wavelength. Somehow, amid the notes of the instrument, he was more likely to receive God's direction.

Many of us play background music during our times with God, but we may not be aware of how greatly it enhances our communication with Him. The connection between God's voice and musical vibrations is stronger than we think. Music may simply seem like an aid to relaxing or getting in the right frame of mind to focus. From God's perspective, it often primes the pump for His truth to flow into our lives—sometimes very specifically and directly. In the midst of any battle or any storm, we can position ourselves to hear God through the sounds that reach our hearts.

Lord, my emotions, anxious thoughts, mental strategies, and momentary moods often block my listening ear, and music removes the blocks. When I surround myself with the language of instruments and rhythm, let it open my spirit to hear the language of Your heart.

APRIL 18

The Spirit of the LORD came upon one of the men standing there. . . .
He said, "Listen, all you people of Judah and Jerusalem! Listen, King
Jehoshaphat! This is what the LORD says . . ."
2 CHRONICLES 20:14-15

Judah was being invaded, and King Jehoshaphat cried out to God. He called for a fast, reminded God of His promises, declared his own helplessness, and appealed to God for defense and direction. Then, as all of the people of Judah assembled, the Spirit came on one of the men standing there. Apparently this was not the leading court prophet or the high priest. He was just a man—a priest with a godly lineage, to be sure, but otherwise just an attendee. And he began shouting, "This is what the LORD says!"

What would happen today if someone in a crowd—even a church crowd—began shouting the Lord's will? We generally look at such things with suspicion or even contempt. But apparently Jehoshaphat had no such reservations. The king staked the future of his people on what this Spirit-inspired man declared in public, even though there was no visible, foolproof evidence that his words were positively from the Spirit. The next day, the king articulated his approach: "Believe in [God's] prophets, and you will succeed" (2 Chronicles 20:20).

The prophecy turned out to be God's voice, and Judah marched out to battle with worshipers leading the way and with the assurance that God would fight on their behalf. The enemy coalition divided and turned on each other, and Judah's army won without fighting.

The point is that Jehoshaphat recognized God's voice and believed it, even though he had no guarantees that the word was legitimate. We have to do the same. We dismiss God's voice far too often, simply because we aren't absolutely certain it is His. But God honors steps of faith—even when we happen to be mistaken about them. He encourages us to hear and respond.

✧ ✧ ✧

Holy Spirit, give me the boldness to take steps of faith. Help me to be discerning without overanalyzing—to trust Your ability to lead more than my ability to miss Your leading.

This foolish plan of God is wiser than the wisest of human plans.
1 Corinthians 1:25

Scripture makes a clear distinction between God's wisdom and our own. In fact, God's wisdom often appears foolish, as Paul points out in referring to the Cross. And human wisdom is often nothing more than foolishness in the eyes of God. Even scriptural wisdom—the maxims in Proverbs that tell us how the world normally works, for example—doesn't apply across the board. What human would have advised Moses to go on an apparent suicide mission into Pharaoh's courts? Or endorsed Hosea's marriage to a prostitute? Or recommended Joshua's circles around Jericho as a viable military strategy? No, God often gives us apparent folly to see if we'll accept it as wisdom, and He often foils the best of our wisdom in order to show Himself wiser.

So when someone advises us to "do what's wise" or to take a live-by-principles approach to life—even when those principles are derived from Scripture—we must insist on the need to hear God's voice, even if He gives us surprising, counterintuitive direction. We may be called fools by many, but the best wisdom comes from hearing God, following Him, and living according to His direction. Eternity will reveal that holy fools were wise and that human reasoning was usually foolish. Only those who are willing to embrace God's absurdities—which aren't absurdities at all, from His perspective—are able to enjoy the adventure of a supernatural life.

Deep down inside, we don't crave a relationship with wisdom or with principles. We crave a relationship with God—a personal, living Being who interacts with us daily. Sometimes His voice will seem wise to us, and sometimes it will seem foolish. If we live by our own standards of wisdom, we will receive the former and reject the latter. But all we really need to know is that we have heard. Then we can follow God anywhere—even if it seems absurd.

Father, I trust Your will—even when I don't understand it, and even when others might think I'm foolish for following it. I embrace Your wisdom, no matter how it appears.

At that time Jesus answered and said, "I thank You, Father, Lord of heaven and earth, that You have hidden these things from the wise and prudent and have revealed them to babes."
MATTHEW 11:25, NKJV

Charles Spurgeon pointed out that in the original language, this verse specifies that Jesus "answered," yet the context doesn't indicate that anyone had spoken to Him. And His answer is addressed to God the Father. Had He just heard from the Father in His Spirit? It would seem so, and it would further imply that Jesus had a continuous conversation with God while the rest of life was going on around Him. If we are to be like Jesus, as Scripture clearly says we should, this has profound implications.

We certainly understand this conversation as it pours forth from our end. When Paul tells his readers to "never stop praying" (1 Thessalonians 5:17), we can instantly relate. Our hearts are frequently conversing with God while we drive, wait in line, have a moment to rest, lie down to go to sleep, and at many other odd moments throughout the day. But hearing from God *unceasingly*? Well, that's another matter. Few of us are confident that we are picking up on His voice that consistently, and most of us have known someone who is much too convinced that he or she is hearing from God reliably. We don't want to be presumptuous.

Yet our great example, the Lord Himself—the one who calls us to be conformed to His image and of whom we are told, "As He is, so are we in this world" (1 John 4:17, NKJV)—heard from God reliably, and apparently in the midst of life and circumstances and conversations with other people. This is our goal: to cut through the clutter of our outward environment and our inward thoughts in order to fix our focus on God's voice. Our prayers should lead us to that depth of fellowship.

✧ ✧ ✧

Father, I want to hear Your voice in the midst of life's circumstances—just like Jesus did. Bring me to that place of listening. Give me the sensitivity to hear and the boldness to believe.

Come close to God, and God will come close to you.
JAMES 4:8

One day early in her mission service in India, as Amy Carmichael sat under a tree studying her Tamil grammar, she had a growing sense of a listener, a presence she could not ignore. She recognized the Lord and listened with Him—to the gaping needs of the country, the blood crying out from the ground, the calling of a people to Himself. Time stood still. The presence was all that mattered.

Of her later work with orphans, young girls serving as temple prostitutes, and boys roaming the streets, Carmichael wrote that she sometimes saw Jesus kneeling alone in prayer for them, and she would go and kneel with Him. She sensed an unspoken communion with Him in His love and compassion for the unlovely, broken, wounded people of the world. No words needed to be exchanged in this spiritual conversation; it was a blending of hearts to accomplish divine purposes. She drew close to God, and He drew close to her.

The voice of God is often far deeper than words, and sometimes even deeper than pictures or images. He has ways of making His heartbeat known to those whose hearts are inclined toward His. The sensitive spirit will not insist on breaking the conversation down into words. Words might interrupt the conversation altogether. Heart-to-heart knowledge goes deeper and must not be cheapened by trying to define it. In God's presence, the best response is simply to embrace the profound work He is doing, to yield our hearts to His impulses, and to accept that His love is indescribable and beyond understanding. In that yielding, He expresses the inexpressible and imparts the infinite flow of His own feelings. And the hearer knows He has spoken, even though He has not spoken a word.

Lord, may I know You to that extent in the depths of my being. Work Your heart into the depths of mine, even when no words can describe what You have placed there. Share Your deepest impulses with me.

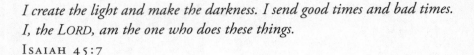

I create the light and make the darkness. I send good times and bad times. I, the LORD, am the one who does these things.

ISAIAH 45:7

FROM THE HEART OF GOD

"You worry about the ups and downs in your life. You long for constant progress and growth, an ability to hear Me without fail, a state of peace and contentment in all situations. Have you not looked at the cycles of this world? I give the plants seasons of hot and cold, wet and dry, barrenness and fruitfulness. They endure dark every night and enjoy light every morning. Every living creature grows fast at some times and hardly at all at others. There are times to plant and to uproot, times to tear down and to build, times to weep and to laugh. As My Word tells you, there's a season for everything under heaven.

"So are there seasons for you. Sometimes My presence is rich and My voice is clear. Sometimes you wonder where I am and why I stopped speaking. I haven't changed, of course, but you grow when things don't come to you easily, so I don't always let them come to you easily. I draw you closer through your hungers—for truth, for revelation, for wholeness, and more. You will seek what you truly love. I let you seek so you will reveal your loves to Me, to those around you, and to yourself. Do not be surprised that your life seems to have ups and downs. It's supposed to.

"When you go through seasons of solitude or darkness or pain, don't be alarmed. Yes, those times can be disorienting, but I haven't left you, nor have I stopped speaking. I am drawing you closer, exposing your truest, deepest desires, and letting you seek until you find. Keep seeking, but don't stress about it. Worry never achieves a thing in My Kingdom. Trust, follow, and come closer. Soon the seasons will change."

Lord, bring me through the darkness and into the light. Let seasons of refreshing come. Give me the grace in the darkness to cling to what You spoke to me in the light.

I was in the Spirit on the Lord's Day, and I heard . . .
REVELATION 1:10, NKJV

What did John mean by being "in the Spirit on the Lord's Day"? Was he talking about a particular day of the week? Probably not—the phrase "the Lord's Day," or "the day of the Lord," is almost always used in Scripture to refer to judgment and is never used to refer to a Sabbath. And what does he mean by being "in the Spirit"? Is he in a vision or a trance leading up to the time that he sees heaven opened? Or is he simply in sync and in deep fellowship with the Spirit? Regardless of these details, we can draw some pretty clear conclusions: John was in some kind of deep devotional or worshipful frame of mind when he heard the Lord speak.

Does that mean we always need to be in some meditative state to hear God's voice? Of course not. After all, there are some rather exceptional aspects to the visions of Revelation; it's not exactly a pattern to follow. It does, however, point to a dynamic that occurs often in Scripture. A well-cultivated, meaningful, worshipful relationship with God creates an environment in which we are much more likely to hear Him speak. He sometimes comes upon the unsuspecting—Moses and Paul are notable examples—but He more often draws near to those who have come near to Him. Just as we recognize the voices of those we spend the most time with, so will we recognize God's voice as we spend ample time with Him. What begins as a whisper grows into a shout if we are in close fellowship with the Holy Spirit.

That ought to motivate us to draw closer in worship, in prayer, and even in just resting in His presence. Time is never better spent than when we spend it in fellowship with God's Spirit. That's where relationships deepen, and deep relationships are where He loves to speak.

Holy Spirit, I offer myself to You—to be "in" You, on any day, and to hear whatever You want to say. Draw me into the closeness of relationship that causes You to want to share Your heart.

To each one the manifestation of the Spirit is given for the common good.
1 CORINTHIANS 12:7, NIV

When we listen for God's voice, our instinct is often to get away and be alone with Him. There's a lot to be said for that instinct; Jesus got away to spend time with the Father often, even when crowds were demanding His attention. Many fathers of the faith found seclusion to be a necessary aspect of following God. There is truly a private side to relating with Him. But in following our instincts, we sometimes forget one crucial detail: God has rigged our relationship with Him to be dependent on other people.

Our faith is a very individual matter, of course, but it isn't *only* that. We can't experience every side of God's nature on our own. For us to be spiritually independent and know God fully on our own, we would have to have every spiritual gift and connect with every aspect of His nature. We couldn't just know Him through our own journey; we'd have to experience *every* journey ourselves. God is too big for that, and too wise. He has made us interdependent for a reason: so that the body of Christ can function as a body. God's nature is to love, and love doesn't isolate. It connects. So He has made our spiritual health and our relationship with Him dependent on connecting with others.

Think about it. No two people reflect God's heart in exactly the same way. No one has had every experience necessary to showcase the fullness of who He is. No one has every spiritual gift. We need each other to experience God's blessings, His expressions, and His voice. Even when we have the gift of encouragement or teaching or wisdom, for example, we can only give them, not hoard them. We still need to receive the fruits of those gifts from other people. And sometimes the best place to hear God's voice is not in privacy, but rather surrounded by people in whom His Spirit lives.

Lord, help me to hear Your voice in others—to see past their flaws and into the place where Your Spirit dwells, and to recognize what You are saying through them.

When [Barnabas] arrived and saw this evidence of God's blessing, he was filled with joy, and he encouraged the believers to stay true to the Lord.
ACTS 11:23

There was a priest from Cyprus named Joseph, but the disciples called him Barnabas—which means "son of encouragement." You don't get a name like that without encouraging someone. In fact, you probably have to encourage people quite often to earn a reputation for it. We see this pattern in Barnabas throughout the New Testament. He bridged the gap between Paul and the other apostles; he journeyed with Paul to teach, encourage, and strengthen churches; and he defended Mark when Paul rejected him as a traveling companion. In Acts 11, Barnabas was sent to investigate the strange happenings in Antioch, when Gentiles began receiving the Holy Spirit through the ministry of people other than the apostles. While some people—particularly those who mistake a spirit of criticism for the gift of discernment—might have quenched or distracted from the Spirit's work in Antioch, Barnabas was able to look beyond traditions and expectations and encourage the believers there. In affirming what God was doing, he expressed God's heart.

We need that. God's default attitude toward His children is to be encouraging, but encouragement is perhaps the voice of God least heard in the church. Some Christians have learned the art of expressing God's heart by cheering their brothers and sisters on, but the gift is far too scarce. Why? Perhaps we haven't tapped into God's heartbeat as we should, or maybe our own false perceptions have portrayed Him as nitpicky and faultfinding, so we act out what we think we see from our Father. But we need to understand that in the absence of outright rebellion, God is kindhearted and encouraging toward us. That's how His voice will sound. We can assume that the oppressive, accusing, critical voice we so often hear is coming from some other place. When God speaks, it will almost always be encouraging.

Father, let me hear Your encouragement often, and give me opportunities to share it with others. Let me be an expression of the goodness, kindness, and gentleness of Your heart.

Jesus answered his thoughts. "Simon," he said to the Pharisee, "I have something to say to you."
LUKE 7:40

Simon the Pharisee observed a sinful woman intruding on his dinner party and tried to make a point about her. He needed a new perspective, so Jesus gave him one—through a story. Jesus could have simply rebuked him or started an argument with this stuck-in-his-ways religious leader; a direct confrontation would have provoked an entertaining and heated discussion. But it would have been a fruitless one. What was the way into Simon's heart? A metaphor. An illustration. A story that the man could relate to.

With this illustration, Jesus made the point that Simon had been looking at this woman through the wrong lenses. As most experts in the law tended to do, Simon's biggest issue in such situations was how to separate between righteousness and sinfulness and, more specifically, how to remain unstained by sin and take a stand against it. Jesus showed him the relationship behind the event. The woman wasn't there to corrupt the guests; she was there to express deep gratitude to the Savior who had cleansed her. Her love for Jesus was entirely appropriate. Simon's attitude toward her wasn't.

This is often how God speaks to us—through stories, metaphors, illustrations, and visual case studies. The circumstances in our lives are frequently much more than just circumstances; they are object lessons in what God wants us to learn. He speaks through them, just as He spoke to Simon. Why? Because this is the language that can pierce the barriers of our hearts. We can understand illustrations. They can give us a radically new perspective—*if* we know to look for a new perspective in them.

Notice what God is saying through the stories around you. Is He making a point? Shedding different light on an old problem? Reshaping your sympathies and expectations? Very often, He is. His voice can be challenging. But if we accept His challenges, they can change our lives.

Jesus, feel free to challenge me like You challenged Simon. I'm open to change. I invite You to reshape my perspective, even if it stretches me out of my comfort zone.

> *[The members of the council] could see that [Peter and John] were*
> *ordinary men with no special training in the Scriptures. They also*
> *recognized them as men who had been with Jesus.*
> ACTS 4:13

Earlier, a crowd in Jerusalem for the feast of Pentecost had marveled that a bunch of provincial Galileans were speaking in diverse languages from across the empire. Now the council of Israel's religious leaders marvels that Peter and John are quoting Scripture and speaking with authority, even though they have no training in Scripture. In both cases, the speakers were filled with the Holy Spirit and speaking God-ordained words. And, in both cases, most of the hearers didn't recognize those words as God's. Why? Because they came from an unexpected source.

That's often how it is with us. God speaks through the people we least expect, perhaps even to see if we can look past the flesh and see the Spirit. If Jesus appeared in front of us and gave us instructions, we would heed them zealously. But what if the Spirit spoke through an outcast on the street or that person at church who never quite seems to fit in? What if the TV preacher who is normally annoying and inauthentic happens to be God's mouthpiece at the moment you're flipping channels and utters a statement meant to travel directly from God's heart to yours? We easily dismiss such moments, yet God uses them to find out if we can see the Spirit through unappealing packaging. Many religious leaders couldn't see Jesus as the Messiah for exactly that reason: He didn't look "Messiah-ish." But He was. God loves to defy expectations.

In listening for God's voice, expect the unexpected. Listen for His Spirit to speak profound guidance, not only through gifted spiritual leaders but through uneducated, common mouths, "unaware prophets," and "unlikely angels." His voice will be surprising—not only in what He says but in how He says it.

Lord, help me to recognize You in the least likely places. When You speak through someone who doesn't seem spiritual or who rubs me the wrong way, help me to look past the surface and into Your Spirit.

Not a single one of all the good promises the LORD had given to the family of Israel was left unfulfilled; everything he had spoken came true.
JOSHUA 21:45

I thought I had blown it. I had clung to God's promise for years, and then I made a momentary decision that could have forfeited everything. Human decisions can't thwart the overall purpose of God, but can they thwart our participation in it? After all, Esau lost his birthright and his blessing, Moses never made it to the Promised Land, and Saul caused God to regret making him king. Had I forfeited my promise too?

I went to church that night with a heavy heart and lots of questions. "Lord, are You ever going to do what You said You're going to do? I don't know if I can hang on any longer. I just need to know. Tell me whether to keep believing or not. I need to know if You're going to do this." I spent two hours pleading with God to speak to me.

It was a night of prophetic ministry, so I asked a team to listen to God for me. They prayed and asked the Spirit to speak. Then one of them said, "I see you hanging on the edge of a cliff and wondering if you can hang on any longer. God wants you to know He's going to do what He said He's going to do. He is so proud of you for hanging on to faith in all these hard places. You don't have to worry that He's not going to do it. He's not going to let you down. It's going to happen."

I was bawling. I can't remember ever needing God's word more desperately, or hearing it so clearly. He not only affirmed His promise, He assured me I hadn't blown it. God does not withdraw His promises, even when we think we've missed them. He encourages us to the end.

Lord, I can agree with Hudson Taylor: "There is a living God. . . . He means what He says and will do all He has promised." Give me faith to believe You will fulfill everything You've ever spoken to me.

[The Lord said,] "I have sworn by my own name; I have spoken the truth, and I will never go back on my word."
ISAIAH 45:23

FROM THE HEART OF GOD

"I have declared again and again how unfailing My words are. I have assured you that I cannot lie. I have sworn not only that all will acknowledge Me, as My words through Isaiah proclaim, but that all My other promises are reliable too. I have given assurances that I'm not fickle, that My words do not shift like the windblown sand, and that I am not a man that I could play fast and loose with the truth. There is nothing more I can say to convince you that I'm faithful and true. Yet many people, sometimes including you, wonder if I will do what I said.

"Does this bother Me? No, not really. I understand your insecurities. I know that when you question whether I've spoken truly, you're really questioning whether you've heard Me clearly. I know that when you hear My promises, you hear them through the experience of having others break their promises to you in the past. I could get angry with you for questioning My faithfulness, but the truth is that you've never experienced such faithfulness from anyone else. It's foreign to you, and it takes time to get used to it. I understand.

"Your questions don't bother Me, but you will eventually need to simply believe. It does no good to ask Me to speak if you're going to question everything I say as if it might not be true. Yes, you can ask for confirmation to make sure you've heard well. But no, you should never question whether what you heard is accurate. It is. It's unshakable. The things I have spoken over your life will certainly come to pass. I have sworn by My own name. No promise could be more solemn, more sacred . . . and more true."

Lord, You are the God of all truth. Your words aren't opinions, suggestions, or speculations. They are fact. Rock-solid certainties. Give me the faith to anchor myself to them and never be moved.

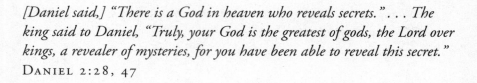

[Daniel said,] "There is a God in heaven who reveals secrets." . . . The king said to Daniel, "Truly, your God is the greatest of gods, the Lord over kings, a revealer of mysteries, for you have been able to reveal this secret."
DANIEL 2:28, 47

King Nebuchadnezzar was in a crisis because of a dream, and Daniel's life—along with the lives of quite a few other sages—was on the line. But Daniel knew that his God was greater than the pressure of the situation, greater than the mystery of the king's dream, and greater than the destiny of nations. The question wasn't whether God knew the secret; the question was whether He would share it with Daniel. Daniel and his friends boldly asked God to reveal it, and God answered.

We often seek God's will on our own behalf, asking for direction and guidance for our personal lives. And while God certainly enjoys guiding and directing us, He often has a much bigger picture in mind. He is looking for people who will listen to Him for the solutions to society's problems. Just as He cared about revealing His will to a pagan king in Babylon, He cares about revealing His will to governments, justice systems, school systems, medical researchers, technological engineers, social scientists, artists and entertainers, media outlets, agricultural planners, and more. When human need cries out for God's response, He doesn't withhold it out of some sense of judgment. He takes the opportunity to show His glory. He answers the hunger of human hearts and accepts invitations into human crises.

The problem is that there are few people like Daniel who are bold enough to believe that God might want to benefit "secular" society—or even a pagan one. But God did just that in Babylon, and it brought glory to His name and benefited His people. He will do so again—if His Daniels will appeal to the revealer of mysteries for His secrets.

❖ ❖ ❖

Lord, You are the revealer of mysteries, and You want Your people to be blessed. Show me Your secrets. Give me Your solutions to the problems around me. Bring glory to Your name by demonstrating Your goodness to those who do not yet know You.

MAY 1

Dear friends, do not believe everyone who claims to speak by the Spirit. You must test them to see if the spirit they have comes from God. For there are many false prophets in the world.

1 JOHN 4:1

When we turn on a radio, we have to tell the radio which signal to pick up. There are lots of signals out there, but we can only tune in to one at a time. That means we have to reject the ones we don't want and focus specifically on the one we do want. We have to be discriminating.

Radio signals may be a matter of preference, but God's voice isn't. There are messages that actually come from Him and many others that don't, and we can't afford to get them mixed up. The hearing ear is in constant need of tuning in spiritually—of finding the right signals and rejecting all the others. Not every message we hear is from God, regardless of what its source claims. Preachers don't always preach the truth, prophetic voices aren't always tapped in to God's Spirit, and even the Bible itself can be read from the wrong point of view or interpreted through false perceptions and motives. Sometimes the voice is clearly not from God, but other times the errors are more subtle. It's possible for the words to be true but to come from the wrong spirit. We have to become well acquainted with spiritual nuances.

That doesn't mean we need to be so "discerning" that we rule out every-thing that might possibly be God's voice. Nor does it mean everything that sounds unusual to us must not be from Him. In fact, we can expect His words to stretch our understanding. He specializes in that. But if we test the spirits—ask for confirmation from God and measure it against what we know to be true from Scripture—He will lead us into truth. His ability to guard us from error is greater than our ability to fall into it.

Lord, give me a discerning spirit and help me to recognize false voices. I trust Your ability to lead me. I want to embrace every word that comes from You.

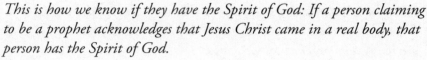

MAY 2

This is how we know if they have the Spirit of God: If a person claiming to be a prophet acknowledges that Jesus Christ came in a real body, that person has the Spirit of God.

1 JOHN 4:2

In the apostle John's day, the most dangerous falsehoods about Jesus centered on whether He was actually human or not. Some teachers claimed He was a spirit who only seemed to have a body; that He had not actually come in the flesh. Therefore, He did not live a human life or die a human death. Whoever suggests such a thing, said John, is speaking from an anti-Christ spirit.

This was not the only heresy to infect the church throughout its history. Many other anti-Christ claims have been taught and practiced. The most serious ones erode our faith's essential foundations: the nature of Jesus (both God and man); the nature of salvation (by grace through faith); or the nature of Scripture (fully reliable and inspired by God). Any voice that undermines one of these important tenets is not from God because it contradicts eternal truth that God has already revealed, and God cannot contradict Himself. He can give different people different instructions, of course—He adapts His methods for specific situations—but He does not change His mind about the nature of His person or His plan. His character and purposes are constant.

That's a key for discerning God's voice. His words will always honor His own character, the divinity of Jesus, the nature of salvation, and the integrity of His written Word. He will not speak blatant contradictions to us, nor will He aim at confusing us. We may encounter mysteries and have to sort them out over time, but we won't hear glaring inconsistencies. God's words are always true to who He is.

Lord, I trust in Your words as an extension of Your character and Your purposes. My spirit joins with Yours to hear and to honor Your truth. Let everything I hear, do, say, and think be a reflection of Your Son and His Kingdom.

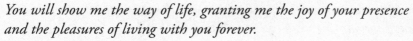

*You will show me the way of life, granting me the joy of your presence
and the pleasures of living with you forever.*
PSALM 16:11

Maybe you think God is mainly interested in getting you to follow instructions.
Perhaps you expect Him to focus on your productivity. Or maybe you are more
aware of His inward emphasis—on conforming you to the image of His Son.
After all, God is very clear in His Word about our obedience and fruitfulness,
and even more so about our character. No one can argue that these are not biblical themes. But according to this verse, there's an even higher destination for us:
pleasure.

If that's hard to believe, it's because of our own sense of unworthiness on top
of two thousand years of church teaching about austerity and deprivation and
mortifying the flesh. In most Christian circles, *pleasure* is a bad word. But what
do we think obedience and fruitfulness and conformity to Christ are all about?
Do we believe that God's ultimate goal for us is changed behavior or a reshaped
character? Those are simply pathways to something much greater. They lead to
joy in our relationship with God, fulfillment in everything He created us to be,
satisfaction in our deepest desires, and glory—that is, God's relentless goodness.
His goal for us, as one translation puts it, is "pleasures evermore." God is leading
us toward having a really good time.

That's why He shows each of us "the way of life," why He speaks to us and
gives us direction. He isn't opposed to our pleasure; He's actually helping us
toward the most thorough and lasting way to experience it. What often seems
like stern resistance to our desires is really God's way of redirecting us into more
fulfilling ones. Every time His words seem difficult, they are offering an acceler-
ated pathway into His joy instead. God really is on our side!

Lord, I long for the eternal pleasures at Your right hand. I know many of them
begin now, and I want to experience them fully. Please honor my attentiveness
to Your words by giving me strong tastes of those pleasures in this age.

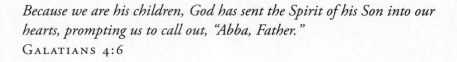
Because we are his children, God has sent the Spirit of his Son into our
hearts, prompting us to call out, "Abba, Father."
GALATIANS 4:6

The Spirit of God puts a child's cry within us. We call out, "*Abba*," an intimately familiar term for "father"—like *Daddy*—in order to talk to our heavenly Father. We are not slaves, as Romans 8:15 assures us, but adopted and favored children in the divine family. We can assume familiarity with God. We can speak to Him on intimate terms. We can come boldly before His throne without cowering before His majesty.

If God's Spirit prompts us to speak to God in familiar, intimate language, it follows that He would speak to us in very familiar terms as well. God calls us with terms of endearment, appeals to the secrets of our hearts, and invites us to sit in His lap and experience His affection. How could He not? If He puts the cry for *Abba* within us, He will never rebuke the intimacy that follows. He allows us to speak personally to Him, and He speaks personally to us with tenderness and warmth. However closely He relates to Jesus, He relates to the Spirit of Jesus within us.

Don't let people formalize your relationship with God by warning you about becoming "too familiar" or "too intimate." They will clothe such warnings with an appeal for "awe" and "respect"—appropriate attitudes, to be sure, but not when they undermine our childlike relationship with our heavenly Father. God, who knows how to open our hearts with just the right words, will often make His words deeply personal. They might sound frivolous to someone else, but they certainly don't to us because we know what they mean. He is speaking to a deep place in our hearts, like a father's play talk can carry enormous weight with a child. In the divine family, that's always appropriate.

❖ ❖ ❖

Abba, my Father, You know that I respect You and bow before You. But I also need to feel Your arms around me and hear Your personal words. Speak warmly, playfully, affectionately. I need my Abba's love.

O Lord, hear their threats, and give us, your servants, great boldness in preaching your word. Stretch out your hand with healing power; may miraculous signs and wonders be done through the name of your holy servant Jesus.

ACTS 4:29-30

A young Christian woman from the Middle East described how persecution was increasing in her region and Christians were becoming uncertain about their future. Many wondered whether they could remain in the country and feared that their churches would be closed or severely restricted. Yet the young woman describing these changes also emphasized the other side of the story. Christians were also experiencing more encounters with God—increased dreams and visions, clearer words of direction, and new strategies for sharing Christ in a hostile culture. And though many were focused on the uncertainty of the future, this woman and many others were focused on a nascent move of God. The Holy Spirit was not going into hiding. His work was increasingly visible.

These conflicting trends—greater persecution along with a greater move of God—have happened often in church history. In the spiritual realm, persecution (a direct attack) and counterfeits (indirect attacks) almost always occur together with the Spirit's work. Sometimes they follow the Spirit's work in an attempt to undo it, and sometimes they may seem to strike first—perhaps preemptively with the awareness that God is about to move. From our human perspective, we may not be able to sense the order or the reasons. Nevertheless, when persecution and deception are abundant, so are the works of the Holy Spirit.

God seems to speak most clearly and give His servants greater boldness in times of distress. Increased access to His Spirit's blessings seems to accompany increased oppression and harassment. Perhaps that's because the intensity of our prayers increases with the intensity of our circumstances, or perhaps it's simply because God gives us everything we need to follow Him well, and we need more when we're under duress. Regardless, He sees our hardships and meets us in the middle of them. He comforts and calms us with the sound of His voice.

Lord, I long for the boldness and power of the early Christians. If I face radical opposition, bless me with radical fruitfulness.

MAY 6

The people will declare, "The LORD is the source of all my righteousness and strength." And all who were angry with him will come to him and be ashamed.

ISAIAH 45:24

FROM THE HEART OF GOD

"I know when you've been angry with Me, even when you are afraid to admit it. I understand that your perceptions are limited and that your circumstances seem to speak louder than I do at times. But you have to understand that no matter what distorted lenses you're looking through, I am always good. I have your best interests in mind, even when you think I'm against you.

"You have help in achieving your distorted perceptions. There's a liar who slanders Me every chance he gets. He spreads lies in your mind and among all the people in the world. Whenever you hear people arguing against My existence or accusing Me of being either unloving or impotent because of all the suffering in the world, you can know they have been influenced by the father of lies, whose mudslinging never ceases. They may have seen part of the picture, but have drawn overarching conclusions, never realizing how skewed their reasoning is. Your challenge in this world is to look past those lies and trust in what is true. Your first parents failed at this, and the darkness ever since has only made things harder. But cling to My goodness, no matter what you see or what arguments you hear.

"Remember, I value your trust much more than I value your understanding. Your understanding can never grasp the mysteries of My ways, but your trust can. You will one day declare with joy and certainty that I am the source of your righteousness and strength. So cling in the darkness now to what you will one day see in the light."

Lord, I confess there have been times when I've been very angry with You. I haven't understood what You were doing—why things You promised were taking so long, or why adversity struck when I was trusting You for good. Thank You for welcoming honesty, but please forgive me for speaking in ignorance. I trust You as my only source of righteousness and strength.

Anyone who hears and doesn't obey is like a person who builds a house without a foundation.
LUKE 6:49

When we say we want to hear God's voice, we need to understand that we aren't just expressing curiosity. We're making somewhat of a commitment. Theoretically, it's possible to ask for God's wisdom or direction and then take it as one of our many options to choose from. But practically, can we really approach God that way? If we hear and then choose not to follow, we have put ourselves in an awful predicament. At best, we've neglected the word of the living God. More likely, we've intentionally and blatantly rebelled. Either way, whether purposely or not, we've set our hearts against His.

We don't want to find ourselves in that position. That's probably why casual seekers often come up dry—and why God rarely rewards them with clear direction. The privilege of hearing Him is wonderful, but the responsibility is sobering. To hear is to enter into a compelling dilemma: either to embrace the wisdom of the all-wise God, or to turn our backs on Him and go our own way. Before we've heard Him on a given issue, we can claim we're doing our best or whatever seems right to us. Afterward, we have only one clear, sensible response. And it may not be easy.

Approach the listening process with a commitment to do whatever God says. He doesn't want us to hear His voice as an option to consider. He wants us to hear Him as the absolute truth. When we come with a commitment to believe what He says, He is much more eager to speak.

Father, my heart is Yours. Whatever You say, no matter how unexpected or challenging it is, I'll do it. My desire is to accept Your will, even before I know what it is. Please share it with me clearly.

MAY 8

When you ask, you must believe and not doubt, because the one who doubts is like a wave of the sea, blown and tossed by the wind.
JAMES 1:6, NIV

Some people ask for God's wisdom without any assurance that they might receive it. The result? They probably won't. That's because any genuine prayer must be accompanied by faith. Otherwise, we'll second-guess the answer until it has hardly any power left.

This pattern is the unfortunate testimony of many. We ask; we hear; then we only think we heard; then we're pretty sure it was just our own conscience/thoughts/desires; then we're more confused on the matter than ever. And while it's always important to be discerning, it's never desirable to be overly analytical. Our minds and hearts can talk our spirits out of just about anything. The result is that we may hear God often but feel as if we rarely hear from Him. We're blown and tossed by the winds and waves of doubt.

God is much more intentional about communicating with us than that, and much more willing to be heard than we think He is. He speaks through the deep fountain of His Spirit whom He has placed within us, through the fellowship of believers, through signs and messages and desires, and through many other means. And of course, He speaks above all through the counsel of His Word. What more do we want? A voice that thunders from heaven? He has been known to do that, too, though rarely. He prefers to converse with us in a deeply relational way, and surely laments that while we have an enormous capacity for having a relationship with Him, we constantly question that relationship. He urges us to come, to ask, and to *believe*.

When we ask to hear His voice, we must believe and not doubt. That's His instruction to us, not our own imaginings. His Word never urges us to over-analyze; it practically pleads with us to believe. Those who ask with assurance are blessed with hearing ears.

Lord, I've asked to hear Your voice; now I'm choosing to believe. I'll trust that You will keep me from error, and I'll accept what I believe You're saying. Guide me into truth.

MAY 9

The LORD sent Nathan the prophet to tell David this story . . .
2 SAMUEL 12:1

David had sinned terribly and lived in denial for months. Perhaps in his mind he thought the scandal was over, but deep in his heart, he had to have known it wasn't. But we know how our hearts can harden, sealing over past secrets and keeping them buried for years. David had buried his secret and refused to own up to its implications. No confession, no plea for forgiveness, no remorse. If the sin were ever to be dealt with, God would have to open the conversation.

So God sent the prophet Nathan to tell David a story—a story about sheep and an unjust owner. This may seem like a random but effective parable until we realize David's background. He had been a shepherd in his early years. He would naturally side with the unprotected lambs. God knew that this story would resonate in David's heart. If anything would move him out of his denial, a jolting parable about a stolen lamb ought to do it.

That's often how God speaks to us. He uses the language of our hearts. He tends not to give bankers metaphors about agriculture, or to give dancers allegories about chemical reactions. Effective communicators know how to reach the heart, and God is the ultimate communicator. He shows us parables that grow out of our interests and resonate with our desires. He encourages us with stories and blessings we can relate to. And when He needs to correct or confront us, He breaks through our barriers by provoking our sympathies. He stirred up David with a story of injustice, and the "man after God's own heart" came to his senses. When we need our eyes opened to reality, God can arrange for the circumstances of our lives and the stories we hear to hit home.

Father, You know how to speak my language. You know what's important to me and where my sympathies lie. Use my heart to Your advantage. Let Your voice pierce all my defenses and change me.

MAY 10

God is not a man, so he does not lie. He is not human, so he does not change his mind. Has he ever spoken and failed to act? Has he ever promised and not carried it through?

NUMBERS 23:19

It begins with a dream in your heart, which then turns into a prayer. In conversation with God, the prayer may turn into a promise, which then becomes a hope and a battle of faith. Somewhere in that battle—filled with delays, twists, turns, and endurance—questions come to mind. Did He really say what I think He said? Do His promises in Scripture come with fine print? Did I blow it by sinning or by not having enough faith? Am I to move forward in faith or wait patiently in faith? Why is it taking so long? Did God get tired of waiting on me and change His mind?

When Balaam, the son of Beor, was summoned by the king of Moab to curse God's chosen people, he had enough sense to ask God for His direction first. God's words were instructive: He is not a human being, so He isn't subject to the whims and fickleness of the human experience. He wouldn't have called Israel if He had simply planned to abandon them or let them be cursed. He sees the end of a matter even from the beginning, so He doesn't speak promises He will later have to renege on. He doesn't lead us into wildernesses that end only in futility and frustration. He follows through on what He has said.

It's true that God "changed" His mind in conversations with Abraham and Moses, but those were both instances of choosing mercy instead of impending judgment, and we get the sense that He had planned to honor their intercession all along. But He doesn't withdraw His promises unless we've shown our hearts to be full of open rebellion. He compensates for our mistakes and sees His word to completion. He will do exactly as He has said.

Lord, my wilderness is long and painful. I've nearly lost faith. But You have never given Your word and then defaulted on it. I choose to trust Your goodness and believe Your promise.

[Agabus] came over, took Paul's belt, and bound his own feet and hands with it. Then he said, "The Holy Spirit declares, 'So shall the owner of this belt be bound by the Jewish leaders in Jerusalem and turned over to the Gentiles.'"

ACTS 21:11

Agabus was known for having a prophetic gift, and he had accurately predicted a famine. Now he warns Paul with a visual illustration and declares that if Paul goes to Jerusalem, he will be arrested.

Some see a couple of minor inaccuracies in this prophetic word—didn't the Romans, not the Jewish leaders, bind Paul, and didn't they rescue him rather than receive him from the mob?—while others argue that the story and Paul's own comments fully support Agabus's accuracy. Regardless of the details, the gist of the prophecy is true. And startlingly, Paul doesn't heed the warning.

Careful readers may point out that Agabus didn't give Paul instructions from the Holy Spirit not to go to Jerusalem. It was the friends hearing this prophecy who pleaded with him to change his plans. Still, Paul accepted the truth of the prophecy and was not deterred. In fact, he seemed to know already that this trip to Jerusalem would come at a heavy price. Even so, it fit with God's will.

If Paul wasn't going to heed the warning, why did the Spirit inspire Agabus to say these words? Perhaps because Paul and his friends would later need the memory to reassure them, after Paul's arrest, that it was foreseen and accepted. Or maybe Paul was being given a genuine choice. Whatever the reason, it's clear that a prediction from God is not necessarily a prescription from Him—that He sometimes gives us information without telling us the application. When that happens, we keep asking, keep seeking, keep pressing ahead with whatever wisdom and insight we have. We can do so with the confidence that God has seen our circumstances and is sovereign over them.

Holy Spirit, when You give me a glimpse of Your will, help me to know how to apply it. When I have only partial guidance from You, give me wisdom for the details. And give me the strength to face whatever is in my path.

MAY 12

[Jesus said,] "Those the Father has given me will come to me, and I will never reject them."
JOHN 6:37

John Bunyan was tormented by guilt. At times, he was comforted by the fact that the apostle Peter was forgiven for denying Christ. At other times, he was distraught over the fact that Esau was rejected even after turning back to the Lord and seeking Him. Was Bunyan a Peter or an Esau? A new creation or a blasphemous sinner? The torment continued until the assurance of Jesus' words sank into his heart: *He will never reject those who come to Him.*

Before his conversion, Bunyan understood the words of God simply as words. Scripture was a book of theological information. But after his conversion, the Bible came alive to him. God's voice was in it. He read Scripture with renewed zeal, its words now being the keys to the Kingdom, shining the truth and love of God on him with wonderful clarity. The Bible had not changed, but his relationship with the Author certainly had. What had once been a stale and condemning religious book became a source of life and fullness.

Many people read the Bible without ever hearing God's voice in it. Others read it with deep conviction that they are receiving the words of God straight from His mouth. What's the difference? Relationship. When we know the Father, we begin to see Him clearly in His Word as well as in our circumstances, the direction of our lives, and the people around us. What once appeared confusing and lifeless now overflows with goodness and blessing. God's voice becomes clear to those who know Him, and the better we get to know Him, the stronger our sense of it grows. When we look at the Bible, we may not grasp who Jesus is. But when we look at Jesus, we grasp everything His Word speaks to us.

Jesus, give me the gift of seeing Your Word with new eyes, as if I'm reading it for the first time every day. Make my vision come alive with new insights every time I gaze into the truth of Your Word.

"We have fasted before you!" [the people of Israel] say. "Why aren't you impressed? We have been very hard on ourselves, and you don't even notice it!"
ISAIAH 58:3

FROM THE HEART OF GOD

"Hearing My voice is not a religious activity, nor is it the result of religious maneuvers and posturing. There are times when I call you to fast, to pray, to discipline yourselves in many ways—but never in order to extract favors from Me. I'm never impressed with your religious activities, only with your heart when you are deeply in love with Me and motivated by that love. If you're looking for a response from Me, there's no need to resort to artificial spiritual gymnastics. Soften your heart and relate to Me at a deeply personal, intensely honest and intimate level.

"You need to understand that I did not create you for servitude. Yes, I want you to serve Me, but I want so much more. I have legions upon legions of angels who serve Me, and they do it far more consistently and automatically than you do. What I want from you is a heart-to-heart connection that cannot be had with any other creature. I want to lower Myself and raise you up to the point where we can have mutual, meaningful interaction. You'll notice in My Word that I have come down further than deity would be expected to come down, and I have exalted you higher than any human would expect to be exalted. Why? Because this is how our hearts can meet. This is where you can hear and respond to what I say, and—as difficult as it is for you to imagine—where I can hear and respond to what you say. I want intimate partners, not groveling slaves.

"Know who you are. Know why I made you and redeemed you. And know what kind of relationship I desire. When you discover that, My words will echo deep in your spirit because it is one with Mine."

Father, lover of my soul, forgive me for behaving like an attention-seeking child. But my desire really is to relate to You truly, deeply, and closely. Let me. Open my heart to receive all of Yours.

Go down to the potter's house, and there I will give you my message.
JEREMIAH 18:2, NIV

God had a word for Jeremiah, but He wouldn't simply tell it to him. He wanted to show it to him. It was a visual message, an illustration from everyday life, a parable that would play out before his eyes. He told Jeremiah to go to the potter's house and observe.

As Jeremiah watched the potter reshape a marred pot into another form, he heard the message clearly. God, the master potter, has every right to reshape His people. He can warn nations of judgment and then turn away from judgment if they repent. Or He can intend good for a people and then reconsider if they turn from Him. All of this was demonstrated by a potter's hand, not by a sermon or an explanation by the Spirit's voice. Why did God choose to communicate this way? Because a picture is worth a thousand words. Or because pictures often can represent truth better than words can. Or because the image of a potter reshaping clay would stick in the psyche of God's people much longer than a lecture would. All of these reasons are true because God knows how to illustrate His point.

God knows how to illustrate His points in our lives too, but we need to learn how to "go down to the potter's house" to get them. In other words, we need to keep our eyes and ears open for the pictures He wants to show us. When we ask God to teach us through the visual illustrations of our lives, He answers. He gives us insights and understanding that we would not have perceived if we were simply listening for words. In the midst of mundane routines, we suddenly grasp spiritual truths by noticing the world around us and spiritually tuning in to what God is saying through it. And everyday life begins to come alive with His voice.

Holy Spirit, speak to me in the events of this day. Teach me something new. Show me a parable of Your Kingdom as I open my eyes and ears to Your illustrations.

Samuel was sleeping in the Tabernacle near the Ark of God. Suddenly the LORD called out, "Samuel!"
1 SAMUEL 3:3-4

God literally woke Samuel up by speaking to him in the middle of the night. But Samuel thought Eli the priest was calling him. It took three attempts for Eli to realize what was happening and advise Samuel to respond to the voice that was calling him. Samuel did, and the course of Israel's history was changed.

But this story is about more than Samuel and Eli and Israel before its monarchy. It's also a picture of how God's voice comes to us. While we're "sleeping" in darkness, He speaks. Like Samuel, we may not at first recognize the voice as His, but when we begin to respond, we discover that He has much to say to us. We may not at first realize the implications of God's desire to communicate with us, but if we engage in the conversation, we find that the courses of our lives—and perhaps of history—are changed forever.

Samuel was near the Ark—in the place that represented God's presence among His people—but he was asleep. Most of us spend a good portion of our lives asleep in God's presence. We know God is with us, but we hardly expect a tangible encounter with Him. The encounter will come, and whether it's tangible or not, it will startle us from our spiritual lethargy. Hearing His voice calls us out of our current posture and into an adventure with Him that can change the world around us. His voice makes us come alive.

Let God's voice awaken you. Just as Jesus raised the dead with the sound of His voice, God will lift you out of whatever darkness surrounds you. Respond as Samuel did—"Speak, LORD, your servant is listening" (1 Samuel 3:9)—and His words will begin to flow. Your heart will come alive, more than ever before, to the sound of His voice.

Speak, Lord. I'm listening. I want to hear whatever You have to say. Call me out of my slumber. Use me as a world changer. Make my heart come alive by the power of Your words.

MAY 16

You can identify [false prophets] by their fruit.
MATTHEW 7:16

We hear lots of voices. We suspect God's voice is in the mix somewhere, but we have a hard time distinguishing the others. Are we hearing our own thoughts? The deceptions of the enemy? The echoes of people who have tried to be our conscience in the past? The voices of temptation? How can we discern God's voice in the cacophony of alternate messages?

Jesus told His followers they would recognize false prophets by their fruit. The same advice applies to false voices of any kind. Clearly, if the messages we hear are enticing us to sin, we know they aren't from God. That's easy enough. But what about the seemingly morally neutral ones? What about when we are asking for direction and every option might be allowed but not necessarily advisable? What about the voices that speak to our identity or our behavior, and that may sound like Scripture, but also may be distortions of it? One key to discernment is to look at the fruit.

Consider the fruit of the Kingdom: goodness, peace, and joy in the Holy Spirit (Romans 14:17); the fruit of the Spirit: love, joy, peace, patience, kindness, goodness, faithfulness, gentleness, and self-control (Galatians 5:22-23); and the fruit of a redeemed mind: thoughts about whatever is true, honorable, right, pure, lovely, and admirable (Philippians 4:8). If the voice leads you toward spiritual fruitfulness, it's probably God speaking. If it doesn't—if it leads to fear, guilt, doubt, anxiety, exasperation, and the sorts of attitudes that don't fit the Kingdom—it isn't God, it's a voice from another source, a counterfeit bearing bad fruit. Knowing the difference will sharpen our hearing and keep our hearts and minds at peace.

Lord, help me recognize Your words by the environment they create within me. You may speak convicting, sobering words, but I know You will never oppress me with guilt, shame, fear, anxiety, or depression. Fill me with joy and peace, lift me up and inspire me, and give me rest with the sound of Your voice.

Take delight in the LORD, and he will give you your heart's desires.
PSALM 37:4

Every human being on the planet has desires, and everyone longs for them to be fulfilled. In fact, this is what motivates most people. We are by nature desire driven. Many Christians want to mature beyond this dynamic and become truth-driven beings, and that's a valid goal. But even when we learn truth and base our lives on it, we still have desires. God has wired us to work that way. The real goal of our faith is not to get rid of desires, but to align our desires with God's purposes.

Whether Psalm 37:4 means God will fulfill our desires or plant the right desires within us may be a familiar discussion, but the outcome is the same: When we delight ourselves in Him, there's an alignment between our hearts' desires and the outcomes in our lives. That's what we want—an end to the frustrating gap between desire and fulfillment, that never-ending sense that whatever we really want isn't going to work out. That gap has led many to view God as someone who gives us only what we need, not what we want—sort of like that great-aunt or -uncle who skips over all the fun items on your Christmas list and gives you socks because that's what you really need. But is that really God's heart?

No, God works through our desires. We have to use discernment, but chances are the long-lasting desires that are consistent with God's purposes are from Him. He wants us to dream with Him, so He speaks through our dreams and desires. That does *not* mean that all our desires reflect His voice. We may have plenty of passions that are misplaced or misinterpreted. But the core of our desires is most likely rooted in a godly impulse, and when the dream takes the right shape and persists over time, it will direct us toward God's purposes.

Notice what you dream about. God's voice is in it somewhere.

Lord, You are the fulfiller of my heart, not the denier of it. Shape my heart to desire Your will. Put Your dreams within me. Speak through the longings that excite me most.

MAY 18

The angel of the LORD appeared to [Gideon] and said, "Mighty hero, the LORD is with you!"
JUDGES 6:12

Marauders from Midian were attacking Israel, and God let them. His people had turned their hearts to other gods, and they needed a wake-up call. But when oppression caused them to cry out to God for help, He answered. He sent an angel to Gideon, who was working hard to keep his grain—and himself—out of sight of the raiders.

The angel called Gideon a "mighty hero," even though Gideon wasn't exactly playing that role. But God's voice normally doesn't point out what we already know about ourselves. He certainly doesn't confirm those accusations we hear from our own guilty consciences or a far more evil accuser. No, He calls out what He knows to be true of us from an eternal perspective. He sees the end from the beginning. He saw Abraham as a man of great faith, even when Abraham was questioning the promise, attempting to help God out, or laughing at the impossibility of the timing. He saw Moses as a great leader, even as Moses was fleeing Egypt in exile. And He saw Gideon as the warrior that Israel needed, even as Gideon was hiding in fear. He sees each of us as the man or woman we will become, no matter how much we're struggling in the process.

Hearing God's voice brings out the best in us. Let Him call you who you are, and don't question His assessment. You may not feel like a mighty warrior, a person of great faith, or anything else He calls you, but He gives His people an unquestionable identity. We are children of the royal household, pure in Christ, kings and priests in His Kingdom, and more. Whatever specific role God speaks to you, it's true, even if it seems unlikely. His words will call you out of hiding and into the glory of your destiny.

Really, Lord? I find Your words about me to be far more lofty than I deserve or expect. Help me grow into the vision You have for me. I am everything You say I am, simply because You say so.

Keep on asking, and you will receive what you ask for. Keep on seeking, and you will find. Keep on knocking, and the door will be opened to you. . . . If you sinful people know how to give good gifts to your children, how much more will your heavenly Father give the Holy Spirit to those who ask him.

LUKE 11:9, 13

Dwight Moody had been crying out to God for His Spirit. He knew he was born of the Spirit, but he also knew his preaching did not have the power of God behind it. He was desperate for greater fruitfulness. Then one day in New York, he had an experience that he described as God revealing Himself, and it was so powerful that Moody had to ask God to stay His hand. He was overwhelmed. Afterward, he preached the same sermons with the same messages to the same kinds of audiences, but everything else was different. Hundreds were converted. Thousands of dollars were now given to Moody's institutions that had previously been failing. His entire ministry was being moved by the flow of God's Spirit.

God had not given Moody any direct words or new messages, but He had given him a personal encounter with Himself. The Spirit had spoken with an overwhelming sense of His love, and that love flowed through Moody with every word of every sermon. Once on the brink of burning out, Moody was now energized with a power that would never leave him. He chose repeatedly to honor the Holy Spirit above all other concerns in his ministry, and the results changed history.

When we cry out for God persistently over time, we will get what we ask for. We will encounter Him and experience His power. That encounter may involve words, as it has for many throughout Scripture and history, or it may simply involve an overwhelming sense of God's nature, as it did for Moody. Whatever it looks like, it will change your life—and very possibly the world around you.

Holy Spirit, I desperately need You—Your touch, Your voice, Your power. Fill me. I yield everything to You in exchange for Your life in me. Flow freely to me, in me, and through me.

[God said,] "This is the kind of fasting I want: Free those who are wrongly imprisoned; lighten the burden of those who work for you. Let the oppressed go free, and remove the chains that bind people."
Isaiah 58:6

FROM THE HEART OF GOD

"Are you looking for ways to show your devotion to Me? Many people do. They imagine long, intense times of prayer; listening to around-the-clock worship music; becoming deeply involved in a ministry that oozes true spirituality; reading the Bible for hours a day and memorizing lots of verses; being poor enough to demonstrate detachment from the things of the world, yet rich enough to put impressive amounts in the offering plate for missions; having great faith, but without taking any foolish risks; and more. Your definitions of devotion may be off sometimes, but I love the heart behind all of these things when you do them in the right spirit, and none of them when you don't.

"Very few people take time to ask some really important questions. They look for ways to show devotion to me, without asking what's really on My heart. What do I desire? What pleases Me? You know I love faith and a desire to fulfill My purposes, but do you take time to think about what My purposes really are? If you're listening for My voice, here are some things you should know: My heart is drawn to the oppressed, those who have been beaten up by the world, whose hearts are broken. I hate the devastation of sin, and I hate its visible manifestations. And I love those who want My purposes and power to flow through them to fix things that are wrong in this world.

"When you listen for My voice, expect Me to talk about this often. Expect Me to give you assignments that no one will notice or honor you for. Expect not only to hear My voice but also to *become* My voice in situations that need to be made right."

Father, I'm so busy looking to satisfy my own heart that I miss the opportunity to satisfy Yours. Open my eyes wide enough to see beyond my own surroundings and into situations that weigh heavily on Your mind.

God is making his appeal through us. We speak for Christ when we plead, "Come back to God!"

2 CORINTHIANS 5:20

Jesus is the Word of God, the *logos* behind all of creation, and the written Word is His revelation. So why would God need us to be His mouthpieces? Because He's an infinite God, and He needs an infinite number of stories if He wants to demonstrate the many facets of His nature. That's one of the reasons He created billions of bearers of His image. We all have the potential to uniquely represent something about God that others cannot. He reveals Himself through a multitude of stories, and each of ours is one of them.

So we make appeals as if we were the voice of Christ, pleading with people to be reconciled to God. We not only speak His message to them; we embody it. We are living testimonies of what Christ has done, examples of His ability to resurrect, heal, redeem, restore, call, and equip. We are stories of His provision, protection, comfort, guidance, and promises. We teach, preach, and live His words. We are a vast multitude of vessels, carrying His presence and His voice into every corner of this world.

Does that sound too ambitious or presumptuous? Regardless of how it sounds, it's true. God has made it clear that His glory will cover the earth, and He does hardly anything on earth that doesn't involve His people. When His glory covers the earth, it will largely be through us. When He speaks, it has almost always come through a prophetic voice or a testimony or a written record of His ways—all inspired by His Spirit but made manifest through a human agent. We need to remember our sacred role. We not only hear and receive God's voice; we are called to express it everywhere we can.

Lord, my story doesn't seem very dramatic or impressive. Yet I know Your hand has been deeply involved in writing it. Therefore, it reveals something about You. May I never be guilty of hiding or minimizing Your glory in my story. I share You well by sharing who I am.

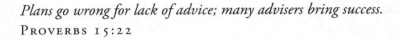
Plans go wrong for lack of advice; many advisers bring success.
PROVERBS 15:22

We wish God would write His words in the sky or speak audibly to our ears. We long for concrete, tangible communication from Him. But God is Spirit, and He communicates spiritually. We can hear Him in the depths of our spirits, and sometimes He speaks more audibly than that. And He has given us His Word as the revelation of His general will for all humanity. Still, we yearn for God in the flesh.

Jesus came as God in the flesh, of course; that's what the Incarnation was all about. But as the time of Jesus' death neared, He told His disciples that it was good for Him to go. Why? Because His Spirit would then come and live inside of us. There would be numerous incarnations as the followers of Jesus became temples of the Spirit of Jesus. Later in the New Testament, the church is called the body of Christ. In this world, Christ's followers become His hands and His feet—*and* His voice. His people are to become the physical expression of His spiritual nature. When we need to hear an audible voice, it will often come through the people around us who are filled with the Holy Spirit.

That's why Scripture tells us there is success in many advisers. In Solomon's time, when most of the proverbs were written, this was perhaps only wise advice to keep a person balanced in his perspective and decisions. After the advent of the Holy Spirit into the inner lives of believers, the advice takes on even greater significance. The people around us aren't simply advisers with a diversity of opinions; they have the capacity to speak words inspired by the Spirit Himself.

When you listen to the wisdom of fellow believers, God's voice will likely be somewhere in the mix. You'll have to discern it, but it's there. Surround yourself with Spirit-filled people and listen to what the Spirit says through them.

Spirit of God, speak to me through Your people. Let Your voice ring true when they speak Your words. I cannot travel this journey alone. Fill Your people with truth.

*When it was clear that we couldn't persuade [Paul], we gave up and said,
"The Lord's will be done."*
ACTS 21:14

Though God encourages us to surround ourselves with Spirit-inspired advisers,
there will be times when we have to stand alone. Not many counselors would
have encouraged Abraham that he should hang on to receive God's promise of
a child at the age of one hundred. Joseph almost got killed for the dream God
gave him. No military adviser would endorse Joshua's battle plan of marching around Jericho. No one would have told Jesus, "Yes, we think going to the
cross is the right direction for You." Nearly all of Paul's friends told him not
to go to Jerusalem after his third missionary journey. Yet in all these cases, the
counselors—both hypothetical and real—would have been wrong. God was
calling each of these people, as well as many prophets and saints throughout
Scripture and history, to follow Him regardless of what those around them
would advise.

Think about it: Abraham, Joseph, Moses, Joshua, David, Job, the prophets,
Jesus, and Paul all had to do or believe something that defied human reason.
At times, they had to go against advice from people who knew God well. The
"many advisers" in their lives sometimes gave good but misguided counsel, and
sometimes they directly opposed God's plan. These faithful people had to know
God's voice well enough to ignore contradictory advice.

We must also learn God's voice that well. We should always listen to Spirit-
inspired people, but we are never to blindly follow their counsel. There will be
times when we have heard God clearly enough that no other voice should be
allowed to influence us. God uses such experiences not to give us an excuse for
our independent tendencies, but to stretch our faith and refine our hearing. In
humility and strength, we must resolve to go where He leads, no matter what
anyone else says.

Lord, give me the discernment to know when You are speaking to me through
Your people and when You are speaking to me apart from them. Give me the
humility to follow advice and the wisdom and resolve to know when to reject it.

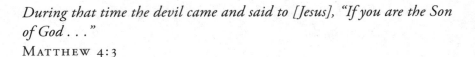
During that time the devil came and said to [Jesus], "If you are the Son of God . . ."
MATTHEW 4:3

A voice from heaven proclaimed, "This is my dearly loved Son." But no word from God goes uncontested, so Jesus was immediately led—by God's own Spirit—into the wilderness, where He would be tempted by Satan. We often see this encounter as a threefold temptation about turning stones into bread, jumping off the Temple, and winning the kingdoms of the world through false worship. But before the devil's first insidious prompt, an even greater temptation came: "If you are the Son of God . . ." It was a calculated strike against the identity that had just been declared. God said Jesus was His Son; the adversary responded, "Oh, really?"

That's an alarmingly accurate picture of the greatest temptations we will ever face. We may be preoccupied with greed, lust, pride, or whatever else, but we will find that the enemy of our souls has two very subtle weapons that are even more effective: (1) he undermines the identity we've already been given in Christ; and (2) he questions whatever God has just told us, daring us to actually believe it.

That's why anytime we learn a great new spiritual truth, we soon find ourselves in a wilderness of contradiction that screams how untrue that truth actually is. Have you learned that you're seated with Christ in heavenly realms (Ephesians 2:6)? Circumstances will soon try to convince you that you are hopelessly earthbound. Have you read that you have authority over the power of the enemy (Luke 10:19)? Life will soon seem to laugh at your impotence. Your response must be like that of Jesus: Cling firmly to what God has said. His voice is true. Faith will prove it—eventually. Your identity as His royal child will be confirmed, and so will all His promises. In the intensity of the battle, never let go of that.

✧ ✧ ✧

Lord, the temptations are fierce. I know what You said, but I see so many contradictions. Give me the strength and the tenacity to hold on. I am who You say I am, and You will do what You said You will do.

We live by believing and not by seeing.
2 CORINTHIANS 5:7

If you are highly skilled at every aspect of your job except one, which aspect will get most of your attention? If you are able to cross off nine out of ten items on your to-do list, which task will you focus on? If your child brings home a report card with five A's and one F, which grade will you focus on? Human beings have a tendency to focus on what's wrong or lacking, not on successes and strengths. We are drawn to whatever needs to be fixed. And an alarming side effect of that tendency is to see things much more negatively than they really are.

That carries over into our approach to hearing God. One word of correction from Him seems to outweigh ninety-nine words of encouragement. And one unanswered question—about direction, desires, or anything else—seems to get more of our attention than all the direction and answered prayers He has already given. The result is an unfortunate bias toward what we see (or rather, what we don't see) and a disbelief and neglect of what He has already said. This inhibits our hearing anything else from Him.

One of the keys to hearing God is *believing* and *acting on* what we've already heard. The good listener focuses on what God says rather than what He doesn't say. We want God to reveal His will to us, and He will. But He gets to choose the chronology and unfold His plan layer by layer. It does not help us to rebel against this process or try to rush it. An obsession with what He hasn't said blocks our ears to what He is currently saying. But an obsession with what He has said and is currently saying opens our ears to discover even more of what He wants us to know. We live by believing whatever we have heard of His voice.

Lord, like faithful priests and prophets of old, I want none of your words to fall to the ground unheeded in my life. I commit to being diligent—not legalistic, but focused—about what You have already said.

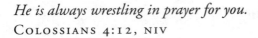
He is always wrestling in prayer for you.
COLOSSIANS 4:12, NIV

A friend was at a dinner party when she suddenly felt an urge to pray for her husband. He was away on a business trip in Germany, and though there was no fear in her impulse to pray, she sensed he needed the Holy Spirit's support. So she excused herself from the table and interceded for him until she felt at peace.

When she talked to her husband later, she understood why the Spirit had prompted her to pray. At that moment, her husband and his traveling companions had been with a group of businessmen who were pressing them to visit the city's infamous red-light district for an evening of entertainment. They were steadfastly resisting, but the businessmen were stubbornly insisting. Eventually, the visitors' refusal trumped the hosts' insistence, and the plans were abandoned. The Spirit provided strength in a time of need.

God often impresses us to intercede for people in danger or distress. Some people who are sensitive to the Holy Spirit wake up in the middle of the night with a sudden urge to pray for a missionary or relative halfway around the world, finding out only later what the urgent need was about. Regardless of why these prayers are necessary for God to accomplish His will, they are apparently effective. Many crises, temptations, and evil threats have been averted at the precise moment when someone prayed without knowing exactly why.

Don't resist sudden urges to pray for someone. If these urges are motivated by fear or panic, they almost certainly aren't the Holy Spirit's prompting; but if motivated by an awareness of intense need, they almost certainly are. Those who are sensitive to these burdens will be called on to intercede at critical moments. And their strategic prayers will greatly influence the Kingdom, even halfway around the world.

Holy Spirit, I would love to be a reliable intercessor in moments of need. Sensitize me to the impressions and burdens You give. I don't need to understand *why*; I need only to know *when* You want me to pray, and I will respond with zeal.

Share your food with the hungry, and give shelter to the homeless. Give clothes to those who need them, and do not hide from relatives who need your help.
ISAIAH 58:7

FROM THE HEART OF GOD

"You worship Me for My mercy. You sing praise songs about how it has saved you, set you free, and met you in times of need. You preach and write books about My mercy and all the many places I've shown it in My Word. Whenever you're in need, you cry out to Me and appeal to My merciful nature. If you were asked under oath in a courtroom if you were aware that My heart is full of mercy, there would be ample evidence to prove your testimony that you were. My generosity of spirit, my magnanimity toward all in need is clear.

"Then why are so many of My people so hard of hearing when I tell them to be merciful to others? Why do so many close their hearts not only to people who have sinned against them, but also to those in need of help? Why do so many of My people not only hold grudges, but also ignore desperate pleas? You have a tendency to become self-absorbed and to stay within your comfort zone, but My voice will never lead you in either of those directions. When I speak, I am leading you away from your focus on yourself and out of your comfort zone. I am calling you to reflect My mercy to the world around you.

"I know you can reflect My mercy only when you've experienced it yourself. I am pleased to give it to you and to respond in your times of need. But I don't stop speaking once your needs are met. I am calling you upward, outward, and forward. I am lifting your perspective beyond your own circle of interests and into mine. Take it all in. See the opportunities to represent Me in this world. Reflect My heart of mercy."

Father, I'm so busy looking for direction that seems relevant that I miss Your pointing me to the needs of others. Lift my eyes to see every opportunity to reflect Your heart.

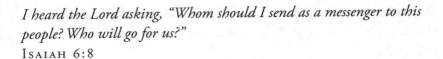
I heard the Lord asking, "Whom should I send as a messenger to this people? Who will go for us?"
ISAIAH 6:8

In Acts, we see the leaders in Antioch "ministering to the Lord" (Acts 13:2, NASB) when God gave them instructions that would shape church history forever. In Revelation, we see John "worshiping in the Spirit" when he heard the voice like a trumpet (Revelation 1:10). In Isaiah, we see the prophet hearing God's questions in the midst of a dramatic vision in the Temple—the place of worship. There seems to be a correlation between our worship and our ability to hear.

This is no surprise. Worship often leads us to an encounter with God and virtually always follows one. And when we encounter God, we not only sense His presence, we also hear His voice. So it stands to reason that when we worship—when we fill our mouths and hearts with His praises—we cultivate an environment in which we encounter God, pick up on His heartbeat, and perceive His words. Certain attitudes create an optimal atmosphere for experiencing God, much like a greenhouse creates a climate in which plants can flourish even amid a harsh, wintry landscape. Worship is first among these attitudes. Not only is it our hearts' right and good expression of adoration, but it also brings us benefits. When our lives reflect God's glory through our affection for Him, we begin to hear Him better.

Cultivate the attitudes that open your ears, and begin with worship. Praise God in all circumstances, even the hard ones. There are few things more difficult than worshiping when life seems to be going against you, but there's hardly anything ultimately more rewarding. Everything—heart, mind, soul, and spirit—opens up to the Spirit of God in an atmosphere of worship. Whatever it takes, develop that atmosphere.

✧ ✧ ✧

Holy God, You are glorious, majestic, and beautiful. I adore Your heart—and Your willingness to share it with me. Let me live with a strong sense of Your presence, an atmosphere in which Your words are abundant and clear. Open my heart and my ears to hear You.

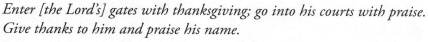

Enter [the Lord's] gates with thanksgiving; go into his courts with praise.
Give thanks to him and praise his name.
PSALM 100:4

An open window not only lets in fresh air, it also lets stuffy air out. An open door not only gives us freedom to go in and out, but it also gives others freedom to visit. Attitudes that open our hearts to give to God also open our hearts to receive from Him. Openness is a two-way street. When we create the right climate within our hearts, we allow God to come to us there.

Gratitude is one of those attitudes that create the right climate. Like a magnet for the divine, thankful hearts draw God's presence and open our ears to His voice. Psalm 100 tells us to enter His gates with thanksgiving, which means not only that it's appropriate to come to Him with an attitude of thankfulness, but that such an attitude is also a *means* for coming to Him. When we bring a sense of gratitude to the gates of God, those gates open for us to enter. Yes, we have access to His throne room through the sacrifice of Jesus and His life within us, but we *experience* that access much more tangibly when we are saturated in thankfulness. Our position in our relationship with God becomes much less a matter of our theology and more a matter of our experience. And in knowing Him more practically, we hear Him more clearly.

Practice gratitude. Don't just thank God for the big blessings. Express appreciation for the little ones too. Avoid the tendency to focus on whatever seems to be going wrong and needs to be fixed; focus on every body part that works right, every circumstance that others take for granted, every good taste or beautiful sight that He allows you to enjoy. The more you tell Him why you love Him, the more He tells you the things that are on His heart.

Lord, thank You for Your goodness to me. Thank You for the joy of existing—for the pleasure You provide, the needs You fill, the opportunities You give. And thank You for speaking when I really need to hear.

MAY 30

Though the LORD is great, he cares for the humble, but he keeps his distance from the proud.
PSALM 138:6

God is repelled by pride. He keeps His distance from self-sufficient hearts that mistakenly assume they don't need Him. Pride is so contrary to God's nature and so resistant to His ways that He simply stays away. The proud cannot enjoy God's presence and are not sensitive enough to hear His voice. Those who are full of themselves cannot be full of Him.

Humility, on the other hand, draws God closer. He loves the humble-hearted because they know their need for Him and are vulnerable enough to invite Him in. Jesus blessed the poor in spirit because they are empty enough of themselves to have room for God. An unassuming, unpretentious soul is a natural fit for the Spirit of God.

Like worship and gratitude, humility creates the right climate for hearing God. If God keeps His distance from the proud but is drawn to the humble, and if hearing His voice is a by-product of His closeness, then humility is a necessary condition for hearing Him. There are exceptions, of course—the proud Pharaoh heard God's words through Moses, and the proud King Belshazzar saw the handwriting on the wall. But these were words of warning and judgment, not messages of compassion or calling. When God wants to speak tenderly and lovingly to His people, His voice resonates with clarity in hearts not cluttered with selfishness.

We tend to think of humility as something done to us—an attitude God works in us rather than one we can create—but Scripture tells us to humble *ourselves*. In other words, we are to choose humility over pride, thinking of others before ourselves. When we do, we position ourselves to receive whatever God says.

Lord, if there is anything in me that hinders Your voice—any pride that causes You to withdraw—point it out and help me deal with it. I willingly forsake anything that obstructs my perception of Your will. I gladly empty myself of me in order to be full of You.

MAY 31

I [Paul] plead with you to give your bodies to God because of all he has done for you. Let them be a living and holy sacrifice—the kind he will find acceptable. . . . Then you will learn to know God's will for you, which is good and pleasing and perfect.

ROMANS 12:1-2

Sacrifices were made often in the days of the Tabernacle and the Temple—morning and evening, on behalf of nations and individuals and families, for sin, for gratitude, and for devotion. Harvest offerings included the first and best of crops, and sin offerings included many kinds of animals. In the Levitical instructions, one gets the impression that blood flowed nearly constantly from Israel's altar. In every case, the sacrifice was just that—a sacrifice. It represented a costly gift to God.

Today, our offerings are usually much less intrusive in our lives and much more monetary. We pay God a sum and consider the offering done. But Scripture urges much more than that. God doesn't demand a compulsory sacrifice, but He invites a comprehensive one given in a spirit of joy. He wants us to offer not just our income or our efforts, but our entire selves to Him.

Unlike the sacrifices of the Old Testament, our offering doesn't die. We continue to live, not under our own direction but under the complete ownership of the one to whom we've given ourselves. We are fully functioning sacrifices, alive and set apart for a specific purpose. But only if we present ourselves as such.

The results of our sacrifices are numerous, but one is the promise of knowing God's will. When we have a hard time hearing Him, it may be because discovering His will is a somewhat obscure and ongoing process, but it may also be because we aren't living sacrificially under His exclusive direction. When we offer ourselves fully to Him, he offers His guidance fully to us.

Lord, You take great pleasure in speaking to the sacrifices on Your altar. I do offer myself to You, but I can't even begin to understand all the implications of that. You'll have to show me over time. Teach me and lead me patiently.

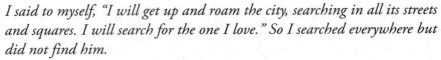

JUNE 1

I said to myself, "I will get up and roam the city, searching in all its streets and squares. I will search for the one I love." So I searched everywhere but did not find him.

<small>SONG OF SONGS 3:2</small>

Words are rarely meaningful apart from the context in which they are spoken. So when we listen for God as a servant listens to a master, we will hear instructions. When we listen for Him as a student listens to a teacher, we will be taught and trained. When we listen for Him as a child listens to a parent, we will be encouraged and corrected. But when we listen for Him as the beloved longs for her lover . . . well, we hear a language of the heart that goes deeper than all other words and rings truer than all other voices.

Few who seek God do so in the context of love, but this is where the deep truths of God's heart are revealed. Yes, He gives information, instructions, correction, and encouragement to any who will seek Him—after all, He promises wisdom to those who ask—but He does not allow just anyone to tap into the desires of His heart. Those secrets are reserved for those who search for Him with the longing of a would-be lover, for those who crave His presence and His touch simply because they are His. This takes us to deeper conversations than others dare to expect.

But it is a search, not a momentary transaction. The beloved in the Song of Songs roams the streets of the city looking for the one she loves—and at first she does not find him. Yet her search will soon be rewarded with a tight embrace. Hearts will cling to each other in unity. And deep, heart-to-heart thoughts, feelings, and desires will be shared freely.

You are the Lover of my soul, and I long for Your embrace. Open Your thoughts to me. Tell me Your desires. What are Your dreams? Share them with me. Take me deep into Your heart.

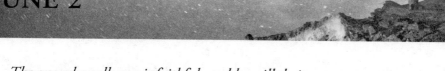

JUNE 2

The one who calls you is faithful, and he will do it.
1 THESSALONIANS 5:24, NIV

Hudson Taylor felt defeated. He had placed his trust in Christ as his Savior long before, but he longed for a deeper blessing, a sense of victory over sin and being set apart for God's service. He knew he could not accomplish spiritual breakthrough on his own; it had to come from God. Taylor was at the end of himself and desperate for God to break the power of sin and give him inward victory. For his part, Taylor promised to forsake all earthly prospects and give himself fully to God's will, whatever the cost. And God answered him powerfully.

Taylor later wrote about the feeling that came over him in that moment. He felt he was in God's presence, entering into a sacred covenant that could never be broken. Something within him seemed to say, "Your prayer is answered; your conditions are accepted." And he was profoundly convinced for the rest of his life that he was called to China.

God has spoken clear terms to many who have been willing to enter into sacred covenants with Him. Hannah vowed to give up her son to God's service if God would open her womb to have a son in the first place, and God accepted and blessed her with Samuel. Hudson Taylor vowed to give himself wholly to God's service if God would accomplish a miracle in his heart. Such vows are not to be taken lightly, but God will clearly acknowledge His acceptance if He plans to fulfill the request. History-making endeavors have begun from such conversations with Him; He uses the deep longings of His people in order to fulfill His purposes. And He who is faithful will honor His Word and bring it to pass.

Lord, I feel that my deepest longings simply must be fulfilled. I have brought them to You to do as You please with them. Use them to accomplish Your purposes in this world. I am fully available to walk out the calling You have given me if You will fully enable me to do it.

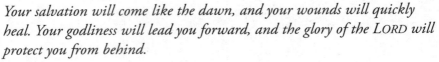

JUNE 3

Your salvation will come like the dawn, and your wounds will quickly heal. Your godliness will lead you forward, and the glory of the LORD will protect you from behind.
ISAIAH 58:8

FROM THE HEART OF GOD

"You've waited for resolution to the problems in your life and for the fulfillment of your deep longings. You've sought My will on these matters, and I've given you some direction on them. But your focus on the things that pertain to you has blinded you to some of the other things I've been saying. If you will widen the range of your hearing—and follow the instructions that don't apply specifically to what you're focusing on right now—the solutions and fulfillments will come. When you learn the art of focusing your prayers and activities on other people's needs rather than your own, you'll look back and discover that I'm giving unusual help to the things that concern you. Getting your attention off of your needs draws My attention to them.

"Sometimes you look to Me for answers while I'm looking back at you for answers. Both of us are asking, 'Why don't you do something?' When you respond to what I've told you, I'll respond to what you've asked Me. That doesn't mean I'm waiting for your perfection, of course. I'm waiting for the leaning of your heart to change. Turn your steps in the right direction and I'll quicken your steps and come running toward you.

"This is one of the hardest practices for you to develop, but it's one that prompts Me to bring your salvation like the dawn. Like a watchman waiting for the morning, you've looked for My help. I can assure you that help will come, but not because you're obsessing about your longings. It's because you've paid attention to Mine. I will demonstrate My power toward those who demonstrate their love for Me."

✧ ✧ ✧

Lord, I desperately long for my salvation to come like the dawn. I have gaping wounds and screaming needs that demand to be healed and resolved. Give me a heart for the world at large, but please rebuild my small corner of it.

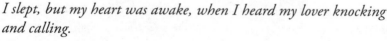

JUNE 4

I slept, but my heart was awake, when I heard my lover knocking and calling.
SONG OF SONGS 5:2

Anyone who has ever been in love knows how it is. One glimpse of her . . . the mention of his name . . . the sound of her voice . . . a brief moment of eye contact . . . all it takes is one hint of a suggestion for your heart to pound, your palms to sweat, your breath to quicken. When you're in love, your heart is awake and alert to your beloved.

Our hearts are always awake to our passions. Even when we're asleep, our spirits seem to be connected with whatever and whomever we love. Some people are stirred by the beauty of visual art but bored by the written word. Some are in tune with lofty, abstract ideas but easily tune out concrete, mundane matters. Some will scream wildly at a football game and fall asleep during a hymn. And everyone brightens up in the company of certain people but wearies in the company of others. Why? Because we are people with passions and interests and deep desires. Whatever can stoke our fires gets the benefit of our full attention.

In the Song of Songs, the beloved's heart is awake to her lover, and she hears him calling. That's because when our hearts are awake, we hear *everything*. We tune in to whispers, hints, and subtle suggestions. We even read meaning into a maybe-normal tone of voice or an otherwise innocuous phrase or a possible pattern of behavior or attitudes. We notice things that no one else could possibly notice. And if our hearts are awake to God, we tune in to every possible hint of His voice.

Pray for an awakened heart—a heart so awake that you will hear God knocking and calling even when you're asleep, a heart fully alive to whatever He might be saying. Be so in love with God that you hear *everything*.

Lord, stir my passion for You. May my heart beat faster at the sound of Your name. Deepen my desire for the sound of Your voice. Awaken my heart to every word from Your mouth.

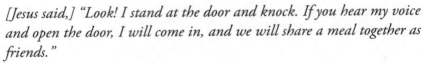

JUNE 5

[Jesus said,] "Look! I stand at the door and knock. If you hear my voice and open the door, I will come in, and we will share a meal together as friends."

REVELATION 3:20

In John's prophetic vision, Jesus has strong words of correction for a lukewarm church. He tells these believers to turn from their indifference and then gives them a profound invitation: Open the door and let Him in. If they hear His voice and respond, He will come into their fellowship and interact with them as friends having a meal together.

This verse is often used in the context of salvation, but that isn't its primary purpose. Jesus is speaking to a church that has shut Him out of their community, especially during the Lord's Supper, which is meant to be an intimate meal commemorating His sacrifice and celebrating His presence and purpose in their lives. If this fellowship of believers would open their ears and invite Him to join them, He would come powerfully into their midst. He is speaking to them primarily about relationship.

Meals, especially in cultures like those of the Middle East, are an occasion for developing deep friendships and lasting bonds. They aren't just about nutrition; they are about closeness. This is what Jesus promises His people, but only if we hear His voice and open the door. We have to accept His invitation and welcome Him in. Our primary motive for hearing His voice is intimacy with Him. Only then are we drawn into the kind of relationship where His will is discovered and His secrets are made known. He shares His heart with those who have opened the doors of theirs.

Above all else in this life, accept this invitation. Don't view it as a one-time acceptance of salvation. See it as an ongoing meal between close friends. Let Him lean over the table of your heart and tell you what's on His mind. There's no greater blessing than this.

Jesus, the door of my heart is wide open. Come on in. Sit with me, eat with me, talk to me. Let me be one of Your closest friends.

[Jesus said,] "My Father in heaven has revealed this to you. . . . Now I say to you that you are Peter (which means 'rock'), and upon this rock I will build my church."
MATTHEW 16:17-18

The voice of God revealed Jesus' identity to Simon, though Simon had heard nothing concrete. He simply came to a realization of the truth, and Jesus said this realization was a revelation from God. But even though this revelation had not thundered from heaven for all to hear—even though it probably seemed to Simon to be his own thought processes—it was enough to become the foundation of the church. God's people would be established on this rock of truth that Jesus was and is the Messiah, the Son of the living God.

Simon had the privilege of calling out Jesus' true identity, and Jesus did something profound in response. He called out Simon's true identity. He told this rash, often-unstable disciple that he was really a rock and that he would be instrumental in the early history of Jesus' followers. He saw the glory and purpose in Simon Peter's calling and declared it openly in front of the other disciples. He affirmed the character that was developing in Peter, even though it was not yet fully formed. Peter would one day deny that he ever knew Jesus, but that didn't prevent Jesus from calling him a rock. He knew Peter's heart and his future. He insisted that Peter would be defined by His words, not by Peter's past.

Acknowledge who Jesus is, and you will hear Him acknowledge who you are. This is a two-way communication, and both the revelation you receive and the revelation you share will build His Kingdom. Your words about Him and His words about you will further His work in this world. His identity and yours are both necessary parts of His mission.

Jesus, I can answer Your question, "Who do you say I am?" You are the Messiah, the Son of the living God. But who do You say *I* am? You alone define my identity. I look to no one else to tell me what role I play in Your Kingdom.

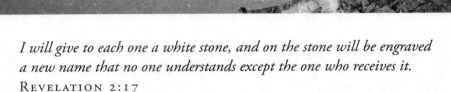

JUNE 7

I will give to each one a white stone, and on the stone will be engraved a new name that no one understands except the one who receives it.
REVELATION 2:17

God enjoys giving people new names. He did it with Abram/Abraham, Sarai/Sarah, Jacob/Israel, Simon/Peter, and others. (Some believe He also gave Saul/Paul a new name, but Paul seems to have continued to use Saul when dealing with a Hebrew audience and Paul with a Greek audience.) God insists on being the one who shapes our identity over all other influences. We are not who we think we are, nor are we who other people say we are. We are who God says we are. And His opinion is the one that matters.

Jesus tells the overcomers in one of His churches that they will receive new names in heaven. For all who believe, this name is more than just another word; it's a definition of who we really are in Him. For everyone who has felt defined by their past, their peers, or their performance, this is good news. The name Jesus gives us will not be based on our baggage, our distorted thinking, or our self-perceptions. It won't be something we can earn or deserve. It won't be based on our profession or accomplishments or failures. It will be rooted in Christ's identity and reflect exactly who we were created to be. His voice alone tells us who we are.

You can go ahead and enjoy the benefits of this new name because the voice of God is already shaping who you are. Perhaps you have accepted the opinions of others—either rejection or affirmation—to shape your identity. Or maybe past experiences and relationships have defined how you think about yourself. But God calls you His child, promises you His inheritance, sees you healthy and whole in Christ, and gives you privileges as a priest and a king. These aren't future descriptions for those who believe in Jesus; they are startlingly current. By His words, this is who you really are, now and forever.

✦ ✦ ✦

Lord, let me go ahead and "be"—in experience—who I really am. Let me live my new name now and enjoy it for all eternity.

JUNE 8

[Jesus said,] "If you don't believe me when I tell you about earthly things, how can you possibly believe if I tell you about heavenly things?"
JOHN 3:12

Jesus has just taught Nicodemus about the necessity for everyone, Jew and Gentile alike, to be born again. It's a divine truth about the spiritual life. Yet a few verses later, Jesus implies that this is an "earthly thing." It's basic revelation. Apparently, there are "heavenly things" that can stretch a human mind much further than this.

That means that one of the deepest truths in the Gospels is, according to Jesus, just the beginning of what He wants to reveal. He is conversant in the realities of both heaven and earth, yet He has to hold his tongue when talking of heavenly realities. Why? Because His hearers can't handle the truth. Not yet. He later informs His followers that He has much more to tell them, but it's more than they can bear (John 16:12). He has to measure out revelation a little bit at a time. Human beings can handle only so much.

God isn't going to speak "new revelation" to us—at least not in the sense that cults and counterfeits have claimed in the past. The Bible is a complete revelation. But it isn't the end of God's speaking and guiding. He continues to give us deeper insights into His Word, greater glimpses of His glory, and hints of how ancient scriptural truths play out in our world today. He isn't unveiling new doctrine, but He continues to unveil Himself in greater measure—a never-ending process for an eternal and infinite God. He never runs out of things to show us.

Will we grasp them? Only if we open our hearts to "heavenly things" that go beyond the "earthly things" that seemed heavenly to us when we first heard them. God's words are always calling us out of our boxes and deeper, higher, further into His heart and His Kingdom. And only those who are willing to be stretched can hear them.

Stretch me, Holy Spirit. Reveal to me the things of heaven. Help me grasp the truths that blow other people's minds.

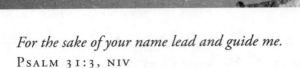

JUNE 9

For the sake of your name lead and guide me.
PSALM 31:3, NIV

The pastor had sensed a transition was coming to his church. He just didn't know the transition would come about because of his departure. He had no intention of leaving, until God began to raise the question in his heart. He asked if he was hearing correctly, but he could hardly believe the direction. Then a friend in another city texted him to say he sensed God was about to move him. And when he traveled to another country for a speaking engagement, the host pastor said, "I see God giving you an exit ramp that you need to take." Another leader in the next city gave essentially the same message. None of these people had heard from each other or from the pastor about this time of transition. They had simply sensed it from God's Spirit. The convergence of the message confirmed the surprising word God had been speaking.

God doesn't typically use the words of other people to inform us of a new direction, but He very often speaks through others to confirm something we've already been praying about. In fact, He sometimes lets us quietly wrestle with a decision until we come to grips with it and choose, and only then will He confirm what we've already arrived at by faith. He doesn't take away the need for faith up front; He lets us flex our faith muscles until He's ready to support us with His affirmation. It's rarely a smooth process, but it's an effective one. He guides us with skillful hands even when we think we're wandering.

Be very cautious when someone says that God has given him or her a message for you that would require a significant change of direction. But if you think God has already been leading you in a new direction and still aren't sure, don't be surprised if He uses the words of others to confirm it. He knows how to guide, and He lets others be part of the process.

✧ ✧ ✧

Lord, I listen earnestly for Your guidance, but You never told me to listen alone. Give me timely words from others—and discernment to know when to heed them.

JUNE 10

When you call, the LORD will answer. "Yes, I am here," he will quickly reply.
ISAIAH 58:9

FROM THE HEART OF GOD

"Nothing opens your ears to My voice better than demonstrating an intent to take what I've said seriously. I have declared that My words will not return to Me void, that they will accomplish all I intend for them to accomplish. I'm looking for people with the same perspective, people who will hear Me and say, 'Lord, Your words will not return to You without accomplishing Your purposes. I am committed to seeing that they are fulfilled.' Are you determined to see them through? When you are fully invested in the power of My words, you will find that the power of My words is fully invested in you.

"I'm not urging you to put My words under a microscope and become legalistic, as religious experts of the past have done. My words are powerful, not oppressive. But you must receive them at a heart level, in the depths of our relationship, handling what I say with a sense of sacredness, showing that My voice is as important to you when it hits your ears as it was to Me when it came out of My mouth. I don't tickle the ears of casual listeners. I move the hearts of loyal friends.

"Friends share desires and passions and interests. Share Mine, and you will find Me unusually responsive to your questions and petitions. I will reply quickly and decisively. You may still go through times of waiting, but you will not go through times of disillusionment. Your prayers will not bounce off the ceiling. You will believe that I am the God who answers you. I will give you ample evidence to know it in the depths of your heart."

Lord, hear me when I call! Your words mean everything to me. Everything. My desires are Your desires. I am zealous about whatever comes out of Your mouth. Let my responses to You, and Your responses to me, be quick and decisive.

JUNE 11

Inside the Tent of Meeting, the LORD would speak to Moses face to face, as one speaks to a friend.

EXODUS 33:11

Arguably the two most prominent figures in the Hebrew Scriptures—and clearly the two most significant in terms of covenant history—are Abraham and Moses. Not coincidentally, they are both spoken of not simply as God's servants or chosen leaders, but as His friends. In both of these men, we see not only reverence for God's majesty, but also the other end of the familiarity spectrum: a boldness to try to challenge or influence God's plan. In other words, they weren't afraid to wrestle with God. And God was not reluctant to engage them in conversation.

One of the hardest things to balance in our relationship with God is the tension between familiarity and awe. Some people emphasize God's majesty and bristle at any thought of intimacy with Him. Others lean the other way, carrying on a casual friendship with God with hardly a thought of falling on their faces before Him. In reality, God is both awe-inspiring *otherness* and a closer friend than we can imagine. When we pursue both sides of that relationship, we find Him speaking in more familiar terms than we might expect.

God spoke with Moses "face to face, as one speaks to a friend," even though the idea of seeing God and relating to Him in familiar terms was practically inconceivable in Hebrew thought. Moses' relationship with God shows us that it's possible. Not only that, but Scripture assures us that we live under a better covenant now, a relationship in which the veil has been torn and we have access to the throne. What could possibly prevent us from running to God and zealously pursuing a face-to-face friendship? Why would we ever be content with not hearing Him well? He invites us into intimate conversation. We should never settle for anything less.

Majestic God, whisper Your personal thoughts to me. Let me know You more deeply than I've ever been taught, more directly than purely religious minds can accept. I want to experience You as profoundly as You have ever allowed anyone to experience You.

> *Afterward Moses would return to the camp, but the young man who*
> *assisted him, Joshua son of Nun, would remain behind in the Tent*
> *of Meeting.*
> EXODUS 33:11

Some of Israel's leaders looked down on Moses' relationship with God and assumed they were just as special as he was. They rebelled against him, and God had to put them in their place. Others might have assumed that Moses' relationship with God was exceptional, far more privileged than they would ever be allowed to experience. They followed him and deferred to his leadership, gladly letting him be the intermediary between themselves and God.

Joshua was different. He understood the extraordinary privilege of Moses' relationship with God, never downplaying the uniqueness of it or treating it as something other than special. But neither did he see it as unattainable. He understood that God's conversations with Moses were unprecedented, but that didn't mean they would be unrepeatable. God does not play favorites, we're told (Acts 10:34; Romans 2:11; Galatians 2:6), which means that when we see how He relates to one person, we can accept that as an opportunity to invite Him to relate to us that way as well. What He has made available to one is, at least in principle, available to all. There may be conditions to meet—such as spiritual hunger and seeking His Kingdom above all—but anyone who meets with God on His terms is qualified to relate to Him deeply.

Joshua demonstrated the kind of spirit that is able to hear God well. He positioned himself for relationship, because he had observed that it was possible. He remained in God's place of presence even after Moses had left. He set his heart on what is most important, and God eventually related to him just as He had related to Moses. If we see what Joshua has done—and if we accept that as an invitation to do the same—we will experience the same kinds of rewards.

Lord, You are just as willing to relate to me as You are to anyone. But I am hungrier than most. I'll sit in Your presence as long as it takes. Fill my heart with Your voice.

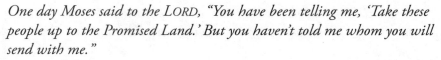

One day Moses said to the LORD, "You have been telling me, 'Take these people up to the Promised Land.' But you haven't told me whom you will send with me."

EXODUS 33:12

There is a hint of accusation in Moses' voice. He has been given an enormous responsibility without the full, visible means to do it. We might tell him simply to "trust God," but even in trusting, Moses needed some practical help. He voiced his complaint to God, and it sounded reasonable: How could he do what God had called him to do if God had not given him the specifics, or His own presence? Why didn't God's equipping come along with His calling? Something was still lacking: Moses needed the assurance that God Himself would go with him to the Promised Land. Otherwise, the trip wouldn't be worth the trouble.

God does not respond in anger or impatience. In the verses following today's Scripture, He responds with assurances and a landmark revelation of His nature. He had earlier rebuked Israel for complaining, and He would have plenty of opportunity to do the same again in the future. But Moses' lament wasn't the problem in this case; it wasn't a complaint. It was a plea for help.

God sometimes sets critical moments like this in our lives. He provokes the kind of tension that will compel us to come to Him with a complaint. When we do—not for the sake of complaining or questioning His goodness, but for the sake of securing His help—He is ready with an answer. Some of the most profound words He ever speaks to us come in the midst of a crisis. Our moments of need tend to open our ears, and He delights in the attention we give Him. Out of our lament, He speaks and deepens His presence in our lives.

Father, use any frustration in my life to draw me closer to You. Hear my words not as complaints but as pleas for more of You. In those moments of crisis, speak to me with Your presence.

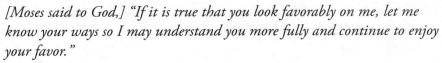

JUNE 14

*[Moses said to God,] "If it is true that you look favorably on me, let me
know your ways so I may understand you more fully and continue to enjoy
your favor."*
EXODUS 33:13

"If it is true . . ." Our theological conscience might cringe over that lead-in, as it
seems to question God's word. After all, God had already made His favor clear
to Moses. He had chosen Moses, called him, used him to lead the Israelites out
of Egypt, delivered him miraculously from the ire of impatient Israelites and a
vengeful Pharaoh, and given him unprecedented revelation at the top of Mount
Sinai. God's favor on Moses was clearly unquestionable. Yet Moses questioned it.

Apparently, in spite of all the revelation God had given him, Moses didn't
sense that he knew enough about God's ways to continue to please Him. He had
seen mixtures of God's power, His love, and His anger, and Moses was still trying to comprehend the strange events of recent history. God had already spoken
with him face to face, already guided him through all sorts of challenges, and
already revealed quite a few laws and expectations for His covenant people. Yet
the heart of this God still remained elusive.

We can know for certain that we'll never arrive at a place of knowing all
there is to know about God. We will always be able to go deeper, to see new
facets of His nature and expect the unexpected. We'll never fully get a handle on
who He is. But we can *trust* who He is and know that He will be reliable. When
we explore His nature, we will get to know Him better. But we will never be
able to define Him.

That's why Moses' prayer doesn't callously disregard what God has already
done for him. No matter how much we've seen and heard, we are right to ask to
see and hear more. And as He did with Moses, God will honor that request with
an answer.

Lord, if it's true that You look favorably on me—and You've made it clear
through Your Son that You do—show me more. Lead me on an adventure
of knowing You more fully every day.

JUNE 15

The LORD replied, "I will personally go with you, Moses, and I will give you rest—everything will be fine for you."
EXODUS 33:14

Many people assume that God's voice will be negative and judging. Perhaps the Old Testament prophets, most of whom ministered during times of national correction and chastisement, have become such an embodiment of God's voice that any other message sounds un-Godlike. In that context, the filter through which we hear Him allows for rebuke but not for encouragement, unless the encouragement happens to be a "one day in heaven" or "at least I saved you from your sin" sort of message—the big-picture consolation that defers hope until later. But help for today's crisis or affirmation for doing well? Many people don't have ears to hear such things.

But God is a God of comfort and encouragement and presence. He is Lord of the "right now" as well as the "one day." Scripture gives us these uplifting messages too, and God takes much more delight in empowering and affirming us than He does in correcting and rebuking. He'll do both, but even His hardest words are cushioned with grace and hope. That accusing voice that is always rebuking us comes from an entirely different source. God wants to lift us up.

That was His message to Moses—"I'm with you, I'll give you rest, and everything will be fine"—and it's His message to us as well. The New Testament makes it clear that His presence is with us, in us, and through us, and it's more profound and commonly enjoyed than it was in Moses' life. The Spirit dwells within, all of the promises of God are "yes and amen" in Christ, and we are a new creation enabled to relate to Him intimately. This is the context in which we hear His voice. And it will almost always be deeply encouraging.

✧ ✧ ✧

Lord, my ears are much more attuned to convicting messages than to affirming ones, but I need plenty of encouragement. Please show me Your smile and let me hear Your uplifting words. I know Your plans for me are good, and I welcome Your sharing them with me often.

JUNE 16

[Jesus said,] "Be sure of this: I am with you always."
MATTHEW 28:20

John Hyde, the famous missionary to India known for his radical life of prayer, used to speak of his conversations with God as one would speak of conversations with any other person. He once came to a meeting claiming that he had been arguing with God the night before about whether to share some of God's dealings with him. On another occasion, he heard the lunch bell ring while he was in the prayer room and asked, "Father, is it Your will that I go?" After a moment of silence, he said, "Thank you," and rose to leave. He continued to converse with people while acknowledging often that God was very much a part of the conversation. The presence of God always seemed to him to be a tangible reality.

Many considered Hyde to be a little odd. Yet, in light of God's many promises never to leave us, Hyde seems to have been more in touch with reality than most of us are. We often have conversations about the subject of God, or His will, with little awareness that He is in the room. But not only is He in the room, He's in the hearts of those who believe in Jesus as their Savior. This may seem like an abstract principle to those who haven't cultivated a deeply personal relationship with God, but in fact the Spirit of our highly relational God is always available for conversation. He may not always stay on the topics we want to discuss, but He will commune with us in the depths of our spirits. He invites us to explore our fellowship with Him from every angle and at every level of our lives. He is with us not just to watch silently; He is actively with us to be deeply involved in our lives.

Jesus, You are with me even as I read this, even as I pray this prayer, and even as I think about all the truths You have revealed. My circumstances, my relationships, and my thoughts are all in plain sight to You. Teach me how to be a good conversationalist with You in every area of life.

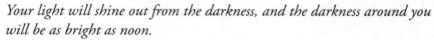
Your light will shine out from the darkness, and the darkness around you will be as bright as noon.
Isaiah 58:10

FROM THE HEART OF GOD

"Do you know why I created you? Do you understand your purpose? You've gotten glimpses of it. Your confessions have captured parts of it. You are designed to glorify Me, and that involves serving and loving Me well. My Son affirmed the greatest commandments as loving Me with everything in you and loving others as yourself. These are all true, but My Word never says they are comprehensive. It only points to greater realities. You haven't seen the full picture. Your words can describe My desires for you, but they can't capture them completely. You have only begun to understand.

"I made you in My image so you could relate to Me at the most intimate levels—*and* so you could embody My nature and shine with My glory. My Son's prayer for you to share My glory gave Me great pleasure. That's My desire. I want you to be smeared with My presence—that's what 'anointing' is about—and saturated in My radiance. I once insisted that I don't share My glory with others, but I was speaking of false gods and prideful human beings. I do share My glory with My children. I want them, all of you, to emanate with the brightness, the brilliance, the display of who I am.

"If My voice ever sounds demanding, this is why. It isn't because I want to hold high standards over your head; I want you to rise higher and fulfill this glorious purpose. My goal isn't to modify your behavior—animal trainers can do that. My goal is to infuse the fullness of My nature into you and let you shine. You have only begun to imagine where you're headed."

Oh, Lord—I can't even imagine. Your purposes for me seem so much higher than I will ever be able to attain. Only You can accomplish this, but I am willing. Let me shine brightly with Your glory.

JUNE 18

Your presence among us sets your people and me apart from all other people on the earth.
EXODUS 33:16

God pulled His people out from among the Egyptians, led them to a mountain in the desert, and gave them a set of laws and teachings that would distinguish them as His own. Yet, during this season at Sinai, Moses appeals to none of that. He doesn't talk about Israel's cultural distinctives or its geographic destiny in the Promised Land. He doesn't bring up their superb, God-given moral code or their unique worship practices or their intensely specific kosher laws. These are not the marks of a set-apart nation. The key variable—the one identifying characteristic that sets this people apart—is that God's presence is among them.

That speaks volumes about our efforts to be separate from the world. God has called us to be set apart for His pleasure and purposes—*holy* is the biblical word for it—but a particular lifestyle can accomplish only so much. A unique lifestyle gives numerous people around the world a sense of identity, but it doesn't set them apart. What sets God's people apart is His presence—and all that His presence entails, including His voice.

Our lifestyle matters to God, of course, but only as it flows out of our relationship with Him. What matters more is our communication with Him, and central to that communication is our capacity for hearing Him and sensing His presence. We aren't distinguished from the world because of our moral code or our theology; we are unique because God lives in us and with us and shares His heart with us. We live by revelation, not by principles. We are guided, not self-directed. We are immersed in a relationship, not an ideology. When we choose to live in full awareness of His presence, our spiritual senses open up to hear and see new things.

Lord, let me never confuse Your voice with mere religious principles and ideals. Help me always focus on Your living presence and Your voice above all else. You are far more than a belief; You are my life.

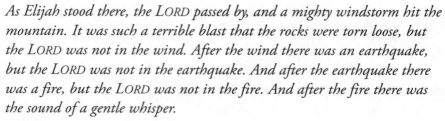

JUNE 19

As Elijah stood there, the LORD passed by, and a mighty windstorm hit the mountain. It was such a terrible blast that the rocks were torn loose, but the LORD was not in the wind. After the wind there was an earthquake, but the LORD was not in the earthquake. And after the earthquake there was a fire, but the LORD was not in the fire. And after the fire there was the sound of a gentle whisper.

1 KINGS 19:11-12

Centuries earlier, God had spoken to Moses amid thunder, lightning, a thick cloud of smoke, and a powerful blast of a horn. There was plenty of drama at Sinai, and quite a few words came out of that encounter with God. Now, at the very same mountain, Elijah experiences similarly dramatic phenomena, yet he hears God's voice only in the gentle whisper that comes afterward. God speaks to Elijah differently than He spoke to Moses, and He makes a point of it.

What statement is God making? Perhaps Elijah, fresh from a victory over the priests of Baal but in exile from the rabid Jezebel, expected God to deal with unbelief and idolatry the same way He had in the time of Moses, and this was God's way of saying, "I have different ways of dealing with people at different times." Or maybe Elijah, who certainly seemed able to hear God's words in the past, was now being trained to hear God's voice in more subtle ways. Regardless, the incident teaches us an essential truth: God's communication is varied. Sometimes when we're watching for an obvious epiphany of His presence and direction, He speaks instead in the nuances of our lives. And sometimes when we're straining to hear the subtle voice, He hits us over the head with His truth. We can't focus on one mode of communication. We have to be ready for anything God wants to say—however He wants to say it.

Lord, help me to remain alert to Your voice in all of its forms. Make my spirit sensitive at all times. Shout to me, whisper to me, speak however You want. I'm listening.

The letter kills, but the Spirit gives life.
2 Corinthians 3:6, NIV

God gave Israel a lot of instructions. We sometimes call them "religious traditions," but the phrase "Thus says the Lord"—or something like it—appears so often throughout the law and the prophets that we can't easily dismiss these instructions as the words of men. God Himself spoke them for the benefit of His people.

So what do we do with Paul's statement that the letter of the law kills? How can something God inspired for our good actually produce death? Anyone with much experience trying to follow behavioral rules that go against human nature will understand. Hearing an external voice telling us what to do may in fact change our behavior for a time, but it doesn't change our nature. It's like putting bars around a criminal or painting a rundown house. The outward appearance conforms to a standard, but the inward condition remains as it was. As soon as the outward restraint is removed, the original state reappears. And it can no longer claim ignorance about right and wrong. That's a recipe for guilt, shame, and ultimately, death.

Asking God simply for information is never enough. We must hear the voice that enables, the living voice that gets inside of us and changes our nature and prompts us from within. When our nature is transformed, we can do what comes naturally. Following God's voice becomes a matter of being who we are in Him rather than attempting to do what we've heard from Him. There is no death in that. We live from hearts that have come alive and can do all that is planted within.

Honestly, Lord, my efforts to do what Your Word says have been frustrating. I can never quite seem to "get there." Please transform me from within by Your Word. Help me be everything Your Word calls me to be.

JUNE 21

The letter kills, but the Spirit gives life.
2 CORINTHIANS 3:6, NIV

No one has to tell a lion to roar. It just does. Why? Because that's its nature. So when we strain to obey God's voice and find it difficult, we are demonstrating something about our relationship to His Word: It's not our nature. Clearly that's often true; we are in a lifelong process of transformation. But this is not ideal. Our goal is to grow out of that condition so that hearing from God is really a matter of being *in* Him. We want to "roar"—or serve or talk or follow His guidance—not just because He tells us to, but because it's our nature.

The letter can't accomplish that, but the Spirit can. Sadly, however, many Christians aren't continually being filled and directed by the Spirit. Most of us tend to revert to living in our own strength. We hear God's Word and set about to do it—on our own. We forget the God-given process. We are to reject our own strengths and abilities, rest in His Spirit, rely on His strength and abilities, become transformed—not by doing things, but by intimacy with Him—and then live "naturally" according to the new nature that God is working within us. That's a deep and weighty process, but it isn't a difficult one. The yoke of Jesus is easy, and His burden is light. He lives within us so we don't have to carry the weight of life ourselves. His Spirit gives us the life we need in order to really live.

That's the difference between religion and relationship—the contrasts we so often point out but rarely experience fully and consistently. We fall back on religion far too easily. But if we can repeatedly and single-mindedly focus on God—if we can develop a Godward gaze and depend on His life within us—our inner nature will be powerfully transformed. And we will experience the Spirit who gives life.

Holy Spirit, plant Your words in me like seeds that spring to life. Let my inner nature flourish. Let Your deepest thoughts become my deepest thoughts. Live strong within me, and let me rest in Your efforts.

The LORD took Abram outside and said to him, "Look up into the sky and count the stars if you can. That's how many descendants you will have!"
GENESIS 15:5

God gave Abraham (Abram) a profound and powerful promise, and Abraham believed it. But many years later, after plenty of visible evidence that the promise might have been an empty one, Abraham was still waiting for God's words to come to pass. The process surely must have seemed cruel, as if God were dangling hope in front of His servant like a master dangles a carrot in front of his donkey to keep him moving. Why didn't God wait to give Abraham the promise until a short time before He was ready to fulfill it? For long years, the word seemed always visible, yet painfully unattainable.

That's often how God works, as Joseph, David, and many others would be able to testify. He speaks, and then life seems to taunt us with contradictions to His voice. We expect a direct process, and it hardly ever is. We expect an immediate fulfillment, and God is usually thinking long-term. We get frustrated, even when we understand this dynamic, and downright disillusioned when we don't. God's word to us is a seed that often takes a really long time to grow.

Handling God's words to us—His guidance, His promises, and His correction or affirmation—is just as important as hearing Him in the first place. He wants us to hold them with faith and patience, even when we don't understand how or when they could possibly be fulfilled. We must continually remind ourselves that God's words don't die. They are planted deep in the soil of our hearts and circumstances, and they will grow up and bear fruit.

Lord, I know Your words will test my resolve. Please help me not only to endure the process faithfully, but also to be strengthened throughout it. May I, like Abraham, end up with faith that does not waver.

JUNE 23

When I heard this, I sat down and wept. In fact, for days I mourned, fasted, and prayed to the God of heaven.

NEHEMIAH 1:4

"Lord, more than ever I need to hear Your voice now. And I need to hear it more clearly than ever before." That was my prayer in a desperate moment not long ago. He had spoken clearly about a matter years before and confirmed it many times since. Now it looked impossible. Life seemed to have dropped a devastating bomb on my understanding of God's will. Everything I thought I had known Him to say seemed to be an illusion. Like Nehemiah, who believed in God's plan for Jerusalem yet heard that the city still lay in ruins, I was distraught. My God-given dreams apparently were not God-given. They had been reduced to rubble.

I accused God of misleading me. (Jeremiah had done the same, so I figured I was in good company.) I railed at how demanding His promises had been, how they had stretched me, how I had clung to them for years in spite of circumstances, and how it now looked as if there would be no reward. But mostly I mourned. I sat down and wept. I fasted for days. And I prayed to the God of heaven who, from all outward appearances, had betrayed my trust.

This time I needed more than general Bible verses (I can subconsciously screen those to suit my purposes all too easily) and more than outward messages, signs, and coincidences. Those would all be welcome, but not enough. I needed the crystal-clear, inward voice of the living God. And it didn't come as I expected. He quietly affirmed what He had already said, yet somehow turned my hope away from a particular outcome and toward Him alone. I can't explain how; it just happened. And all without a "voice," though surely He had spoken. Broken, I still knew He was—and is—walking me through a valley. The details weren't the story. His presence and guidance were.

❖ ❖ ❖

Lord, I don't have to understand what You're doing in order to trust You. I don't have to hear details to know I've heard You. Just walk with me. Please.

JUNE 24

*The LORD will guide you continually, giving you water when you are dry
and restoring your strength. You will be like a well-watered garden, like an
ever-flowing spring.*
ISAIAH 58:11

FROM THE HEART OF GOD

"Some people believe I guide them sporadically—that I will give direction
on an emergency basis, but not day by day. And those same people believe I
give times of refreshing sparingly, only after seasons of hardship or barrenness
when refreshing is particularly needed. Those are, in fact, the experiences of
many, but they are not necessary patterns. Life with Me doesn't have to be
this way. I'm much more willing to be in your life day by day—even moment
by moment—than you might think.

"The reason people don't experience Me as often as they want is because
they aren't convinced that they can. They make assumptions about apparent silences and withdraw rather than pressing in. They develop theological
arguments to explain why I let them experience dry and difficult times. They
don't realize that if they had persisted in faith and patience—requirements
for everything in My Kingdom—they would have broken through to a new
depth and consistency in knowing and hearing Me. My guidance would have
become clearer. My times of refreshing would have come sooner. Those who
settled for less of Me would have gotten more.

"My desire is for you to be a well-watered garden and an ever-flowing
spring. I may let you go through dry times, but they aren't meant to last,
and they aren't meant to drive you away. They are meant to draw you nearer,
to keep your face turned toward Me, to keep you asking for the things I
already want to give you. If you will ask, seek, and knock, you will find.
Consistently."

Lord, You desire to guide and refresh me continually, yet I experience dry and
confusing times. I know better than to try to figure out why; You value my trust
much more than my understanding, and You haven't designed me to figure out
everything. Please help me trust. And persevere. And experience Your continual
presence every day.

We are confident that he hears us whenever we ask for anything that pleases him. And since we know he hears us when we make our requests, we also know that he will give us what we ask for.

1 JOHN 5:14-15

For most of us, the normal pattern of prayer is to ask God to accomplish certain things and then wait to see what He does with our requests. There's nothing wrong with that approach; any kind of conversation with God qualifies as prayer. But those petitions are almost like shooting an arrow and hoping it hits the bull's-eye. Is it His will, or isn't it? We'll have to see when—and if—the results come in.

According to biblical promises, God means for our prayers to be more confident than that. His Word tells us that a prayer of faith often is answered when a tentative prayer would not be. But in order for us to pray in faith, we have to know up front whether our petitions are consistent with God's will. When we pray and only hope He will answer if the request happens to fit within His will, it's hard to pray in faith. We trust God, of course, but we don't have much confidence that our prayer will be answered. In order to have specific faith for what we ask, we need to know that what we ask fits God's purposes.

This is one of the areas in which it is crucial for us to hear God's voice. We know His general purposes through His Word—clearly we can be confident about some requests that further His Kingdom. But the personal requests about direction, provision, healing, and more—not to mention the deep longings of our hearts—are always tentative unless we've heard from Him. He invites us to ask what His will is—and then, when we've heard, to pray that His will be done. Confidently.

Father, if you tell me my prayer is consistent with Your will, I will maintain unwavering faith until the answer shows up. Help me pray Your desires and mine in confidence.

JUNE 26

Those who are controlled by the Holy Spirit think about things that please the Spirit.
ROMANS 8:5

God is working within you. He is shaping your character, your desires, your feelings, your sense of direction, your vision of the future . . . everything. While you are listening for an external voice to guide you, God is renovating your heart and mind internally. He may speak through an external voice, but not independent of His Spirit's internal work. According to Romans 8:5 and Philippians 2:13, God is busy shaping your thoughts, your will, and your works for His good pleasure.

Most Christians are deeply suspicious of their own desires, and we have some basis for that. Our desires can be selfish and misdirected. But our tendency to crucify all of them isn't the answer. If God is working within us to shape our will, and we try to crucify everything that qualifies as "our will," aren't we then at odds with the Holy Spirit's work? If God has planted many of our desires within us, it will do no good to try to crucify those desires. Though many people assume that if they want something it must not be God's will, we can assume that if we want something it very well might be God's will. He is cultivating us to want what He wants for us.

Don't be afraid of the work God is doing within you. Don't assume that your pleasures and His are at odds with each other. He is working His pleasure into you, helping you desire what He desires and pursue His purposes. When your will and His will align, it may feel like you are simply seeking your own interests. But you are seeking His interests too. And both you and He will be satisfied with the results.

Holy Spirit, are my desires really okay? Have You put Your desires within me? Help me discern which ones are Yours and which have flowed out of my own selfishness. Satisfy me with the fulfillment of every desire that fits Your purposes.

> *He urged them to ask the God of heaven to show them his mercy by telling them the secret. . . . That night the secret was revealed to Daniel in a vision.*
> DANIEL 2:18-19

Nebuchadnezzar had made an unreasonable demand with potentially dreadful consequences. The pressure struck terror in the sages of Babylon, but it compelled Daniel and his friends to pray. Instead of despairing at the impossibility—after all, who among us would really expect God to reveal someone else's dream to us?—Daniel took the impossibility to God. He didn't resign his hope to the God who works in mysterious ways, or assume that God had already revealed His Word centuries before and therefore wasn't interested in a pagan king's dreams today. He appealed to the living God whose voice spoke all of creation into being.

So Daniel and his friends counted on God's mercy and boldly asked Him to tell them a secret. That night, God answered by revealing the secret in a vision. As it turns out, the pagan king's dream had been given by God in the first place. This wasn't a psychological outworking of a disturbed mind, the fruit of a guilty conscience, or a demonically inspired thought of an idolater. Nebuchadnezzar did not believe in God; in fact, he worshiped false gods. Yet the God of heaven spoke to him in a dream, and then revealed the dream and its meaning to Daniel in a vision. The "revealer of mysteries" (Daniel 2:47) was very vocal about what was happening because He had authored the mysteries to begin with.

This story ought to stretch our understanding of how—and to whom—God speaks. We know He has spoken in Scripture, but Scripture itself tells us that He speaks in a multitude of ways. God has not put Himself in a box. He can speak to anyone at any time for any reason—and reveal any mystery that confounds us.

Lord, You gave Daniel a vision simply because he asked and didn't limit You with his expectations. I relinquish my expectations too. Please give me insight into the problems of my life and of my world.

JUNE 28

He gives wisdom to the wise and knowledge to the scholars.
Daniel 2:21

Daniel asked God for revelation, and God answered. Even in his asking, Daniel affirmed God's nature as the provider of wisdom and knowledge. God didn't create the world in order to withhold Himself from it. He didn't give us inquisitive minds simply to abandon us to their fallen instincts. He didn't establish the beauty, order, and intricate designs of creation in order to hide them from us. And He doesn't callously watch us struggling with huge issues while hoarding the solutions in His own mind. No, He not only has all wisdom and knowledge; He is predisposed to share it with us.

But usually only if we ask. It's true that we can gain limited knowledge and insight through experience, discovery, and education, but that doesn't always help us with immediate needs, and it's usually tainted with misperceptions anyway. But those who want to access God's wisdom for current situations are invited to ask in confidence that He is the source of truth and that He wants to impart it. We are not left in the dark to deal with life on our own.

When we pray for revelation—for wisdom, insight, solutions to problems, words of guidance, or visions of truth—we need to pray in faith, without doubting, that God has the answers we need and that He is willing to share them with us if we will open ourselves to Him. James 1:5-6 is emphatic that God is not reluctant to share His wisdom. Any holdup is more likely in our lack of confidence in asking and hearing. But if we ask in faith, God will give us the wisdom and knowledge we need.

Father, it's Your nature to share what You have. That's what love does. And You have all wisdom and knowledge. I need guidance and solutions to problems. My eyes and ears are open, and I'm asking in faith. Fill me with Your truth.

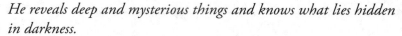

*He reveals deep and mysterious things and knows what lies hidden
in darkness.*
Daniel 2:22

A well-known hymn declares that God moves in mysterious ways, and it's true.
We don't always understand what He's doing—or when or why or how. But the
overwhelming testimony of Scripture is that He reveals His mysterious ways
to His people. We aren't fatalistically relegated to ignorance. Throughout the
pages of Scripture, God works in the lives of those who love and trust Him,
while interacting with them along the way. It's true that we may go through long
seasons of mystery, understanding each turn of events only in retrospect. But
for most of the people of faith in the Bible, God punctuated those seasons with
words of encouragement, correction, or instruction. And usually those words
were quite specific.

Think about it: Abraham went twenty-five long years between a promise
and its fulfillment, not knowing for most of those years exactly how or when
the promise would be realized. But each time God spoke, the promise—and
Abraham's understanding—got more specific. The same could be said of Jacob,
Moses, and David. God rarely lays everything out up front, but He also rarely
withholds all communication until the end. In between those two extremes, our
interaction with Him is a process that unveils His mysteries piece by piece. And
those who experience the greatest unveilings seem to be those who ask for them.

There's a fine line between trusting God for the details (which reflects faith)
and assuming He doesn't want to talk about them (which doesn't reflect faith).
Finding a balance isn't always easy, but it involves seeking revelation zealously
while being content when God chooses to let some things remain veiled—
without losing heart in the process. When the time is right, He will help you
discover things that have been hidden in darkness.

Revealer of mysteries, no secret is hidden from You. You know every corner
of every heart and every situation in this world, including mine. Let me never
judge or limit the ways You speak or the secrets You reveal. Guide me in every
way I need to go.

JUNE 30

Faith is the confidence that what we hope for will actually happen; it gives us assurance about things we cannot see.
HEBREWS 11:1

Rees Howells, a man known for his life of intercessory prayer, found himself on a train platform without any money to get to his next destination. He was led there by faith, believing God would provide, yet the time had come to catch the next train, and he still had no means to buy a ticket. At that moment, the Holy Spirit spoke to him: "If you had money, what would you do?" Howells responded that he would go ahead and get in line for a ticket. The Spirit then said, "Have you not been preaching that My promises are equal to current coin? You had better take your place in the queue." So Howells obeyed.

There is nothing ambiguous about this conversation. It was a clear exchange of words. As Howells waited in line, he also had a clear conversation with the enemy, the tempter; apparently Howells was well versed in the language of the spiritual realm, regardless of his conversation partner. In our age, we might be inclined to call this an imaginary discussion between competing thoughts in our own minds, yet there was nothing at all imaginary about the fruit of this discussion. God provided money for Howells's ticket at the last moment through a bystander who had no knowledge of the need. Howells's faith was rewarded rather concretely. The conversations about the terms of his faith had been very real.

Many of our thoughts are more than just thoughts. They are an exchange of words between us and the Holy Spirit, or sometimes between us and an unholy spirit of darkness. Far from "just our imagination," they are concrete communications. Through eyes of faith, we can recognize them as such and act on them. Our minds very often think the thoughts of God, and our hearts can learn to discern them.

Spirit of God, You've told me I have the mind of Christ. Teach me to recognize which thoughts are His. I wholeheartedly invite You to be thoroughly present in my mental conversations.

JULY 1

Some of you will rebuild the deserted ruins of your cities. Then you will be known as a rebuilder of walls and a restorer of homes.
Isaiah 58:12

FROM THE HEART OF GOD

"Most people know Me as a personal God, the God of the individual. Some understand My love for the church, the bride I am setting apart for Myself. But few understand My love for cities and nations. They see My love for individuals in cities and nations, but they don't see My zeal for the social structures and community life of all people, not just those who believe in Me. My desire is for you to have safe places to live, healthy and whole families, balanced lifestyles, and peace on every side. I want the world to be a place of blessing.

"That's how I originally created the world to be. Many have thought that I'm simply waiting for this present world to pass away so I can take you to heaven to experience My Kingdom forever. But have you noticed how many times I've urged you to repair your life *on earth*? Do you remember the prayer My Son taught you about My Kingdom coming *on earth*? Have I not instructed you to pray for people in places of authority so that life might go well for you *on earth*? I've never said, 'Ignore the world because I'm soon taking you out of there,' yet so many of My people behave as if I have. I don't just redeem; I restore. Few have understood how concerned I am for your well-being.

"You will not hear Me directing you to isolate yourself from the world. I will lead you not into hiding, but into civic organizations, run-down neighborhoods, schools, recreation programs, broken families, community clubs and activities, and more. If I'm going to bless the world through you, you will have to go into the world. There is no other way. You are called to restore, rebuild, and let My blessings flow."

Lord, I don't know how to rebuild my city—or even how to bless my own neighborhood. Give me ideas. Show me opportunities. Let me be an instrument of restoration in the world around me.

David asked the LORD, "Should I chase after this band of raiders? Will I catch them?" And the LORD told him, "Yes, go after them. You will surely recover everything that was taken from you!"

1 SAMUEL 30:8

It should have been obvious to David that God was on his side. David had inquired about attacks before, and would surely inquire again. If anyone had a right to assume a *yes* from God, David did. And in this case it wasn't simply a strategy decision; a horrible injustice had been done. Of course God would want David to pursue the raiders, rescue the wives and children of his men, and secure justice. Even so, David asked.

Many of us assume that one-time direction from God implies a general policy that we can follow thereafter, but that's a careless assumption. When God guides us, He isn't saying, "This is how I speak and where I will lead you from now on." What we hear from Him usually applies to that specific situation. The next time we need direction, we'll have to listen again, even if the situation is similar to the last time. God doesn't give us formulas or patterns. He gives us Himself—His presence and His ongoing voice.

David seemed to understand that. He brought each situation to God as if it were the first and only time He was listening for guidance. He knew that God had different plans for different situations, and that even when His general will is known, the timing and methods for how to proceed aren't always clear. We may be confident of what God wants to accomplish in our lives, but we still need direction about how and when He wants to accomplish it, as well as what role He wants us to play in the process. We can never assume that what He said last time applies just as clearly this time. In every situation, we need to ask.

Lord, let me never be presumptuous about Your will. Your character never changes, but there is no end to the variety of Your methods. I'm depending on fresh guidance in every situation of my life.

You are a chosen people. You are royal priests, a holy nation, God's very own possession.

1 PETER 2:9

This statement from Peter is either true or (as far as we know) potentially true of everyone we meet. Even the most hardened criminal or twisted psychopath is a candidate to become a chosen, royal priest and a child of God. But in attempting to share God's Word, many Christians focus on the sin in people's lives. Some of us have a tendency to point out where others are falling short of God's standards. We don't focus on their potential in God's Kingdom; we focus on their experience outside of it.

That isn't God's voice. It's true that the Spirit convicts of sin, but He rarely needs us to help with that. We aren't called to point out each other's faults. No, when God speaks through us to other members or potential members of His body, the voice is not condemning. It's full of hope. We are to see the treasure He has put in others and to call it out. If we ask God how He sees the people around us, He will show us His love for them and what they will look like in Christ. He will point out their gifts or their fruitfulness in the Kingdom. He doesn't reveal what we have no business knowing. He urges us to bless the good that He is cultivating in others.

Paul told the Corinthians that prophetic ministry among believers is for strengthening, encouraging, and comforting (1 Corinthians 14:3). If you're sensitive to the Spirit, that's what you'll hear: words that build up and bring hope. Ask God what's on His heart that He wants to share with others, and He will give you glimpses of the treasure He has placed within them. And you will be able to affirm what He wants to do in their lives.

Lord, give me hope-filled words. Show me the treasure in Your people. Let me see them through spiritual eyes and bless what You are doing in their lives.

[Paul wrote,] "Timothy, my son, here are my instructions for you, based on the prophetic words spoken about you earlier. May they help you fight well in the Lord's battles."

1 TIMOTHY 1:18

Paul doesn't tell us what the prophetic words were that were given to Timothy, or who gave them. They aren't scriptural words, but they were an accurate expression of God's heart and His will for Timothy when they were given. They may have been spoken by Paul or one of his associates, the community of believers in Timothy's hometown, or any other combination of people. And apparently they were sufficient to fuel Timothy's calling and keep him focused.

God's words have that kind of power. When we hear them, whether directly in our spirits or through other believers, we have a divine invitation to cling to them and let them shape our focus. With all the distractions and obstacles that come against us, we need that. We won't stay on a direct course or have the energy to keep following it if we're questioning how we've been led in the past. We have a nearly limitless capacity to second-guess ourselves, and many of us constantly reconsider whether we're heading in the right direction. Confidence in what God has said gives us the clarity we need.

Listen well to what God has told you. You will go into battle with it later. Paul urged Timothy to fight with the words he had been given, likely knowing that both Timothy and the people around him might have a tendency to question his calling. Prophetic words that have given you direction in the past become an anchor when you begin to question that direction in confusing times. In God's Kingdom, when the going gets tough, the tough will use God's past words as weapons against every misleading thought, suggestion, distraction, and obstacle. His words yesterday are your key to victory today.

Lord, I'm clinging to what You said. I won't depart from it, no matter what contradictions I hear or think. Help me pursue only the calling You've given.

JULY 5

One night Joseph had a dream, and when he told his brothers about it, they hated him more than ever.

GENESIS 37:5

From a human perspective, Joseph's journey looked like a tragic mistake. God had spoken to him, and he had indiscriminately told his brothers about how one day they would bow down to him. This seemingly arrogant sense of having a superior destiny enraged them, and they retaliated first with a plan to kill him, then with a revised plan to sell him into slavery. As we know in retrospect, this was the path to the fulfillment of the dream. But for years it looked like the opposite.

When God gives us a glimpse of our calling and then circumstances seem to take us in the opposite direction, we're usually very disoriented. We cry out, "Did You tell me only to frustrate me? If it was going to take this long, why didn't You wait until closer to the time to tell me?" But what looks like an overdone lesson on faith and patience is really God's mercy. He didn't give us a glimpse of our calling to frustrate us during the delays and obstacles. He gave us the glimpse in order to prepare us to persevere. At confusing and disappointing turns in the journey, we will need to hang on to those words. They become our anchor of truth in the midst of shifting messages from the world around us. They give us direction and hope when it's hard to tell which way is up.

Joseph's dreams may have seemed like an unnecessary part of the story—God could have accomplished everything in his life without giving him a preview—but he likely held on to those dreams through years of darkness. Psalm 105:19 tells us that the Word of God tested Joseph until it was fulfilled. It would also encourage him. When God speaks a "yes," He is giving us something to cling to when everything else says *no.*

Lord, I'm clinging to the words You have spoken to me. They are my anchor, my encouragement, my food for living in hope. Help me always to see them as larger than my circumstances.

He will proclaim justice to the nations.
MATTHEW 12:18

We live in an age of personalized Christianity, in which each person has his or her own relationship with God, and the individual is paramount. When we speak of Jesus' relationship with social structures, it's most often in terms of the church. That's because the church is His body, and we assume everything else is "secular" or "worldly" and beyond His focus. We're well acquainted with the fact that He sends us into nations in order to share the Good News with people everywhere—individuals again—but we forget how often God thinks in terms of entire nations in Scripture. And we also forget that He is interested not only in evangelism but also in justice.

Though modern evangelical Christians have an aversion to "social gospel" movements of the past—and it's true that the gospel can't be reduced simply to social improvement—Jesus nevertheless is zealous about the welfare of society. Injustices bother Him. He is always seeking those on the margins of society who need help. His Kingdom will do away with national policies that fuel gross inequities. He wants His creation to be spiritually, emotionally, psychologically, physically, and materially whole.

We can expect God's voice to speak to us about injustices wherever we live and work. If His heart is for those who are oppressed and disadvantaged, His followers will be moved to do something for them. He will not tell us, "Don't worry about that; I'll set everything right when I come." He's much more likely to say, "Before I come *for* you, I'm going to come *through* you." We are meant to reflect His heart in this world. And reflecting His heart means we will seek justice for the nations.

Jesus, if You proclaim justice to the nations, I need to proclaim it too. If this is part of Your message, I need to hear it and then live it. Help me align my life with the truth of Your agenda in this world.

JULY 7

How good is a timely word!
PROVERBS 15:23, NIV

A member of our group asked for prayer for her mother, who was suffering from a terminal disease and increasingly unable to walk. Several times a day, her mother stumbled and fell, and the family would rush to her side. Mother, daughter, and everyone else in the family needed God's support.

After we prayed, we read through a preselected psalm, Psalm 145, with each person reading two verses aloud. When it came to the woman who had requested prayer for her mother, she began reading the verses that fell to her in the rotation: "The LORD upholds all who fall and lifts up all who are bowed down" (Psalm 145:14, NIV). She barely finished the words as the tears began to fall. God had directly acknowledged a personal need and promised to walk with this family through their trial.

God is the master of timely words. He knows the seating order of a group before they sit down and read. He knows years in advance which Bible passages and which devotionals will be read on a certain day, and He has a supernatural ability to coordinate them to speak directly into the events and issues of the reader's life. He knows how to direct us out of our normal patterns to listen to a message, read a passage of a book, or even overhear a casual comment that speaks profoundly into our hearts' desperate needs. He knows how to time His voice to get our attention and fit our circumstances.

Never hesitate to ask God for timely words. When you're discouraged, ask Him for encouragement. It always comes, usually sooner rather than later. When you need guidance or wisdom, ask Him to express His will in the messages you will hear through your conversations, readings, and exposure to His Word. Whatever your need, He has something to say. And He knows the perfect timing to say it.

Lord, impress upon me the folly of seeing timely words as "coincidences." You are the Master of my circumstances, and Your timing is impeccable. You coordinate the things I hear and see. Help me recognize Your voice in them.

JULY 8

*Keep the Sabbath day holy. Don't pursue your own interests on that day,
but enjoy the Sabbath and speak of it with delight as the LORD's holy day.*
ISAIAH 58:13

FROM THE HEART OF GOD

"Why do you read My Word? Some read only to find out what I require. Others read to discover what's on My heart. Do you see the difference? It's possible to search for My requirements without having a relationship with Me or even caring that a relationship is an option. But no one tries to discover what's on My heart without wanting a connection with Me. Your goal when you read My Word will determine what you do with it.

"That's why many throughout the centuries have seen the Sabbath as a demand, an obligation to fulfill rather than a blessing to receive. The result is severe restrictions and a lot of guilt for failing to adhere to them. But do you see My heart in this command? I want you to rest and be refreshed. I designed you not only for everyday connections with Me but for a focused time each week to enjoy My presence. I crafted you to need pauses from your routine. I gave you a built-in excuse to take a break from your normal responsibilities. I mandated this break because I know your tendency to rationalize your overwork. No one will fault you for defying the expectations others place on you. You can blame Me for your time of peace and rest. You can come away with Me guilt-free.

"Remember this: Every instruction I give you is relational. Like the Sabbath rest, none of my instructions are about fulfilling requirements, but all of them become a reflection of the state of our relationship. If you do them, it must be because you care—because My desires matter to you. That's the reaction My voice is meant to provoke in you, and it's the only reaction I want from you. Hear Me with your heart."

Lord, may I never hear Your voice without connecting with Your heart. As I take time to be alone with You, meet me with Your presence, power, and love. May everything I do be an extension of my relationship with You.

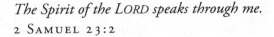
The Spirit of the LORD speaks through me.
2 SAMUEL 23:2

These are among the last words of David—not David the priest or David the prophet, but David the shepherd-turned-king. The thought that a young son of an ordinary family, looked down on by his brothers, would somehow rise from the shepherd's path to the royal palace seems too farfetched to be true. But that's the course David's life took, demonstrating for us that a heart for God is the only real prerequisite for an extraordinary life. And apparently it qualifies a shepherd to speak God's words.

That's the kind of person God chooses to speak through. He doesn't share His voice exclusively among the religious elite—the seminary-trained ministers of any given era. Yes, He has established a priesthood at times, eventually calling all believers to function as priests toward each other. And yes, He has chosen prophets to carry specific messages at particularly critical times in history. But He has also chosen to speak through shepherds and farmers, warriors and kings, servants and slaves, and even a donkey and a burning bush. We're told that even stones can cry out in praise of God, so presumably any common vessel is able to bear His messages. All that's required is a life that is yielded to Him.

David lived such a life, being chosen specifically because he was a man after God's own heart. If we want the Spirit of the Lord to speak through us, that's really our first and only requirement—to live with passionate love toward Him, to pursue Him above all other affections. The Spirit of the Lord is more than willing to speak through those in intimate fellowship with Him. In knowing His heart, we are qualified to express it, and He is eager to give us the words to do so.

Spirit of God, David was no more qualified to speak for You than I am, as long as my heart is zealous for You. So cultivate the right heart in me. Draw me close to You and let Your words flow through me.

His words are upon my tongue.

2 SAMUEL 23:2

In the movies, God's voice thunders from heaven. It's deep, calm, and authoritative, though it contains hardly any emotion. But at least it's clear. No one questions what God says when Hollywood portrays His voice.

But apart from a few rare exceptions in Scripture, that's not normally how it works in real life. We can hear God in a variety of ways, but very often He will speak to our hearts through other people. That's what He did in the Bible every time a priest, prophet, king, apostle, ordinary believer, or any other willing vessel expressed His Spirit. David was able to say God's words were on his tongue because that's God's normal mode of speaking. Those who are close to Him can translate the inaudible thoughts of His Spirit into audible words that everyone can hear. We can put human words to heavenly sounds. We are translators of the universe's highest and holiest language.

In God's wisdom, this is better than thundering His voice from heaven. It requires faith. It separates casual hearers from zealous seekers because it takes time and effort to discern the spirit behind a message. It demands a depth of relationship in order to distinguish the good from the bad, the true from the false, and the holy from the common. If God's voice were all thunder, the world would cower in obedience, but would not be drawn into His love. But when His voice comes through those who are made and re-created in His image . . . well, that's a different story. We can be filled with His truth and love. And when we are, we very often find that His words are upon our tongues.

Lord, when I hear Your voice through others, help me to be neither hypercritical nor under-discerning. Let me rightly distinguish what comes from Your heart. And when I speak Your truth and love, may it always be received by those for whom it is intended.

When you are arrested, don't worry about how to respond or what to say. God will give you the right words at the right time.
MATTHEW 10:19

Few of us in the Western church today would expect Jesus to begin a sentence with, "When you are arrested," but we would certainly rejoice at the instruction that comes afterward. And though the context narrows the audience to those living under persecution, the principle applies to all of us. There are times, particularly under pressure, when we don't have to focus on getting all the words right. God Himself will speak through us.

The great comfort of this verse is not that God is always inspiring our words—we have enough experience with slips of the tongue to know that isn't true—but that He can fill us with His words at any moment. He doesn't possess us and control us, so we shouldn't wait for some different state of consciousness to take over. He does, however, fill us with His Spirit and His own nature and desires, so at times we will notice that we seem more energetic and insightful than usual. Then we wonder whether it's the Holy Spirit at work in us, and after reflecting on the experience, realize that it must have been. That's how it usually plays out—not a distinct experience of Spirit-possession, but an intertwining of God's Spirit with ours, and with some sort of fruitful result to prove it. At critical times in our relationships, we become a mouthpiece of the Lord, who happens to use our mouths and personalities in the process.

Most Christians have, at some point or another, been a mouthpiece for the Lord, often without even being aware of it. But whether we recognize it or not, God speaks through us. And when we rely on Him without worrying about our words, He speaks most freely.

Holy Spirit, give me the words to say—not just in pressure situations, but in every relationship I have. Let my words be seasoned with Your grace, truth, and power. Use my mouth as You wish.

It is not you who will be speaking—it will be the Spirit of your Father speaking through you.
MATTHEW 10:20

Jesus told His followers that the Spirit would guide them into all truth and tell them about the future (John 16:13). Paul assured his readers often that Jesus lived in them—willing, working, and speaking the things of God. Peter told his readers to speak as if they were speaking the very words of God (1 Peter 4:11). In Matthew 10, Jesus gives His followers a glimpse of what that will look like. There are times when they will speak—with their voices, their thoughts, and seemingly their words—but it will actually be the Spirit speaking through them. They will be the speakers, but God will be the source.

Few people today are apt to claim divine inspiration when they speak, but that comes more from humility than from biblical conviction. It also comes from a lack of faith in what God has promised, as well as too much sensitivity to pharisaical critics. Often when someone in the church today claims to have heard from God—or more daringly, to have spoken His words—hypervigilant "defenders of the faith" will declare such audacity to be practically heretical. But these kinds of critics, in defending the Bible, have forgotten what the Bible actually says. They have ignored the words of Jesus or redefined them to apply only to one generation of disciples or apostles. Meanwhile, those who have heard God's voice are intimidated into thinking they haven't.

Jesus was emphatic that the Spirit speaks through His followers with the Father's own words. It isn't heretical to believe that truth. In fact, *not* believing it falls far short of God's purposes. Instead, we are invited to let the Spirit rise up within us and speak boldly through our mouths in the situations around us—not arrogantly, not presumptuously, but confidently. The Spirit loves to make Himself heard through His people.

Holy Spirit, I know You are speaking, and I trust that You are speaking to me and through me. You give me permission to declare what I've heard from You to others. Help me make the most of every opportunity to do so.

Your new life will last forever because it comes from the eternal, living word of God. As the Scriptures say, . . . "The grass withers and the flower fades. But the word of the Lord remains forever."

1 PETER 1:23-25

God doesn't speak transient words. He has enough foresight not to say something that isn't going to prove true. He knows the effects His words will have, and who will and won't accept them, and He speaks them with full knowledge of their impact. He offers us eternal life through words that won't pass away, and He makes promises knowing they will come to pass if we believe them. He doesn't speak things He will regret or take back. When He speaks, He speaks with the authority of permanence.

That doesn't mean God never adds to His words or tells us we haven't lived up to them. He does that at times in Scripture, giving the impression that He can change His mind—or at the very least, redirect the specific details of His overall purposes. But though God may allow people to disqualify themselves from experiencing His truth, He doesn't change His truth. He doesn't reject His own words. He declares His will without reservation.

That means if God said something yesterday, we don't have to ask Him to say it again today. We don't need to worry about whether His promises still apply or if He has changed His mind about the good things He is doing in our lives. When He has given us a long-term vision, we don't need to ask about short-term visions that are inconsistent with it. He isn't a wishy-washy God who keeps changing His mood and retracting rash statements. His words endure. His purposes are eternal, and His words to us are based in those purposes. Whatever He tells us will endure.

Eternal God, the words You spoke to me years ago are still true, even long after I've forgotten them or chosen to neglect them. And the words You speak to me today will not fade away. I trust them—for as long as it takes to see them come to pass.

JULY 14

[Paul and Silas] headed north for the province of Bithynia, but again the Spirit of Jesus did not allow them to go there.
ACTS 16:7

George Müller tried several times to become a missionary, but the doors always closed. His father opposed his plans, a war broke out on one of his intended fields of service, and a mission agency declined his application. Many years later, he would travel the world as a speaker, but for decades, he was limited to his adopted home of England—where he began orphanages and developed a ministry with a huge impact on society. His closed doors led to fruitful, life-changing work where he was.

Nearly everyone has experienced a time when we've sensed God's leading and then found opposition at nearly every turn. Sometimes that opposition is from the enemy, but sometimes it's from God. Paul's work was redirected by the Holy Spirit, who would not allow him to go farther north into Asia, and he was then given a vision of a Macedonian pleading for him to come to Europe. In Revelation 3:7, Jesus is depicted as the one who opens doors no one can shut and shuts doors no one can open. Doors can shut emphatically on our plans, even when we thought they were God's plans. And if He is the one who shut them, no attempt to open them by faith will work.

God often speaks to us through the open and shut doors of our lives. We have to be discerning; many open doors are temptations, and many closed doors will open like the Red Sea if we believe and move forward. But when God firmly shuts us off, we will always be able to find Him leading in another way. That may take time, but new doors inevitably open. He will direct us down paths we never knew existed. And He will open opportunities that are far better than the ones we thought we understood.

Jesus, You are the Master of my doors. Father, my times are in Your hands. Holy Spirit, You promise to direct my paths. I trust You to close every door that isn't Your will, open every one that is, and give me discernment to recognize the difference.

JULY 15

Whoever has ears to hear, let them hear.
MARK 4:9, NIV

Like most people who are familiar with the Bible, you may have experienced a strange phenomenon. After reading the same passage or verse for about the hundredth time, it suddenly looks remarkably new. A lightbulb comes on in your mind, an "aha" comes to the surface, an "I never saw it that way before!" sinks into your heart. An old, familiar, and possibly even bland piece of your Scripture knowledge suddenly fits your experience in a fresh way. You see what you've never before seen, even though it has been right in front of your eyes.

That's God's voice. Yes, it's partly how the human brain works and partly how our shifting needs shape our receptivity, but it's also how God manages to apply His timeless words to our time-specific circumstances. When we're reading Scripture, especially as part of an ongoing conversation with God—with questions on our minds, issues to deal with, and ears to hear—He finds ways to lead us to truth that jumps off the page. Amazingly, He can fit the portion of a reading plan that was scheduled months or years ago to coincide with our problem of the day. Or He can send us on scriptural rabbit trails that land us in exactly the right spot. Or He can prompt one of His people to post one of His verses on Facebook exactly at our time of crisis, or inspire a pastor to preach a message that addresses a momentary concern, or use any number of other seemingly serendipitous message alerts to let us know what He is saying. His Word is unchanging, but His methods are more varied than we can imagine and more individually applied than we expected. God knows how to communicate.

Don't dismiss those moments as coincidence or as a function of your own psychological quirks. Embrace them as the voice of God speaking personally through His Word. These are moments when He has opened your ears to hear.

✧ ✧ ✧

Holy Spirit, let me read Your Word as if reading it for the first time. Unveil its meaning and apply it to the moment. Please carry our conversation forward.

JULY 16

The word of God is alive and powerful.
HEBREWS 4:12

God breathed His words through human beings. That's what *inspired* means: "breathed into." So the Bible is a mysterious mix of the divine and human, with the divine guiding the thoughts and expressions of humans who encountered Him and spoke and wrote what they experienced and learned. When the Word was written, it was under the specific guidance and supervision of the Holy Spirit.

The Word is also inspired when it is read and heard today. The Spirit's activity didn't end once the words were on ancient scrolls. He is working even now, causing specific messages to jump off the page into our hearts, provoking our minds to encounter truth and wrestle with it, encouraging our hearts to believe and grow, and imparting truth and wisdom into our spirits. Yes, it's possible to read Scripture purely from the mind, with human thoughts and skepticism and motives filtering the words to the point that they have little power. But when our spirits are open, the voice in the Word comes alive. Scripture still speaks.

We often strain to hear God's voice while our Bibles lie smoldering on the shelf, waiting to breathe God's words into us. And though He speaks through a multitude of messengers, we hear best when Scripture is an integral part of our hearing process. The Word is the necessary context for all other hearing. When we forget that, we're likely to get skewed messages from spurious sources. But when we feed on the Bible—which is still very much alive and powerful—the voice of God simmers and stirs within us. He fills us with truth.

Don't just read the Bible. Saturate yourself with it. Savor it. Let it shape your heart, your mind, and your spirit. When you do, it will open your ears.

Holy Spirit, breathe Your words into me. Don't just teach me Your truth; fill me with it. Let it shape me in every way so I can hear Your voice in it, through it, and by the light of it.

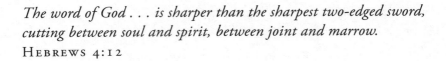
The word of God . . . is sharper than the sharpest two-edged sword,
cutting between soul and spirit, between joint and marrow.
HEBREWS 4:12

The Spirit who lives within us influences our thoughts and inspires our inner
senses. But we also know that we generate other thoughts—self-directed desires
and logic based on human wisdom—that can't be described as inspiration from
God. Once we are born of God's Spirit, our inner lives become a strange mix
of human and divine, and while the difference is sadly clear at times, there are
moments when we have difficulty discerning which source is at work. It's hard
to know if our thoughts are from God or from ourselves.

How can we tell the difference? The Word of God, the Scripture He has
given us, is masterful and powerful at dividing between truth and error. It's true
that we can find verses to justify almost anything we want to justify, but if we
read the Word with an open heart and mind, asking for wisdom and guidance,
God will use it to affirm us, correct us, challenge us, convict us, and inspire us.
Those questions we have about whether we are hearing Him correctly or not
will be answered as we saturate ourselves in His truth. The direction we think
we need to pursue will either be confirmed or revised as we read Scripture and
let it breathe into us. The Word divides between our minds and spirits, separating between our various motives and leading us into God's will.

We won't experience this power if we read the Word only to find justification
for our own agendas. We are masters at rationalization, and it isn't difficult to
bring the Bible into the rationalizing process. But that doesn't mean Scripture
will always oppose our thoughts and desires. If God has put them within us, the
Word will confirm them and strengthen us to hold them tightly in faith. The
sword of the Spirit will always point us toward the thoughts of God.

Spirit of truth, I invite You to sharply and decisively divide my own thoughts
from Yours and distinguish Your voice within me. Let Your words burn powerfully
in my heart and mind.

We never stop thanking God that when you received his message from us, you didn't think of our words as mere human ideas. You accepted what we said as the very word of God—which, of course, it is.
1 THESSALONIANS 2:13

Paul, speaking not only for himself but also for Silas and Timothy, was aware that their words weren't entirely their own. They were expressed in their own style and speech patterns, according to their distinct personalities, but the message itself was from God. These were not human ideas coming out of the mouths of these men. They were the very words of the Father. And the listeners in Thessalonica were somehow able to recognize that.

Few audiences today will recognize any divine origin behind human words. We're far too sophisticated and skeptical for that. We may acknowledge that a message is consistent with God's Word, but can we accept that it might actually be the very words of God? Most of us are far too suspicious of personalities and motives to hear God's voice through a human mouth. Yet God's own Word has made it clear that people are able to represent His voice.

We are right to be discerning, but wrong when discernment turns to blanket skepticism. We overestimate God's work in people when we elevate them to some false ideal of holiness and perfection, but we underestimate His work when we assume that the words of people filled with the Holy Spirit are only human words. He speaks through human mouthpieces. He fills hearts with truth. He inspires thoughts and messages and even specific words. We're fond of seeing ourselves as His hands and feet in this world, so it's only logical that we can hear ourselves and others as His voice. That voice must always be measured by His previously revealed truth, but if it's from God, it will measure up well. We can accept the proven words of His servants.

✧ ✧ ✧

God of truth, You know how to express Yourself through flawed human beings and fill us with Your Spirit in order to communicate. Help me see Your mind and heart in everyone who speaks Your truth.

JULY 19

This word [of God] continues to work in you who believe.
1 THESSALONIANS 2:13

When God speaks and hearers reject His words, His words will not be effective in those hearers' lives. We know this to be true in matters of salvation; those who reject the Good News will not experience its promises. But the same is true in matters of following God, growing in Christ, receiving His blessings and answers to prayer, and more. In many aspects of relating to God, what He speaks only takes shape when we believe what He said.

Faith is the currency of God's Kingdom, just as surely as dollars and euros and renminbi are the currencies of the world's systems. We need faith to receive. Jesus said "*if* you believe" far more often than we want to admit, which implies that His promises about prayer and the blessings of the Kingdom don't apply if we don't believe. "Anything is possible if a person believes" (Mark 9:23), for example, tells us that many things aren't possible at all for those who don't. "You can pray for anything, and if you believe that you've received it, it will be yours" (Mark 11:24) tells us that if we don't believe, it won't be ours. Whatever promises God has spoken, whatever assurances He has given, they are there for the taking—by faith. They fall to the ground without effect if we don't believe.

Never make the mistake of thinking that hearing God's voice is the same as believing it. Many hear what He says and then are disillusioned when it doesn't come to pass or doesn't prove true. But many times, they have heard without believing, only waiting to see if it might have been God who spoke. Faith requires letting our hearts step out of their comfort zones, banking on the assurance of having heard. The message that God delivers to us, whether of salvation or some aspect of following Him thereafter, will powerfully work in us—when we believe.

Lord, I have heard Your voice; help me believe it. May I fully embrace everything You have spoken so I can see the reality of it fully manifested in my life.

JULY 20

The rain and snow come down from the heavens and stay on the ground to water the earth. They cause the grain to grow, producing seed for the farmer and bread for the hungry. It is the same with my word. I send it out, and it always produces fruit. It will accomplish all I want it to, and it will prosper everywhere I send it.

ISAIAH 55:10-11

Some of us speak with little expectation of our words being heeded. Parents give instructions, sometimes repeatedly, knowing that their children may forget them or choose to ignore them. People speak of their future dreams without much confidence that they will come to pass. Counselors give advice, realizing that their advice will only sometimes be followed. To many of us, words are just words.

The result is a culture of language in which "all talk and no action" is a frequent lament. We tell people to put their money where their mouth is and describe their inaction and empty promises as "only words." But with God, there is no "only" about words. His words are as good as done. Like seeds sown into fertile ground, they will yield a harvest. When He issues an order, it will be carried out. When He gives a promise, it will be fulfilled. When He declares His purposes, they will be accomplished. As some versions of this passage say, God's Word will not return to Him empty. It will result in what He wants it to do.

Understand that when we hear God's voice, it's a weighty matter. He isn't just suggesting an option; He's declaring His truth. We can't afford to listen to Him simply out of curiosity. We have to listen with a sacred resolve to align with His words. If they are instructions, we will carry them out. If they are promises, we will believe them. If they are encouragement or correction, we will accept it. Whatever He says, it's true. It will not return to Him without fulfilling His purpose.

Lord, if all creation heeds Your voice, so must I. Let the distance between my ears and my actions be short. I respond with *yes* to whatever You say.

JULY 21

To another the same Spirit gives a message of special knowledge.
1 CORINTHIANS 12:8

"Do you have pain in your right knee?" one man asked another for no apparent reason. "Yes, as a matter of fact, I do," said the other. The man who asked the strange question then offered to pray for the pain to go away, and permission was granted. When he prayed, the pain began to subside.

The gentleman who received prayer for his knee marveled that anyone might be able to pinpoint his aching joint. He hadn't mentioned it. They had both been sitting, so the stranger couldn't have observed a limp. "How did you know?" he asked. The first man explained that he suddenly felt pain in his own knee. Having well-trained spiritual sensitivities and no history of knee problems, he assumed that God was giving him a message. He had learned that when something began to hurt for no apparent physical reason while he was talking to someone else, that person might have physical issues there. God was prompting him to pray for healing.

Most of us instinctively begin to wonder what's wrong with us when we have a physical symptom or a sudden mood change, and our focus turns toward ourselves. But when that happens, we may be picking up a signal from the Holy Spirit. He isn't limited to words, after all; He can speak through our senses. He has alerted many prayer warriors to other people's symptoms by giving them a brief, mild, and otherwise inexplicable pain in the area of need—a neck, a heart, an eye or ear, or anything else. "God told me your [neck, heart, ear, etc.] needs healing" is not an appropriate approach to the situation, but a polite query followed by an unassuming offer to pray is never out of line. When we invite God to speak this way, He uses us to show His goodness to people in need.

Lord, alert me to Your gentle nudges to represent You to others. Make me aware of the creative ways You speak. Teach me to ask, "What are You saying?" before I ever think, "Why is this happening?"

JULY 22

You cried to me in trouble, and I saved you; I answered out of the thundercloud and tested your faith when there was no water at Meribah.
PSALM 81:7

FROM THE HEART OF GOD

"The place of Meribah is a place of quarreling; it was given that name because My people quarreled with Me. Moses said they tested Me there, but I was also testing them. Their hearts were full of accusations against Me, thinking I had neglected them and forgotten to take care of their needs. But I was testing their trust, giving them an opportunity to remember My past faithfulness from the Red Sea and apply it to their present situation in the wilderness. And in spite of their complaints, I answered their cries.

"Did you notice that? I abhor complaining, but I still answer the pleas of the complainers. When you are in trouble, I listen and, sooner or later, come to the rescue. I may use the time between the prayer and the response to filter some attitudes out of you, but I still respond. I will not leave you in the wilderness without any provision.

"There have been times when you thought I was unresponsive. You wondered why you cried out and no one answered. You heard explanations of My sovereign will that implied I rarely speak, but those were the opinions of human beings, not the testimony of My Word. You may have wondered if I was withholding My mercy because you had departed from My will or sinned against Me somehow, but My Word makes it clear that even when I discipline My children for sin and rebellion, I am still there to meet their needs. Your faithfulness will allow you to experience more of My favor, but the absence of it does not cause Me to leave your needs unmet. Mercy compels Me. When you cry out, I will answer."

Lord, I am so unworthy. I have complained against You. I have grumbled about My circumstances and wondered if I've forfeited Your favor. But I'm exactly the kind of person Your mercy was meant for. I'm crying out. Let me hear and see Your answers.

JULY 23

The Lord went ahead of them. He guided them during the day with a pillar of cloud, and he provided light at night with a pillar of fire. This allowed them to travel by day or by night.

Exodus 13:21

We long for such concrete guidance. If only God would post arrow signs in the direction we need to go, or roll out a carpet in the direction of our next steps, or open our spiritual eyes to see His gestures showing us the way, we would follow Him everywhere He leads. This is the kind of guidance Israel got on its way out of Egypt and all the way to the Promised Land. They wandered for a generation, but it wasn't because they got lost in the Sinai wilderness. The cloud and fire were clear to all. They knew exactly where to go, day or night.

Why was God so clear with them and yet is so seemingly vague with us? Perhaps it is because they were in a critical, monumental moment that would affect the rest of history and illustrate God as Deliverer, Provider, Protector, and more for generations to come. But we have crisis moments too, and we need to hear His voice. We can rest assured, even when we don't see a cloud by day and fire by night—or arrow signs or a carpet on the path or visible gestures—that He will show us enough to keep us moving forward.

Visible direction is the exception, not the norm. God is generally much more relational with us, leaving a huge gap of unknowing that compels us to search deeper into His presence in order to hear. Cloud and fire give information, but they don't cultivate a sharing of hearts. Even so, God will patiently lead us—on a very circuitous path at times, but with a purpose—as we come close to Him. He is determined to get us through whatever wilderness we face.

Lord, You have led me on such a winding path that sometimes I'm not sure I'm headed in the right direction. I long for Your cloud and fire, but I'll cling to whatever guidance You give. Please get me through this wilderness safely.

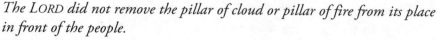
The LORD did not remove the pillar of cloud or pillar of fire from its place in front of the people.
EXODUS 13:22

In the Chronicles of Narnia series, the lion Aslan rarely makes his presence known, except at critical moments of need. He closely watches those who are loyal to him, but without their awareness. He is there, behind the scenes, always knowing, but only occasionally revealing himself. Even so, in spite of his hiddenness, he makes sure the children get where they need to go.

It isn't difficult to recognize in this illustration the nature of God in the ways He guides and protects us. We receive His direction daily, but often when we aren't even aware of it. God governs our steps, even though we think we're the ones taking them. His voice is prompting us, even though we think it's our own thought processes. He is the guardian behind the scenes, letting us travel but rigging the path and the circumstances to steer us in the right direction. Even when we make mistakes or rebel against Him, He has ways of getting us where we need to go. We are hearing Him even when we think we hear nothing. He does not remove His sovereign guidance from our lives.

God is relentlessly committed to your journey, whether you realize it or not. He is not surprised by any turn you take, even the ones that are eating you up with regret. He accounted for them and perhaps even ordained them. As you strain to hear His voice, He is content with the fact that He already put it within you and has been using it to lead you forward. You may not hear the footsteps beside you, but they are always there. Your steps may be uncertain to you, but they are never uncertain to God. He will never remove His cloud and fire from your life.

Lord, I submit my every step to You. I invite You to direct my path with or without my awareness of it. Give me understanding when I need it, and trust when I don't understand. Lead me into the land of promise You've designed for me.

Whenever the cloud lifted from the Tabernacle, the people of Israel would set out on their journey, following it. But if the cloud did not rise, they remained where they were until it lifted.

Exodus 40:36-37

We have decisions to make, so we ask for guidance. We wait for it. We remind God of His promises to give wisdom to those who seek it. And when He lingers . . . well, very often we don't let Him linger. We assume that if He hasn't spoken quickly, He must be leaving us to our own discernment to make the best decision we can. We go ahead and move forward, not because we've heard His voice but because moving forward seems to be the only option. We use our best judgment and trust that it fits with His will.

Sometimes God wants us to move forward in the wisdom and discernment we already have, but our decision-making process should never be reduced to that alone. We are in such a rush to make decisions that we act as if meeting a deadline is more important than hearing specific direction from God. When He lingers, He is waiting to see if we will fill the vacuum by seeking Him or by using our own logic and sense of urgency. Far too often, we fill the gaps with our own assumptions. We make decisions before we've heard God's directions.

When the Israelites were following God in the wilderness, they waited until the cloud rose and led them. If the cloud didn't rise, the people didn't either. They stayed, sometimes long beyond their own comfort level, until God led them. That isn't easy to do, but it's an essential exercise in faith and listening. In most significant decisions, God wants us to ask and wait. And wait some more. And wait even more—until we've heard. No time is wasted in this process; when we follow the "cloud" of direction, God gives us a direct path into His will.

Lord, You direct my paths, sometimes much more methodically than I want. Give me a patient spirit; help me not rush to judgment; undo my assumptions. And when I've heard from You, I'll follow with confidence.

Do not rebel against the LORD, and don't be afraid of the people of the land. They are only helpless prey to us! They have no protection, but the LORD is with us! Don't be afraid of them!

NUMBERS 14:9

Moses sent twelve spies into the Promised Land, not to find out if it was possible to take it, but to provide information that would be helpful once Israel got there. But ten of the spies came back with a discouraging report: The people of the land were big and strong, and taking the land from them would not be possible. Only two spies, Joshua and Caleb, objected to this report, and they were treated with contempt by the naysayers. Their faith was seen as foolish.

Faith often looks foolish, and "realistic" people are quick to offer more practical wisdom. But Joshua and Caleb remembered something that most of Israel had forgotten: The Promised Land was actually the *promised* land. The God who cannot lie had assured them it was theirs. Moses and others had heard His voice, and the faithful ones among them believed Him. They knew that when He spoke, He told the truth, even if circumstances made the truth seem impossible. We serve a God who does what He says He will do. He follows through on His words.

When God gives you His promises in Scripture and helps you apply them to your specific situations, don't let them go. Circumstances will tempt you to question whether His promises are actually possible, and your mind will reason that perhaps you misinterpreted what He said or applied His words inappropriately. Entire doctrines have been developed to explain why God didn't mean what He seemed to have said. But when His words become personal in your specific situation, they can be trusted. Cling to them. Whatever God has spoken to you, don't let the obstacles around you persuade you otherwise. Never let go of His promises.

Lord, it is so difficult to believe Your promises when circumstances and the "wisdom" of others dictate against them. But Your words are bigger to me than the giants around me are. I choose always to believe what You have said.

Believe in [the Lord's] prophets, and you will succeed.
2 CHRONICLES 20:20

When Jehoshaphat and the people of Judah were surrounded by threatening armies, they cried out to God in desperation. They knew they were powerless; they needed a word from Him. In response, God inspired Jahaziel to speak the truth to them about the situation. The people believed and worshiped, and then prepared for the battle the next day.

It isn't unusual to be fully inspired and encouraged by God in the evening and wake up the next day with a deflated spirit. So when morning came, Jehoshaphat reminded the people that this battle belonged to God, as had been prophesied, and that they could face their enemies without fear. How could he be sure of such a thing? He had heard God's voice coming through one of the priests. The Spirit of the Lord seemed to have come upon this man. Jehoshaphat was confident that the key to success was believing in God's prophets.

If you ask people if they believe there are prophets today, many will say no. But ask if they believe God speaks through His people, and many of those same people will say yes. What they mean is that they believe the era of the infallible Old Testament prophets who wrote Scripture is over. But that doesn't imply that God no longer uses His people to express His voice. As He did with Jahaziel, God's Spirit comes upon His people and inspires them to convey His thoughts about a specific situation. And when He does, the difference between success and failure is whether we believe what He says through them.

Those who see God's voice as alive and active are able to follow His instructions for success. Those who see His voice as too mysterious to understand will never be certain about His guidance in the first place. Believing His prophets—those who share and declare His thoughts—is the key to victory in any area of life.

Lord, what are You saying to me through Your people? If I err in understanding, may it be on the side of belief rather than skepticism. Show me the path to success in all Your purposes.

JULY 28

The promise is received by faith. It is given as a free gift.
ROMANS 4:16

John Wesley was born into a Christian home, knew the Bible well, and had served as a missionary in colonial Georgia. Even so, he wasn't convinced he had saving faith, and thus, with the help of some Moravian friends, he sought it with all his heart. One morning, he opened his Bible to see 2 Peter 1:4, a promise about participating in the divine nature. And later that day, he opened again to the phrase, "You are not far from the Kingdom of God" (Mark 12:34). In the afternoon, he heard in a church service a hymn with powerful words about redemption. And that evening, he went to a meeting on Aldersgate Street—"quite unwillingly," he would later write. Yet at that meeting, as Luther's preface to Romans was being read and Jesus' ability to change a heart was being explained, Wesley felt his heart "strangely warmed." He knew at that moment that he did trust in Christ. He understood that Jesus not only saved sinners; He had saved *him.* The general work of Christ became very personal.

In that highly subjective experience, Wesley found Christ to be his Savior. It was more than a momentary feeling. It changed his life and affected the course of Christianity for generations to come. God had spoken in the depths of Wesley's heart, and this burned-out, depressed former missionary zealously served God for the rest of his life.

God hounded Wesley's heart through testimonies of other Christians, Bible verses, hymns, and the fellowship of believers until Wesley was able to respond. That's often how God speaks—not rudely, but very persistently. When He calls, He doesn't let the message go until the hearer truly hears. And when that happens, the once-objective information suddenly becomes deeply and warmly personal. It lights a fire in the heart that cannot be quenched.

Lord, I beg You—light a fire in my heart. I would love to be "strangely warmed" by Your presence and Your words. I need to know not just that You love the world but that You love me personally. Hound me until my heart awakens fully to You.

[The Lord said,] "Open your mouth wide, and I will fill it with good things."

PSALM 81:10

FROM THE HEART OF GOD

"Hear My open invitation. Is there any hint of reluctance there? Any sense of scarcity when I speak of My resources? Any lack of generosity on My part? No, I have demonstrated My ability and My willingness to deliver, provide, and heal. I have lavished My love on those who have loved Me in return. I have given grace and mercy and plenty of material blessings. I have promised that in My Kingdom, you will not suffer lack. I am your Shepherd; you shall not want for anything. There's only one condition: You have to open your mouth wide.

"What does it mean to open your mouth wide? It means living with a sense of expectancy. Like a hungry child who has never missed a meal, open up with the certainty that you will be fed. Don't be one of those people who wonder whether My patience or generosity or extravagance has reached its limit. Always expect to receive more.

"Open your ears, too. Never ask Me to speak to you 'just this once.' Don't plead with Me to give you 'a little bit' of direction or counsel. You are not praying to a reticent God. I'm never at a loss for words. I may give you seasons of silence, but you will never go long without hearing from Me if you are persistently listening. I have made a commitment to you to keep you in My will. And I never fail on My commitments.

"Open your arms, too. Never say, 'All I'm asking is . . .' I don't want you to ask reluctantly, as if I'm stingy with My gifts. I want you to ask extravagantly—big, audacious prayers. Don't just bring Me possibilities; bring Me all your impossibilities. In every request, assume My willingness to give. This is faith. Know the heart of the one to whom you pray."

Lord, forgive me for thinking too small. Fill me with hope and faith for everything You want to give, whether big or small, possible or impossible, conventional or extraordinary. You are the God who gives—and says—good things.

JULY 30

[The Lord said,] "I am watching to see that my word is fulfilled."
JEREMIAH 1:12, NIV

Countless people are holding on to what they believe is a God-given dream, vision, or purpose—and are thoroughly frustrated by how long it's taking to happen or how many detours they have had to take. It can be extremely painful to live between a promise and its fulfillment, wondering whether it has been lost, forgotten, forfeited, thwarted, or eternally delayed. It often seems as if God speaks and then sits on His words without doing anything about them.

As frustrating as this is, it's normal for God. He gave Joseph dreams and then took long years and a very winding path to make them manifest. He anointed David as king and then let obstacles to his throne stand in the way for a confusingly extended time. Abraham, Moses, Caleb and Joshua, the captives of Babylon—all of them waited far longer than they expected to. God has a confounding tendency to speak long before He plans to fulfill.

Even while we wait, God is working behind the scenes. And during the process, our faith is stretched seemingly beyond its breaking point, though in the end, we find that it hasn't broken. We wrestle with God, ask many questions, cry out in desperation, and exercise more spiritual muscles than we thought we had. And it's terribly uncomfortable. But it's necessary. This is how God develops His people and prepares them for the weight of their calling.

Don't give up on the things God has spoken. It may seem that He has forgotten them or chosen another direction, but He hasn't. He had enough foresight to speak only what He intended to accomplish. If He has said it, He will act on it. He is watching to see that His words are fulfilled.

Lord, I don't understand why Your process takes so long, nor why the path is so indirect. But I trust You. I know Your words are true, even years after You've spoken them. I'm choosing to cling to them in faith.

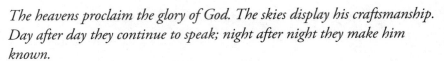

The heavens proclaim the glory of God. The skies display his craftsmanship. Day after day they continue to speak; night after night they make him known.

PSALM 19:1-2

Every aspect of the universe tells us something about God. His invisible attributes—wisdom, glory, love, and much more—are seen in the visible world. The design of creation points to the Creator.

But creation can speak even more specifically than that. God has filled our lives with symbolic gestures—meaningful sights and sounds and smells that bring up memories or suggest a significant event we've experienced—and these gestures speak to us at surprisingly relevant moments. We see a symbol of wisdom at a moment when we're desperate for wise counsel, or we hear a song that was meaningful in one situation when we're now stuck in a similar situation, or a unique phrase that guided us in the past is suddenly brought into our present predicament. These "coincidences" are God's way of speaking to us through His creation, pouring forth His voice to make His purposes and His love known to us at critical times.

Everyone's "God language"—the specific symbols and gestures that become common in conversations with Him—is unique, based on our unique meaningful experiences. The particular words and pictures will vary from person to person, but the dynamic of this God language developing through ongoing communication with Him is universally available. We learn the language like any other: through hearing, interpreting through trial and error, and asking questions when meanings are unclear. Over time, we become fluent in hearing and in speaking back to God. More and more, we encounter His voice in everything around us. We find that the heavens, the skies, and even our everyday interactions with creation proclaim His glory.

Lord, the work of Your hands tells the whole world about who You are. It also often tells me what You want to say to me. You are sovereign over every word, name, sight, sound, symbol, song, creature, and message I perceive. Help me become familiar with the language You use in my life.

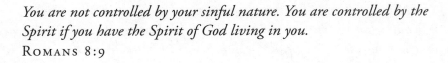

AUGUST 1

You are not controlled by your sinful nature. You are controlled by the Spirit if you have the Spirit of God living in you.
ROMANS 8:9

"I'm a sinner saved by grace." That's the declaration of nearly every Christian who understands the nature of salvation and embraces humility. And it's true; we've all come out of a sinful condition and been saved purely by grace through faith in Jesus. But it's possible to focus so much on our fallen background that we forget the glory of our current condition. Yes, we were sinners; and yes, we still sin sometimes. But that isn't God's final statement about us, and neither should it be ours. We are raised up and seated with Jesus in heaven (Ephesians 2:6) and filled, directed, and empowered by His Spirit. That's who we are.

We will never be confident in hearing God's voice unless we know this. If we focus on the fact of our sinful condition, we will always assume that our inward thoughts and impulses are of sinful origin, not prompted by the Spirit of God. We will never trust that we are being inspired and empowered by the Spirit—that it's God working in us for His pleasure (Philippians 2:13). Recognizing His voice requires recognizing the desires and thoughts He puts inside us. In order to believe He is inspiring us, we have to believe that He, not our sinful nature, is the dominant force in our hearts.

Never acknowledge the depths from which you came without also acknowledging the heights to which God is taking you. To emphasize the former above the latter is to underestimate and even dishonor God's power and promises. He did not save us at such great cost in order for us to remain broken sinners. He only showed us that side of ourselves so we would come into His Kingdom and experience His power and life.

Spirit of God, I don't trust myself, but I trust that You are working in me in power, and speaking to me and through me according to Your will. Some of my thoughts may be sinful, but many others are directly from You. Help me to trust the Holy Spirit inside me.

The Holy Spirit prays for us with groanings that cannot be expressed in words. And the Father who knows all hearts knows what the Spirit is saying, for the Spirit pleads for us believers in harmony with God's own will.

ROMANS 8:26-27

Sometimes we know exactly what to pray for. We understand enough to make specific requests that are consistent with God's will. Other times, we want to pray but don't know what to say, so we turn our prayers into wishes and hopes and never really voice them. But if we pray anyway, even if those prayers come out as incoherent thoughts or heartfelt groans, we are participating in a divine phenomenon. The God who lives within us appeals to the God who is above us. He joins Himself with our spirits and births His desires within us, moving us to pray His will—even when we don't consciously know what His will is.

This is a different dimension of experiencing God's voice than we normally expect. Not only does the Holy Spirit speak *to* us, He speaks *through* us; and not only does He speak through us to others, He speaks through us to the Father Himself. Somehow we get caught up in a conversation among members of the Trinity. They could have this conversation without us, but for some reason God has chosen to work through human agency to get things done in the world. Human beings need to ask and believe. And we need lots of help doing that.

The Spirit helps us in our weakness, praying the things we didn't know to pray. Sometimes that comes out of our mouths in unexpected words, sometimes it rises as sounds and groans from our deepest needs, and sometimes we pray seemingly normal prayers that the Spirit takes and reinterprets for the Father's purposes. However it works, it's a sacred process. We receive the heart of God and are enabled to pray it back to Him.

Holy Spirit, thank You for pleading on my behalf—for taking my incoherent longings and lining them up with what You wanted to do all along. Please tell the Father everything that my words are insufficient to express.

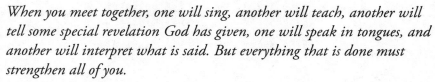

When you meet together, one will sing, another will teach, another will tell some special revelation God has given, one will speak in tongues, and another will interpret what is said. But everything that is done must strengthen all of you.

1 CORINTHIANS 14:26

The voice of God was being expressed in all sorts of ways in Corinth. Paul had to put some guidelines around the expressions, but he never told the Corinthian believers that they were only pretending to hear God's voice or that they were mistaken in what they heard. He questioned the motives and timing surrounding their spiritual gifts, but he affirmed those gifts as legitimate. And he ascribed to them a unifying purpose: spiritual gifts must strengthen the church.

Many people don't seem to realize that. They claim to speak for God, but major on doomsday predictions, alarmist tactics, and faultfinding attacks. Instead of emphasizing what God is doing, they panic about what remains to be done. Instead of commending believers for their gains, they point out how far we fall short. Instead of testing movements to see what's true in them, they dissect them to find out what's false. They claim to be discerning and biblical, but instead they are skeptical and legalistic. In forgetting to strengthen the church, they quench the Spirit.

When you hear voices that claim to speak in God's name, but that criticize, condemn, or tear down, you can reject them. God wants to encourage and build up. That's His heart's desire. When He speaks, this is the effect His voice will have. He will remind you who you really are in Him, point out the treasures He has placed within you, and urge you to step higher and deeper into His Kingdom. He will correct you when He needs to, but He will saturate all of His messages with love. His words through others, if they are truly His words, will build you up.

Lord, forgive me for accepting critical and condemning words as Yours. I know Your voice heals and strengthens me, even when You correct me. Help me to discern who Your messengers are by the love that motivates them.

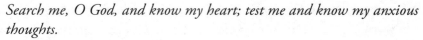

AUGUST 4

Search me, O God, and know my heart; test me and know my anxious thoughts.
PSALM 139:23

In a reasonably good mood, I walked into the meeting room to see several people. Yet I suddenly had a strong sense of discouragement. I hadn't been discouraged before I came into the room, and no one there seemed discouraged. I had neither seen nor heard anything negative. So why did I feel discouraged all of a sudden?

Apparently, this is sometimes how God speaks to us about the needs of those around us. As it turns out, one of the smiling faces in that room was masking a deep inward pain. He wasn't the type to share his feelings openly, at least not in that context. But he needed someone to ask him how he was really doing, to pray with him, and to express support. Just for the moment, God put into my heart a glimpse of the other man's feelings—not to expose him, but to draw me to him. God was alerting me to a person in need.

When our mood suddenly shifts, our tendency is to look inside at our own condition, but sometimes God is sending a message about someone else's inner state. He knows what is in each person's heart. Why wouldn't He at times reveal that to a safe person who can help? He would never do so to embarrass a hurting person, but He would certainly do so to alert one of His people to have compassion and to pray. The one who knows all hearts reveals some of them discreetly.

Be aware of sudden mood changes. They may be your own shifting feelings; they may be the feelings of God flowing through you toward someone around you; or they may reflect the inward condition of the person you're talking to. If led to do more than pray, ask cautious, not intrusive, questions. And be available to respond as a vessel of God's encouragement.

Lord, if You are to make me an instrument of Your peace, surely You will give me inside information at times when someone is not at peace within. Help me recognize that information and pray or act on it with compassion.

[The Lord said,] "Oh, that my people would listen to me! Oh, that Israel would follow me, walking in my paths!"
PSALM 81:13

FROM THE HEART OF GOD

"Many people cry out to hear My voice, but they aren't really listeners. I speak, and they dismiss My words as their own imagination, coincidence, or subjective experience. Some even dismiss the Bible as not being My voice to them because it didn't apply specifically to them when I first spoke those words, or they don't think that context is relevant to their lives. They place higher standards on themselves than they do on My prophets, who were bold enough to act on what they thought they heard. Skeptical hearers can talk themselves out of virtually anything I say, even though they begged Me to speak in the first place. They want to hear, but they don't want to listen.

"Most people don't realize that while they are crying out to hear My voice, I am calling out for them to listen. I have no shortage of passive hearers in My Kingdom, but I'm looking for active listeners. I want you, like stewards who refuse to bury their talents, to take some risks. If you think you probably heard Me, don't play it safe. Assume that you did. If you pursue My voice and aren't certain you heard, the way of faith is to believe I answered your request rather than believe I didn't. I want you to trust My ability to communicate more than you trust your ability to be deceived. Listen and step out on what you've heard.

"Don't be afraid. I don't punish those who dare to have faith. If you fall, I will pick you up and put you back on the right path. If you make a mistake, I won't condemn you. My grace is more than generous for those who follow Me boldly and passionately, even at the risk of being wrong. Don't just hear with your ears. Listen with your heart."

Lord, I know You value discernment, but You value trust even more. You urge me to walk by faith, not by sight. I commit to listen intently; fill me with holy boldness to act on what I hear.

Jesus gave her no reply, not even a word.
MATTHEW 15:23

A Gentile woman was pleading with Jesus to deliver her daughter from demonic torment, so much so that the disciples were bothered and wanted Him to make her stop begging. Jesus surprisingly responded to her by not responding. In her time of desperate need, He didn't say a word. Why? We know it wasn't because He was unwilling because a few verses later, after her persistence, He commended her for her great faith and delivered her daughter. It wasn't because of any lack of mercy or compassion because He demonstrated gentle and extravagant love on so many other occasions. His silence at first was no reflection of His unwillingness to help or a coldhearted nature. Apparently, the delay offered some benefit to the woman or to the onlookers. It prompted her to draw closer. In the end, her persistence proved her faith.

When we ask to hear God's voice and then don't, it isn't because He is reluctant or unmerciful. Many people walk away at this point, assuming they are wrong for expecting to hear Him clearly. But perhaps He wants our persistence to prove our hunger. Or more likely, maybe His silence is intended to provoke movement in us. When we don't hear from Him, it isn't a snub. It's an invitation to come closer.

Sometimes that's a frustrating invitation, but it's only in the frustration that we persist in exploring deeper nuances of His character and His ways. Many Christian thinkers have discovered profound insights in the midst of an uncomfortable or even painful search for God's will. We tend to learn from Him only what we need in a given moment, and if that process is brief, our knowledge of Him remains superficial. But when we have to keep asking and keep searching, we dive deeper into His depths. And when He eventually speaks, we find that we know Him better than we did before.

Jesus, my hunger for Your voice is enough to make me persist through Your silences. Please draw me closer in these times. Let me discover the depths of Your nature when I'm searching and waiting for Your response.

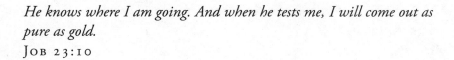

AUGUST 7

He knows where I am going. And when he tests me, I will come out as pure as gold.
Job 23:10

It's comforting to realize that God knows where we're going because there are times when we clearly don't. Our circumstances can be very disorienting, even when we think we've followed Him closely. We know where we've been and how we got into our current situation, but we don't know how to proceed. How does this happen?

When we're listening for God's voice and following His lead, He gives us enough to go on, and we follow as best we can. And when we've done all we can do, we find that sometimes it still isn't enough. God leads us straight into an unknown wilderness and then seemingly leaves us there alone. We cry out for more guidance, wondering where the Lord has gone. Has He abandoned us? Is something wrong with our hearing? Did we follow the wrong path in the first place? These are the questions we ask, and we think something is wrong. But it isn't. This is perfectly normal. This is how God works. His seeming silence is a test to refine our faith and define our resolve, to let us experience the mystery of God's ways while clinging to them relentlessly, to see if we will wander in hope or wander in resignation. He stretches us beyond comfort. And when the test is over, we will come forth as pure as gold.

Don't give up in the wilderness. God's silence is not abandonment; it's affirmation. It means you were on the right course and now you're in a testing phase. When God speaks, follow. And when He doesn't, keep your gaze on Him anyway. He is separating you from dependence on your circumstances and assumptions and turning your only hope toward Him. Times like these aren't comfortable, but they are good. They prepare you for the deliverance, the direction, and the fulfillment that God is going to give you.

Lord, it's painful not to hear Your voice, to wonder why I'm here and where You've gone. You know the path I need to take. I don't. Until You lead again, my eyes are fixed on You.

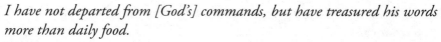

I have not departed from [God's] commands, but have treasured his words more than daily food.

JOB 23:12

No one can honestly claim to have never departed from God's commands, but Job wasn't saying he had never made a mistake. He was saying he had not willfully rebelled against God's ways. Even so, he found himself in a dreadful situation, having suffered the loss of property, the death of his children, and the ravages of life-threatening illnesses. Now his friends were assuming that his calamities were the result of his sins. Clearly, God wouldn't deal with a faithful servant so harshly, would He? Therefore, Job must have offended Him. That seemed to be the only explanation for the suffering of an apparently godly man.

But Scripture tells us the story behind Job's trials, and he wasn't to blame for them. He was right: He had treasured God's words more than daily food. He had been careful to follow all God had said, relentlessly clinging to the divine will. He was a model of submission to God's written Word.

What does Job's situation tell us about hearing God's voice? That it's possible to follow the revealed will of God and still have no insight into His hidden purposes. God wants us to heed Scripture faithfully, but that doesn't mean we'll always understand what He is doing in a given situation. Job spent a lot of time lamenting his trials and defending his reputation, but instead of looking at his past and his peers, he might have better endured by focusing entirely on the behind-the-scenes heart of the Father. Even in God's silences, He can be sought. Even when we've read the Word, we can search out the heart behind it. Even when we've been obedient to God's instructions, we can explore His ways more thoroughly. And when we do, we find treasures we never before imagined.

Father, let me never waste my pain. Use it to draw me deeper, to show me hidden treasures of Your ways and Your Kingdom. Give me glimpses behind the scenes of my life.

AUGUST 9

Order the Israelites to turn back and camp by Pi-hahiroth between Migdol and the sea. Camp there along the shore.
EXODUS 14:1-2

The Israelites fleeing from Egypt were following the cloud and the fire of God closely. They had not deviated from His path. And where did it get them? They were led to an extremely vulnerable position at the edge of the Red Sea. There was no way to move ahead because of the sea, and no way to retreat because of Pharaoh's pursuing army. God led them directly into a seemingly unsolvable predicament.

That sounds just like Him, doesn't it? He may sometimes make us "lie down in green pastures" (Psalm 23:2, NKJV), but He rarely leads us on smooth paths when He's taking us somewhere. The way can be treacherous. If we followed our own logic, we would always make the seemingly wise decision to ensure our safety. But when we're following God, we find ourselves walking in what appear to be unreasonable directions. God doesn't always lead us away from visible dangers, though He promises to keep us safe. He doesn't always lead us on a straight path, though He promises to get us where He wants us to be, no matter how many zigzags we take. From our limited perspective, God's paths often have no rhyme or reason—until we look back on them, when we see how they made perfect sense. Just as the Israelites eventually celebrated their deliverance from an impossible situation, so will we. But we have to be led into impossible situations for a miraculous deliverance to happen.

Don't make the mistake of many who assume that unreasonable guidance isn't from God. Apparent absurdity may very well be a mark of His leading. Not all unlikely paths are from Him, but much of His direction will certainly seem unlikely. The God whose ways are far above ours enjoys being unconventional. He thinks "outside the box" because boxes can't contain Him. Surprising directions are His specialty.

Lord, I'm listening for Your voice, and I'm not ruling out anything unless it contradicts Your character. No twist in the journey is beyond Your nature. Lead me into—and out of—any predicament You choose.

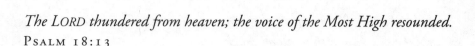

AUGUST 10

The LORD thundered from heaven; the voice of the Most High resounded.
PSALM 18:13

David was in a terrible predicament. He had been pursued by enemies for years, surrounded and outnumbered at times, and hiding in caves and at oases at others. As he always did in seemingly hopeless situations, he cried out to God. And as Psalm 18 describes, God answered with power and a flair for the dramatic.

It's the ultimate answer to prayer: A child of God cries out and God answers with thunder and lightning and earthquakes. The rescuer God rides in on a heavenly chariot and routs the enemy. In words reminiscent of the Exodus and the deliverance at the Red Sea, David applies God's power to his own situation, which on the surface wasn't nearly as dramatic. But in the behind-the-scenes war, it was just as significant. David survived his enemies and became king because God went to war using the power of His voice.

That's how God fights. Just one word from His mouth can turn a situation around completely. The mountains and seas and all the forces of nature are at His command. His angels respond decisively to His every word. When God speaks, things happen.

We long for such answers to prayer. When we cry out for God's voice, it isn't just so He will give us direction; it's also for Him to speak into the situations of our lives to change them. We can ask Him to issue commands and utter decrees that shape our circumstances and turn our predicaments into opportunities. We can even give audible voice to His promises and decrees, speaking His words into the predicaments of our lives. Under God's authority, all creation must respond to His voice. When we speak His words, creation must respond to us, as well. The thunder of God's voice changes the world around us.

Lord, let Your words resound for me, in me, and through me. Speak into my situation. Just one word from You changes everything, and I need change. Ride into my battles in the power of Your word.

AUGUST 11

No prophecy in Scripture ever came from the prophet's own understanding, or from human initiative. No, those prophets were moved by the Holy Spirit, and they spoke from God.

2 PETER 1:20-21

Isaac of Syria, a bishop of Nineveh who left his service in the church to live in solitude, spent years meditating on Scripture. He is considered a mystic, yet he anchored his encounters with God in the context of biblical truth. His advice to those who study God's Word is profound: "Do not approach the mysterious words in the Scriptures without prayer and without asking help from God, saying: 'Lord, grant me to perceive the power that is in them.' Deem prayer as the key to the insight of truth in Scripture."

God can speak at multiple levels through His Word. He has embedded nuances and shades of meaning into it, even in the languages and cultures in which it was written. One phrase can have several different implications and apply to many situations. But that doesn't mean the Word can say whatever we want it to say. Mystical encounters with God and subjective experiences with His voice can be thoroughly genuine, but they can't be genuine if they are violations of His nature or His Word. His voice is expressed in many ways and in many contexts, but it is never the private property of the hearer to be abused or distorted. It expresses only what God means to say.

Follow Isaac's advice. Approach Scripture with prayer to perceive the power within the words and to understand the insights of the Spirit. Never let your own mind and heart be independent interpreters of truth. Submit your faculties to the Holy Spirit and take time to let Him inspire, reveal, and lead. When you read the words of the Father, which testify to the Son, in the power of the Spirit, your understanding of the Word will come alive.

Lord, who can grasp Your thoughts unless You enable, inspire, and interpret? My experiences and intellect are not enough. I need the wisdom of Your Spirit as I read and meditate. Unveil Your truth to me, in me, and through me.

I am sending you to say to [the nation of Israel], "This is what the Sovereign LORD says!" And whether they listen or refuse to listen—for remember, they are rebels—at least they will know they have had a prophet among them.
EZEKIEL 2:4-5

FROM THE HEART OF GOD

"I am the living Word. I speak. I cannot be silent. Even though the Bible is complete, My sheep still need to hear My voice and know My guidance in specific situations. My church is full of well-intentioned teachers who falsely declare that no one can claim to have heard My voice with certainty. Even My own people wonder if it's presumptuous to say I've spoken to them, in spite of My many instructions to listen to and declare My words. I am not silent, yet to many of My people, I might as well be. They have ruled out the possibility of hearing My voice and telling others what I've said.

"It isn't presumptuous to be a prophetic voice if I've told you to be one. It's only presumptuous if I haven't actually spoken to you. I'm not asking you to write Scripture, as the prophets of old were inspired to do. I'm asking you to be in sync with My heartbeat and represent Me to the world. I'm sending you to portray My ways and My purposes to the people around you. I'm expecting you to embody My nature and declare what you hear My Spirit saying. I intend to maintain a voice in this world, and for many hearers, you're it.

"Does this frighten you? It shouldn't. It should frighten you more to neglect My calling. You should have a sacred awe of the task, but My love casts out all fear. I will speak clearly to those who are willing to declare what they have heard. Get in touch with My heartbeat, and I will send you on a mission to demonstrate it."

Sovereign Lord, were your words to Ezekiel really for us, too? Your Spirit fills all of us who believe, not just a select few, so it must be true. Give me words to say, feelings to portray, and thoughts to convey. Fill me with the heart of Your mission.

[Jesus said,] "I am the good shepherd; I know my own sheep, and they know me."
JOHN 10:14

Most Christians are familiar with the verse that says the sheep follow the shepherd "because they know his voice" (John 10:4). But here Jesus declares that His sheep know *Him*. They can sense His presence, interact with His personality, understand His ways, and recognize His work. This knowing isn't a mental process of discernment; it's an intuitive, spiritual familiarity. The sheep pick up on the scent and the voice and the mannerisms of the Shepherd.

We tend to try to sort out this familiarity with logic. We think it through. We look for steps to develop it. We read and memorize Scripture in an effort to improve our understanding. All of these efforts are good, but our knowledge of the Shepherd isn't an intellectual exercise; it's a spiritual awakening. He puts this sense of the familiar in all of His children, even when we're encountering Him for the first time. It may be covered up with normal thought processes and emotions, but it's there. We know Him because . . . we just do.

The biggest part of hearing God's voice is recognizing what in your life is from Him and what is not. All things are under His sovereignty, of course; it isn't as if there are aspects of your life that are beyond His control. But the messages you receive from your circumstances, the people around you, your own thoughts—and even the various interpretations you derive from His Word—are a mixed bag of perceptions. Some are true, some are not. Some are God's leading, some are distractions from His leading. How can you sort it all out?

Look for the deep, intuitive, spiritual "knowing" of the Shepherd. Even new experiences and ideas will feel, smell, and taste strangely familiar in the depths of your spirit when they are from Him. They carry His personality and look like His work. Deep within every sheep, the Shepherd's voice rings true.

Jesus, I'm not even going to try to figure it out. Help me sense, deep in my spirit, Your presence and voice. May everything in Your Kingdom and in Your heart feel like "home" to me.

I tell you the truth, the Son can do nothing by himself. He does only what he sees the Father doing. Whatever the Father does, the Son also does.
JOHN 5:19

Some people see Jesus as the exception. Others see Him as their example. Though it's true He is rather exceptional, He came to us as a human being to show us how we are to live and relate to the Father. Philippians 2:6-7 says that Jesus gave up the privileges of deity to live among us, meaning that He shows us what is possible for us if we live in perfect obedience to God's Spirit. So if the Son can do nothing by Himself but only does what He sees the Father doing, what does that say about us? We too are meant to do nothing independently, but to follow the lead of the Father. We are to hear Him and respond as a way of life.

How can we see what the Father is doing? We have to learn to notice what He's doing, where He's working, and when He's setting up a situation for His glory. That might sound hard, but it really isn't if we ask Him to heighten our spiritual senses to His activity. He will alert us to His presence, His work, and His words as we choose to consciously watch and listen. Every time we ask, "Lord, where are You in this situation? What are You up to?" He will answer by speaking deep in our hearts or making His movements clear. Because He wants us to live with constant awareness of Him, He will make constant awareness a real possibility.

Become a noticer. Ask the Father what He's up to. Watch where He's working. Align yourself with His activity and do what you see Him doing. Hearing His voice isn't nearly as difficult when we're aware of His activity and partnering with Him in it.

Lord, imitation may be the sincerest form of flattery, but it's also the sincerest form of worship I can offer You. Heighten my spiritual senses to recognize Your footprint everywhere You go so I can do what You're doing.

AUGUST 15

[Solomon] could speak with authority about all kinds of plants, from the great cedar of Lebanon to the tiny hyssop that grows from cracks in a wall. He could also speak about animals, birds, small creatures, and fish.

1 KINGS 4:33

The sages of Israel believed that God's wisdom was liberally infused in His creation. So observing created things was not just a matter of curiosity or science. It was a peek into God's ways. That's one reason the writer of 1 Kings, in describing Solomon's wisdom, goes on to declare his insights about animals, birds, small creatures, and fish. It's also why Proverbs is filled with lessons from the industriousness of ants, the unity of locusts, the craftsmanship of spiders, the strength of lions, and more. (See Proverbs 30:15-33 for a few examples.) By observing the things God has made, sages believed they could learn some things about God's ways.

We can too. God has filled creation with illustrations of His ways and His attributes. Scripture speaks of Him in terms of light, water, dew, thunder, wind, and more. It encourages us to emulate the best traits found in the animal kingdom. We can get illustrations of God's work from the fields of agriculture, medicine, technology, arts, media, government, physics, astronomy, history, and many more. No single illustration is perfect or complete; God is infinite and beyond our full understanding. But each example provides an illuminating picture of God's nature. That's why the study of any field of inquiry is worthwhile, and why anyone who studies anything in truth and depth can eventually find evidence of God in what is studied. God has written Himself into His world.

Live with curious wonder about the world around you. Though fallen and distorted, it nevertheless offers innumerable glimpses into the divine. The physical reflects the spiritual more often than we imagine. And in that reflection, we can hear the voice of the one who made it.

Lord, I would love to recapture the curiosity I had as a child, and I know I would learn more about You and Your ways if I could. Fill me with an inquisitive spirit that seeks out Your truths in the forms and functions of Your world.

Your sons and daughters will prophesy. Your young men will see visions, and your old men will dream dreams.
ACTS 2:17

On the day of Pentecost, when God poured out His Spirit on all the believers who were gathered, Peter quoted the prophet Joel about the "last days." But clearly, Peter wasn't talking about some future end-times era. He was pointing to that very day as the fulfillment of Joel's word. The clear implication is that the people of God were entering into a time in which men, women, and children of all ages would be able to hear from God themselves. Their encounters with Him would include visions, dreams, and other prophetic sensitivities. God would no longer have to speak through a small group of prophets and priests. He would speak to them directly.

If that was true during Peter's days, and Joel called them the "last" or "latter" days, then we must still be living in that era. There have been varying degrees of the Holy Spirit's activity in church history; sometimes He moves in dramatic ways, and sometimes we have seemed to live in spiritual dark ages. But His gifts have always been fully available since Pentecost, and so has His voice. Ever since the Holy Spirit came to live inside God's new creation—this means anyone who belongs to Christ, according to 2 Corinthians 5:17—all things are possible. God is accessible. No one has to say, "Know the Lord," because all are able to know Him already (Jeremiah 31:34; Hebrews 8:11). He is no longer an obscure God.

It's true that we go through dark and confusing times when God seems to be silent, but it's important to know these are temporary, not normal conditions. Over time, God means for us to know Him. We must pray, pursue, and press in to Him, but He will make it happen. We live in an age of open communication with the divine.

✧ ✧ ✧

Spirit of God, I long for clearer expressions of Your truth. Let me see visions and dream dreams, whatever that looks like and however You want to shape them. May the free-flowing spiritual environment of Pentecost be a reality in my life today.

AUGUST 17

The LORD says, "I will guide you along the best pathway for your life. I will advise you and watch over you. Do not be like a senseless horse or mule that needs a bit and bridle to keep it under control."
PSALM 32:8-9

You've prayed for guidance and pursued the direction you thought you heard from God. But now you've encountered not only obstacles or delays—those can be overcome—but a firmly closed door. Apparently this wasn't God's direction after all. So you start back at square one and hope that God eventually leads you to the right path.

It happens all the time, doesn't it? And it can be terribly frustrating. Yes, sometimes the process is just as important as the destination, and bouncing off of closed doors has a purpose. But sometimes the process makes us feel like nothing more than a pinball. We're clueless about where we're going; we just bounce from obstacle to obstacle until we land in the right place. And everything in us wants to cry out, "Lord, is this really what You mean by a relationship?" We crave a tangible conversation up front in which He tells us what to do, not an after-the-fact wondering where we went wrong.

Though it's true that God often leads us simply by opening the right doors and closing the wrong ones—and that after-the-fact wondering can have a deep spiritual purpose—there are times when God also longs to communicate with us *before* we take the first step. He wants us to hear Him first, not butt our heads against a closed door later. There's no shame in the latter—the Bible is filled with examples of people who started out in one direction and had to be redirected—and the key is to be responsive as we go. But God promises to lead us sometimes before we even start. He will guide, advise, and watch over every step.

Lord, neither You nor I want me to be like a senseless animal. I'm tired of bouncing from door to door. Please speak clearly and tell me which way to go. My heart's desire is to hear what You say and respond to it.

*This is the way to have eternal life—to know you, the only true God,
and Jesus Christ, the one you sent to earth.*
JOHN 17:3

Blaise Pascal called it his "night of fire." Whether or not it was his conversion—
he had had some sort of conversion experience a few years before—it was the
most profound event of his life. For two hours, he was shaken to his core in a
vision of God. When he died eight years later, a description of this vision was
found sewn into his jacket. Pascal felt that before this vision, he had known
through his intellect only the God of the philosophers and scholars. Afterward,
he knew he had met the God of covenant, the God of Abraham, Isaac, and
Jacob. He had moved from mental understanding of a Creator God to personal
knowledge of Jesus Christ. His belief in God was no longer an argument; it was
a relationship.

True encounters with God always have this effect. To know His presence or
to hear His words is to be drawn into His covenant. Grasping at words to record
his vision, Pascal quoted John 17:3: "This is the way to have eternal life—to
know you, the only true God, and Jesus Christ, the one you sent to earth." He
realized that a relationship with God is just that—a relationship. No one can
have a genuine experience with God that simply results in greater understanding
or new insights. God is much more personal than that. Encountering Him
begins conversations, establishes accountability, and further designates terms
of His covenant and calling. It deepens our connection with Him.

Never seek God's voice simply for the information He provides. When you
hear Him, the information is no longer the primary issue. The relationship is.
Our response to the conversation becomes bigger than the conversation itself.
We are intrinsically bound to the one who speaks.

Father, Your words are my life. Your truth demands a response and draws me
into an unbreakable bond with You. Implant Your life within me through the
power of Your words.

AUGUST 19

The voice said to [Ezekiel], "Son of man, eat what I am giving you—eat this scroll! Then go and give its message to the people of Israel." So I opened my mouth, and he fed me the scroll. . . . And when I ate it, it tasted as sweet as honey in my mouth.

Ezekiel 3:1-3

FROM THE HEART OF GOD

"My words were written on scrolls, but they are more than ink on parchment. They are alive and powerful, always accomplishing their purpose and expressing My heart. They aren't simply vehicles of communication; they are vessels of My Spirit. To embrace My words the way they were intended is to embrace Me.

"When I speak to you, I want My words to become part of who you are. Ingest them. Digest them. Become one with them. Don't let them go in one ear and out the other. Don't treat them simply as commands or suggestions or instructions. If you see them as requirements, they will affect only your behavior. But if you see them as food, they will change your nature. As you're fond of saying, you are what you eat. When you eat My words, you become one with Me.

"My words are difficult to obey, but they are easy to digest. I never intended for them to remain external, where you would have to follow them without having a heart equipped to do so. My desire is for them to sink so deeply into your spirit that you can fulfill them simply by acting naturally. That's why I gave you a changed nature and put My Spirit within you—so My voice would find a home in your heart. The words that were once bitter on the outside are now sweet when you've consumed them. Savor them well."

Living Word, is this why following Your voice has always been so hard? Put Your truth in me; let me consume with my mouth whatever comes out of Yours. And help me embody Your voice and speak to others the words that come straight from Your heart.

AUGUST 20

The LORD asked [Moses], "What is that in your hand?"
EXODUS 4:2

Moses raised all kinds of objections to God's call—apparently a burning bush wasn't convincing in itself—so God had to prove that His power would accompany Moses back to Egypt. God could have sent Moses to find a special rod with magical powers from a secret hiding place in the wilderness, but there was no need for such theatrics. The particular rod wasn't the issue; God could demonstrate His power in the rod Moses already had. So when He told Moses to throw down the rod, and then it became a serpent—and then a rod again when Moses picked it back up—the symbolism was profound. God's power accompanies what we already have in our hands if we use it according to His direction.

Your life is filled with assets: your natural gifts and talents, spiritual gifts, material resources, education and experience, job, geographic location, and more. These aren't a random collection of memories or coincidences. They are collateral for the work of God's Kingdom. That means you can often discern God's voice from what He has already put into your hands. Whether it's possessions, positions, or knowledge and experience, you have things that God has probably long intended to use. His voice will likely tell you to throw it down before Him and see what He does with it.

That doesn't mean God always aims for the status quo in your life. In fact, He rarely does. But He also tends to build on what He has already given you. Whatever you hear from Him as you seek direction, it will probably include some things that are already in your hand. As you "throw them down"—offer them to Him for His use—some of them will come alive in ways you've never experienced before. What He has done in your past very often points toward what He will do in your future.

Lord, the past You have guided me through is speaking to me about the future You are guiding me into. Show me what You can do with the things in my hands. All I have is Yours to use.

What he opens, no one can close; and what he closes, no one can open.
REVELATION 3:7

Sometimes we attempt to go through an open door, and God shuts it. And sometimes we come to a closed door, and God opens it. So neither an open nor a closed door initially tells us anything about God's will. But when those doors remain open or closed, even after we've prayed with faith and patience, it may be time to consider whether God is using those doors to direct us.

God may speak through the opportunities set before us. His voice is often in the opening and closing of doors. Not every open door is His will, nor every closed door a denial—after all, the Red Sea was a tightly closed door when Israel first came to its shores, as were the walls of Jericho when the people came toward the city. We have to be careful in making assumptions about situations that seem impossible.

God orchestrates the circumstances of our lives to lead us down the right path. He may direct us toward a closed door, but He will open it in His timing if it's His will for us to go through it. Our eyes may light up when we see an open door of opportunity, but God will close it in His timing if it isn't the opportunity He means for us to pursue. As much as we long to hear His voice before we move, we sometimes have to move and find out on the way whether we can pass through or not. He speaks through the doors of circumstance, and we can learn how to discern them.

Take great comfort in the fact that you can't force your way through a door that God has closed nor be blocked from a door He has opened. No one can undo His will for your life if you are trusting and following Him. He will open the right way for you in His time.

Lord, please open every door I should go through and close every one I shouldn't. And if I find more than one door open, give me the wisdom to know which one to choose.

Tell [the leaders of Israel], "This is what the Sovereign LORD says: The people of Israel have set up idols in their hearts and fallen into sin, and then they go to a prophet asking for a message. So I, the LORD, will give them the kind of answer their great idolatry deserves. . . . And if a prophet is deceived into giving a message, it is because I, the LORD, have deceived that prophet."

EZEKIEL 14:4, 9

It's a frightening prospect. The God of truth, the God who cannot lie, the God who has promised to guide His people—this is the God who tells idolaters that He will deceive prophets to set them up for failure. If they have craved false direction in order to satisfy their misplaced desires, they will receive it. He will lead them in a way that fits their wandering hearts.

As people who know the fickleness of our own hearts—we each have some inclinations toward idols at times—we tremble that God might mislead us. What if we are those people Jesus talked about, the ones who will be deceived by false prophets (Matthew 24:11, 24)? What if all those people who say we're wrong for claiming to hear God's voice are right? What if we are the faithless generation that is always looking for signs and hearing only what we want to hear?

It's good to check ourselves with these kinds of sovereigns, but not to obsess over them. Jesus spoke of false prophets who would claim to be the Messiah or who would offer alternate ways of salvation, not simply people who sought to hear God's voice. Ezekiel writes of an extremely rebellious generation that stubbornly set up altars to false gods, not of sincere lovers of God who struggle with typical idolatrous tendencies, as all human beings do. Yes, we aren't perfect; but if we aren't in outright rebellion, we can hear God. He promises. He will never mislead those who sincerely seek Him with submissive hearts.

Lord, I fear getting it wrong. I know my own heart. But I'm not listening selectively or to feed my idols. Guide me into truth—whatever Your truth entails for my life.

This is what the LORD says: "Stop at the crossroads and look around. Ask for the old, godly way, and walk in it. Travel its path, and you will find rest for your souls."

JEREMIAH 6:16

Our quest to hear God always brings us to an intersection of the new and the old. The new is God's personal direction for this moment of our lives. He opens up new insights into His Word and reveals specific steps we should take. The old is what He has already shown us about His nature and His ways. He will not give us new doctrine, only insights into eternal truth. He will not lead us in ways that contradict His character or purposes, but only those that fit our relationship with Him and our role in His Kingdom. To sort it all out, we sometimes have to stop at the crossroads and look around. And we may need to take our focus off of getting "new truth" and put it on what God has already said.

Thousands of years of revelation have been laid out behind us. We can't depart from it. It was true when spoken, and coming from the mouth of an eternal God with no lack of foresight, it is true now. He changes His methods from time to time and even person to person—the Bible itself gives us a multitude of means by which He spoke, as well as situational instructions—but His nature and His ultimate purposes do not shift with the times. His work progresses from generation to generation, but His character does not. Much of hearing God's voice, especially in Scripture, involves discerning the difference between His eternal purposes and His momentary methods. We have to see into His heart.

Make that a priority. Knowing God's heart is the better part of hearing His voice. His heart is ageless and has not changed. Stop at the crossroads and look at where He has been. Then you will know where He is going and be able to fall in step with Him.

❖ ❖ ❖

Lord, give me deep, rich insights into Your Word. Show me ancient paths and eternal meaning. Let me see into Your heart.

*I posted watchmen over you who said, "Listen for the sound of the alarm."
But you replied, "No! We won't pay attention!"*
JEREMIAH 6:17

Both God and Jeremiah were frustrated. Jeremiah lamented that no one listened when he spoke (Jeremiah 6:10). His message wasn't popular. Now God affirms Jeremiah's lament. In spite of the fact that He had posted watchmen (prophets) among His people, the people had shut their ears and determined not to pay attention. They were open only to certain messages, things they wanted to hear that turned out to be false. They missed God's voice because they tuned it out.

The number one obstacle to hearing God is a calloused heart. Those who ask, seek, and knock will receive, find, and walk through open doors; but we live in a world full of people who set their own agendas and are not asking to hear from God. Even God's own people had shut Him out in Jeremiah's time—as well as in many other eras of history—and did not want to hear. They ignored warnings, listened to flattery, and clung to their own agendas. They chose spiritual deafness.

Always approach God with a willingness to hear the exact opposite of what you want to hear. Nevertheless, don't approach Him with that expectation; He is usually much more encouraging than that. But there's a vast difference between expectation and openness, and though we expect affirmation from Him, we need to be open to hear correction or direction that goes against our surface desires. Listening to God selectively has a tendency to cultivate spiritual deafness; when we refuse to hear in one area, we limit our hearing in other areas too. But when we open ourselves to anything God wants to say, He can say anything. When He has our attention, He is much more generous with His.

Lord, there are things I don't want You to say to me—things that don't fit with my dreams and desires—yet if they are Your will, I need to hear them. My ears are open even to Your correction. I am paying full attention to You.

AUGUST 25

I will give you shepherds after my own heart, who will guide you with knowledge and understanding.

JEREMIAH 3:15

"That which people trample upon must be thy food." George Fox, founder of the Quaker movement, heard those words as he walked by a church, and he knew God had spoken to him. He believed other ministers were feeding upon empty words and neglecting the message of the blood of Christ. He knew their words could not give life. Long before, Fox had searched desperately for a way to be set free from the fleshly works of death and be prepared for life-giving ministry, and he found none from the ministers he knew. He had heard a voice then too: "There is one, even Jesus Christ, that can speak to thy condition." He found freedom and life in Jesus alone, and this would be His message. God spoke to him to call him away from ministry practices that were bearing no fruit.

God's people have departed from His truth in numerous eras throughout history, but God eventually speaks to those with hearing ears to bring His people back. That's why God raised up prophets in biblical times and why church history is marked with repeated reformations and revivals. When God speaks, His words are often corrective. That can be true not only of individuals but also of generations of His followers. If the shepherds of His people do not fulfill their responsibilities in truth, He will get their attention or raise up new shepherds. His words have the power to reform.

When the Spirit is not freely flowing in the people around you, look to God alone to speak to your needs. He may direct you somewhere else, but He will often call you to *be* the reformation you desire. He will lead you into truth, even when truth is not flourishing around you. You will hear His voice guiding you into freedom and life.

Lord, my experience with You is not dependent on the people around me. It depends on You alone. You can feed me with Your truth anytime, anywhere. Give me eyes to see You above any human wisdom or teaching.

Son of man, let all my words sink deep into your own heart first. Listen to them carefully for yourself. Then go to your people in exile and say to them, "This is what the Sovereign LORD says!" Do this whether they listen to you or not.

EZEKIEL 3:10-11

FROM THE HEART OF GOD

"I have many servants who think they are expressing My will simply by passing along the information that's in My Word. But My truth is more than information; it's life. That's why I tell you to let My words sink in and listen carefully for your own benefit. There are enough hypocrites in My Kingdom who are trying to implement My words in the lives of others before implementing them in their own. But this produces death, not life. My desire is for you to embody My truth and then just be who you are.

"You have no idea how much pleasure it gives Me when you savor My words not because you think you have to, but simply because they are Mine—because you want to understand Me, My thoughts and feelings, My work and My ways. This world is full of people who want My Word because of what's in it for them. There are very few who want to savor it and consume My Word in order to become one with Me. I am inviting you to be one of those few. You will be surprised at how close I draw to you and how strong I show Myself to be on your behalf. I want you to do it because you love Me, but I also want you to experience the benefits of My love. I want to bless you, and this is how I can.

"When you do this, you will share My desires and see them fulfilled in your life. You will embody My truth and impart it to others. You will become more than a servant. You'll be a friend."

Lord, I want that. Whatever benefits and blessings there might be, I want to become one with You, not only in principle but also in experience. I want to embody who You are—in Spirit and in Word.

I [Ezra] proclaimed a fast there at the river of Ahava, that we might humble ourselves before our God, to seek from Him the right way for us and our little ones and all our possessions.
EZRA 8:21, NKJV

Some translations say that Ezra proclaimed a fast to ask God for a safe journey, and certainly that's true. But he also seems to be asking not only for the safe way back to Israel's homeland but also the *right* way. There was no way to know which roads would provide the best travel conditions; thieves and dust storms were not predictable, except to a God who sees the future. So Ezra and the people fasted and prayed, listening for God and asking for His protection and provision.

Many modern Christians don't understand the purpose of fasting, but it's nevertheless a well-founded biblical practice. Depriving oneself of food for a time has a way at first of focusing our attention on physical discomfort and cravings, but then our focus shifts to the reason for the fast and raises the intensity of our prayers. Fasting is a decisive declaration that we are not enslaved by the physical world we live in, but are dependent on God alone. It's a statement that His voice and His presence are more important to us even than the food we need to survive. It's a tangible and conscious shift in our priorities.

Sometimes the best way to hear God's voice is to shut out all other needs, cravings, and desires in order to focus all attention on Him. When our routine is so radically violated, we are compelled to keep the purpose in the front of our minds. All we think about is our lack of food and the reason for it. In so doing, we cry with intensity to the God we long to hear from. And He loves to respond to such cries.

Father, for a time, I forsake my physical senses in order to heighten my spiritual senses. Amplify Your voice during this time. Hear my cries. Lead me in the right way.

One day as these men were worshiping the Lord and fasting, the Holy Spirit said, "Dedicate Barnabas and Saul for the special work to which I have called them."

ACTS 13:2

Men from the church at Antioch were worshiping—some translations say "ministering to the Lord"—and they heard directly from the Holy Spirit. We don't know what that sounded like, or whether it began in the spirit of one man or in several simultaneously. We only know that this group collectively sensed a leading that they could attribute definitively to the Holy Spirit, and that it resulted in the beginning of missionary journeys to far reaches of the empire that would dramatically influence world history.

What exactly did these men hear? We know what the Spirit said, but did He speak in an audible voice? Did He influence hearts with the deep "knowing" that can't be clearly explained by those who have experienced it? Whatever the case, His words were specific and undisputed. The men knew they had heard from God.

Perhaps the bigger issue is not *how* they heard, but *what they were doing* when they heard. They were worshiping and fasting, ministering to the Lord, focused on His desires and purposes rather than their own. They weren't asking for guidance or seeking His will. They hadn't come with a particular agenda of what they would like to accomplish in the world. As far as we can tell, they had nothing on their to-do list other than caring for God's heart. And that created the right environment for them to hear world-changing instructions.

One of the keys to hearing God's voice is to take a break from seeking it sometimes. It's more important to Him for us to know and love Him than it is for us to get information from Him. But when we make the relationship the priority, the instructions come. Those who seek His heart will discover what's truly on it.

Holy Spirit, I want to hear Your voice just as the men in Antioch did. But more than that, I want to express my love through worship. You are always my highest priority.

It seemed good to the Holy Spirit and to us.
ACTS 15:28

"It seemed good to the Holy Spirit." On one hand, that doesn't seem very definitive. The council in Jerusalem had listened to the various opinions about Gentiles coming to Christ and had prayed about what to require of them. Clearly, the Holy Spirit had not sorted it out for them with an audible voice. All the church leadership could say was, "It seemed good." On the other hand, the Holy Spirit was clearly involved. Most of us would say after a long discussion about various options, "It seems good to us." We wouldn't want to pin our own thought processes on the Holy Spirit or speak presumptuously about His will. Yet, without hearing a clear, audible voice, James is able to say that this decision seemed good to the Spirit. The Spirit had not given any of these participants an unsettled feeling or a clear objection about the outcome. They were convinced that He had led them.

That's how most of our Spirit-led decisions will come to us—somewhere between a clear, audible voice and our own independent thought processes. We ask for the Spirit's leading, pray for Him to fill our hearts and minds with His will, hear all sides of the issue, discuss the options, and then trust the wisdom He gives us. That may not involve an audible voice from God, but it's still a voice. He is involved in the inner workings of our decisions when we invite Him to lead and seek His agenda alone.

Somehow, the participants in this discussion in Jerusalem made a radical transition. The meeting began out of a heated argument between factions and ended with a unified policy that affected the entire future of the church. Certainly there were dissidents thereafter, but the key leaders of the church were generally united in their mission. The Spirit speaks powerfully even when He speaks quietly.

Holy Spirit, please influence my thoughts, my discussions, and my decision making. I choose to trust Your leadership even when it only *seems* that I've heard You. You are my all-sufficient, always-present Guide.

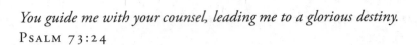
You guide me with your counsel, leading me to a glorious destiny.
PSALM 73:24

Something in us deeply longs to hear God's voice. Yet, something else in us deeply dreads it. Why? Because many of us hold on to a lingering doubt that we would like what God says. *His will is always difficult,* our assumptions whisper to us. *He only gives us what we need, never what we want,* our suspicions say. *Full surrender to His purposes will be all cross and no resurrection,* says the skeptic within us. We don't fully trust God's goodness toward us, wondering if our spiritual diet in this world is meant to be always vegetables and never dessert. We retain something of a split spiritual personality.

Intellectually, we know how false these suspicions are. God is good all the time, and He always wants the best for us. According to today's verse, as well as many other passages and stories from Scripture, God is leading us into a glorious destiny. Sometimes the path to that destiny is difficult, but sometimes it's thoroughly enjoyable. That glorious destiny certainly includes the Kingdom of Heaven after we pass from these bodies, but it isn't limited to that. Though our tendency is to think of our destiny as "there and then" rather than "here and now," Scripture doesn't make such clear distinctions. It's true that life in this world will never go entirely smoothly, and many will suffer unspeakable pain. But God is leading us into His Kingdom glories, and the Kingdom has already come into this world. It is continuously growing. God's glory can be experienced now.

Don't assume that God's will is always hard or painful. It isn't. It may not always be easy, but we need to cling to the hope that He has glories planned for us. There is nothing to lose in hearing His voice—and everything to gain. His words are always good for those who love Him and are called into His purposes.

Lord, I relinquish any suspicions I have of Your will. Your voice is always music to my soul, and my destiny—now and forever—is glory. Tell me everything I need to know to step into that destiny.

AUGUST 31

You must be careful to obey all the commands of the LORD your God, following his instructions in every detail.
DEUTERONOMY 5:32

God's voice is not just a voice. It's a mandate. That doesn't mean He's a dictator who compels us against our will to do whatever He says. Far from it. But when He speaks, He speaks absolute truth. There is no reasonable alternative to what He says. He isn't simply one voice among many others to choose from. We can find other options if we want to, but none will serve us better than what God has said. His voice is the only one worth following.

That's the nature of absolute truth—and the difference between asking to hear from God and asking to hear from a human being. We normally weigh the voices we hear—experts on a given subject carry more weight than casual opinions—and then consider our options accordingly. But when we hear from God, our normal processes for seeking advice don't apply. The only reasonable response to absolute truth is to follow it.

We need to remember that when we ask to hear from God. We have to know that we aren't seeking suggestions or advice or a thoughtful opinion. We're seeking authoritative words, and we should be prepared to respond to them as such. God loves a good discussion, but He has no need to ask for a rebuttal from us, no matter how well reasoned. He invites our thoughts, feelings, and desires, but in matters of instruction, He doesn't really need our wisdom. He knows what He is saying, and it's as true as truth gets.

Respond with diligence to all God has said. His words are more than helpful; they are exactly what we need to know for our own well-being. If we treat them casually, we do ourselves harm. But if we are careful to follow all that He says, He assures us that we will experience life in all its fullness.

Lord, forgive me for treating Your words casually. They are my absolute truth, my only anchor in this world. Help me follow You from my heart.

SEPTEMBER 1

God knows how much I [Paul] love you and long for you with the tender compassion of Christ Jesus.
PHILIPPIANS 1:8

I felt an overwhelming surge of compassion for the woman I'd just met, and I didn't even know why. I didn't know her story—nothing about her needs, experiences, problems, or relationships. Her expression may have subtly revealed some discouragement, but there was no striking indication that she needed sympathy. I simply felt compassion. And I had an almost irresistible urge to act on it.

Sometimes we sense God's emotions for someone else. When we can't put our finger on why we feel encouraged, loving, concerned, joyful, or anything else that might come from God's heart, we may be picking up what is actually in His heart for that person. An unexplained sense of anger, condemnation, or judgment may come from an entirely different source, but God's compassion flows through His people toward others. Why? So we'll act on those impulses and show His compassion. He wants us to represent His goodness to the world, and sudden shifts in emotions or attitudes may be a divine nudge to display what's in His heart.

Don't assume that all feelings are simply your own. If you are a vessel of the Spirit's presence, it only makes sense that He would move you through His desires and attitudes. He is a ministering, missionary Spirit who wants to draw people to the Father through the Son and lavish His goodness on His people. Any urge to bless likely comes from the influence of God's Spirit in your heart. It may be there simply for your awareness, but more often it's there to move you to some sort of expression or action. The tender compassion of Christ—as well as His encouragement, His favor, His forgiveness, and more—is on display in His people.

Jesus, I long to express Your heart to people. Help me recognize the movement of Your Spirit within me—the swells and impulses and attitudes—and give me opportunities to respond to them. Put Your heart on display in me.

[The Lord said,] "I have appointed you as a watchman for Israel. Whenever you receive a message from me, warn people immediately."
EZEKIEL 3:17

FROM THE HEART OF GOD

"Am I calling you to be an ardent evangelist and warn sinners of their ways? I do choose some to do that, but your watchman role is bigger than that. I have called you to be sensitive to My heartbeat and express it to others. I've given you ears to hear My voice, and the spiritual insight to know what I'm doing so you can help others interpret the circumstances of life. I share my purposes in the world with those who listen and wait for Me to speak. I have put you in a position to know the truth behind the scenes.

"Most people in this world live in constant confusion about their circumstances and about the direction of history. They don't know My plans for them today, and they don't know My plans for the world. Everything appears random to them, and they play the odds the best they can. But if they had glimpses of My ways and My work, they would begin to align themselves with My plans. Their lives would begin to synchronize with My purposes.

"That's your role as a watchman. You are an interpreter of the times, someone with your finger on the divine pulse. I have given you that responsibility and invite you to step into it. It doesn't matter if you don't know how; I will teach you. I will begin to sensitize your spirit to Mine and show you things you do not know. I will unveil My purposes so you can help others step into them and know where I am leading them. I will use you as a voice in the wilderness around you, a spring that waters and refreshes the weary, and a signpost that redirects the wayward. Ask to receive messages from Me, and I will give you opportunities to share them."

Is this really possible, Lord? I don't know many who think this way—or who really expect to hear from You concretely. If this is true, show me clearly. Show me what's on Your heart, and I will share it.

Let the message about Christ, in all its richness, fill your lives. Teach and counsel each other with all the wisdom he gives. Sing psalms and hymns and spiritual songs to God with thankful hearts.
COLOSSIANS 3:16

Heaven is full of God's voice. Angels obey the sound of His voice, worship Him, bask in His glory, and proclaim His will. Multitudes declare His goodness around His throne. No one in heaven needs to sort out the voices to determine which is from God and which is not. No one questions what His purposes are. It's an openly God-saturated environment.

Here in our realm, however, things aren't as clear. Lies swirl around us, discouragement and fear and unholy agendas seem to dominate the atmosphere, and most people have a hard time telling which end is up. We strive to find truth and meaning, live purposeful lives, and have healthy relationships, but we often find ourselves confused and disillusioned. Yes, we Jesus followers cling to the truth that has been revealed, but we struggle desperately to apply it to the difficult situations in our lives. Our environment is not nearly as heavenly as we want it to be.

The words of Colossians 3:16 can make an enormous difference. Many of us say we want to hear God's voice, but then we fill our hearts and minds with things that would never fit in a heavenly environment. We want the clarity of heaven, but take deep breaths of the polluted air of the world. We willingly tune in to mixed signals and then complain about not being able to discern God's voice.

If we want the clarity of heaven in our lives, we need to saturate ourselves with heaven's atmosphere. Our spirits will be much more sensitive to God's voice when we've surrounded ourselves with the things His voice inspires. Worship-saturated, glory-permeated souls hear God more often and more clearly than those steeped in unholy messages.

Jesus, I know I'm thoroughly in the world, but You never meant for me to be influenced by it. Please, I need tastes of heaven—even full banquets—that will open my soul to Your voice. Help me fill my atmosphere with Your words and songs.

> *Moses and the people of Israel sang this song to the LORD: . . . "With your unfailing love you lead the people you have redeemed."*
> EXODUS 15:1, 13

If our spirits hear a voice that sounds demanding, compulsive, or impatient, it is almost certainly not God's. He may be firm and persistent, but His approach is personal and respectful of the relationship. He isn't manipulative because manipulation isn't appropriate in healthy relationships. He's a leader, not a pusher. He doesn't drive us against our will; He draws us into agreement with Him. Like a consummate gentleman, He woos and beckons and counsels.

Sometimes we forget that. Whether through a guilty conscience or a pattern of dysfunctional relationships with other people, we tend to hear God's voice with an expectation that He will command us like slaves or compel us to do what we don't want to do. We forget that He works through our desires more often than He works against them, bringing us into alignment with His will rather than forcing it on us. He is not a hard master; He's a persuasive leader.

Avoid the pessimism of those who believe God will almost always tell you what you don't want to hear or that His words will always crucify you—or at least be hard to hear. Yes, we are to submit our wills to His, but His will is usually appealing and uplifting. If He inspires prophecy to strengthen, encourage, and comfort (1 Corinthians 14:3), His voice will certainly sound that way when we hear Him directly.

Listen carefully today. God's words are not to be feared or avoided; they are to be eagerly sought and consumed. Whatever your situation, even if you're in the dark depths of a crisis, God knows the way out. He always leads His people into places of peace and victory.

Lord, I've heard that demanding, manipulative voice before, and sometimes I've wondered if it's Yours. Help me discern the tone of Your voice and recognize Your gentle ways. You lead well; let me follow well too. I choose to listen to You with the expectation of goodness in everything You say.

SEPTEMBER 5

Everyone spoke well of [Jesus] and was amazed by the gracious words that came from his lips.
LUKE 4:22

Jesus visited his hometown synagogue and read the weekly Scripture passage for the Sabbath gathering. Then He sat down—probably in the "Moses seat" from which the sermon was normally delivered—and added some commentary implying that He was the fulfillment of the verses he had just read, found in Isaiah 61:1-2. His audience couldn't have fully understood the implications, but they understood enough to marvel that this son of a carpenter was speaking knowledgeably and eloquently on prophetic Scriptures. They found His words to be gracious and surprising.

That's one way we can recognize the voice of God. Fresh, inspiring thoughts that are new to us are likely to have come from His Spirit. Some people marvel at how sharp and creative they are when they have new insights, but most of us realize we aren't as brilliant as we'd like to think we are. We know we have a deep well of revelation to draw from, and it isn't anything we ourselves could produce. It has been put into us by the Holy Spirit, who has far greater wisdom and understanding than we have. When those gracious, inspiring, and surprising thoughts come to the surface, they must be from Him.

Ask God to give you unexpected insights. Ask for illustrations, parables, connecting ideas, and angles on biblical passages that you haven't seen before. Pray as Paul did that the eyes of your heart would be flooded with light so you can rise to new levels of wisdom and understanding (Ephesians 1:17-18). Learn to recognize sudden ideas and inspiration not as products of your own mind but of the Spirit who lives within you. And thank Him for the gracious words He has poured into your life and will continue to speak in the days and years to come.

Jesus, Your words are truth. I expect them to stretch me, inspire me, fill me with hope, and counsel me with deeper wisdom than I have on my own. Give me fresh ideas and insights. With the ears of my heart, help me recognize the words You speak.

SEPTEMBER 6

When they heard this, the people in the synagogue were furious.
LUKE 4:28

Jesus infuriated the crowd at the Nazareth synagogue when He began telling them about the tendency of hometowns to reject their own prophets. They had just marveled at His gracious words, and now He was predicting their rejection of Him before they had actually rejected Him. Stories like the one Jesus told about God's sympathy for loathsome outsiders like Gentiles will do that. They didn't endear this speaker to His audience. Jesus' listeners suddenly found Him offensive.

We can assume that a voice that criticizes us, harasses us, makes impatient demands on us, or instills fear or anxiety in us isn't from God. But His voice might offend us from time to time—or at least stretch us beyond our comfort zones. His perspective will often defy our deeply held assumptions and challenge our biases. We are more shortsighted, narrowly focused, and exclusive than He is. When He speaks, He will frequently give us a bigger vision, a broader focus, and a more inclusive worldview. That can be pretty uncomfortable.

Most perceptive Christians who have encountered God's voice have then had to rework their religious practices, political views, or social expectations. It's unreasonable to think that when we hear Him, we'll remain pretty much unchanged. God doesn't come into our lives to take our side in human arguments; He comes to establish His will and His ways. If we expect otherwise, we'll be disappointed and, very possibly, offended.

That's why many of Christian history's greatest saints were somewhat offensive to their churches and their peers. They heard God, and what they heard didn't fit in with their religious culture. In retrospect, God was calling His people to new perspectives, but at the time, His voice simply seemed unfamiliar and therefore unwanted. We hear Him best when we accept that He will offend our sensibilities when He needs to.

Go ahead, Jesus—offend me if You need to. I know how limited my views are. I would be foolish to think my finite mind won't be stretched by Your infinite truth. Challenge my assumptions whenever, wherever You please.

> *[Prophets and priests] offer superficial treatments for my people's mortal wound. They give assurances of peace when there is no peace.*
> JEREMIAH 6:14

False prophets are known for telling people what they want to hear. So it stands to reason that true prophets would be known for telling people what they don't want to hear, right? Well, sometimes. But even though biblical prophecy gets a bad rap for being negative, that isn't a very accurate assessment. True prophets tell the truth. Sometimes their words express harsh warnings, as in the time of Israel's captivity, but even then they are balanced with hope. God always declares the redemptive side of His plan, even when the truth hurts.

We need to find that balance. Some people assume that anything God says will tickle their ears. Others assume that anything God says will reek of disapproval. Anyone expressing either of those extremes is not representing God's true voice. He will be honest with us, but there will always be hope in what He says. That was true in what He spoke through Isaiah, Jeremiah, Ezekiel, and virtually every other biblical prophet. Even the harshest warnings, rare in the course of redemptive history, were precursors to a positive end. Why? Because God knows where His people are headed, and it's all eventually good when they choose to listen to Him.

Don't fall for the lie that God will tell you yes to everything that crosses your mind. But don't fall for the opposite lie that He will never say yes to what you truly desire. His ultimate purpose is to bring us into His joy and lavish on us the extravagant blessings of His Kingdom, now and forever. He will never speak peace to us when there is no peace. But He will speak peace every chance He can do so truthfully.

Lord, help me learn to recognize Your voice by the balance in it. You sandwich Your hardest words between comforting, strengthening affirmations. I want to hear words of peace when they are really from You and ignore them when they aren't. Help me take every word of Yours to heart and fully live the ones You've spoken.

SEPTEMBER 8

Through everything God made, they can clearly see his invisible qualities—his eternal power and divine nature.
ROMANS 1:20

In his poverty, Nicolas Herman enlisted in the army to earn a living and fought in the Thirty Years' War. One winter during his term of service, he came upon a barren tree. Because it was winter, the tree had no leaves and no fruit, but in the spring it would be resurrected and flourish again. As Herman stared at the tree, he grasped the gospel with unusual clarity. He realized the enormity of God's grace and the certainty of resurrection. And feeling barren like the tree, Herman knew he could look forward to the change of seasons that would bring fruitfulness to his life. God's providence would grant him life.

Perhaps not many people come to Christ based on a visual picture in nature, but the message was clear enough for Herman to see the gospel story: death, resurrection, and the sovereignty of God. He was profoundly changed. After his military service, he joined a monastery as a low-ranking servant and took the name Lawrence of the Resurrection. We know him today as Brother Lawrence, a man who practiced the presence of God so profoundly that even cardinals and bishops came to listen to his wisdom.

Some people dismiss the idea that God might speak through nature, but Paul was right about God's invisible attributes being clearly visible in the things He has made. His creation is His expression, so naturally He can speak through it. Nature is full of parables of God's story and His purposes, and discerning eyes can discover them: caterpillars, cocoons, and butterflies; rainbows; water falling from heaven to produce fruit; seed sprouting differently according to the soil it falls in; and many more. Ask Him. He'll show you a multitude of messages in the things He has made.

Lord, give me eyes to see Your parables and promises in the beauty and intricacies of Your creation. Your glory really does cover the earth. Speak to me through what You have made.

SEPTEMBER 9

[The Lord said,] "Get up and go out into the valley, and I will speak to you there."
Ezekiel 3:22

FROM THE HEART OF GOD

"If you want to encounter Me, go where I tell you. Sometimes I whisper to you in the moment, right where you are. Sometimes I meet you in your normal routine. But sometimes you need a change of location. My Son would go to a mountaintop or withdraw from the crowds. Ezekiel had to go to a place where I could show him My glory more fully and privately and then send him back into his normal surroundings. Jeremiah went down to the potter's house so I could give him an illustration. I often put My friends in places that will be relevant to the word I am about to speak, or put them in a strategic spot in order to speak a specific word to them. I have many reasons, and I rarely explain them fully. But when you hear Me telling you to go somewhere, get up and go. When I speak, sometimes location matters.

"I am not bound by geography, but I often use it to make a point. The topography of the Promised Land is full of subtle messages about My purposes. The paths I led My people on are rich with symbolism. My physical creation and My spiritual truth go hand in hand. If you understand this, you will begin to learn lessons and hear messages in the ways and the places I lead you. I have already filled your life with deep symbolism, and you will begin to notice it. And when you find solitude and privacy, I will unveil Myself more noticeably. Your location can affect what you hear.

"Don't resist the impulses I give you to position yourself to hear. I will make them clear to you, but you must follow them. You will encounter Me in places you never expected."

Lord, I would go to the ends of the earth to hear Your voice. But I don't want to wander aimlessly. Take me where You want me to go and speak to me there. If you need to change my view to show Your glory, I'm all for it.

SEPTEMBER 10

I [Paul] pray that God, the source of hope, will fill you completely with joy and peace because you trust in him. Then you will overflow with confident hope through the power of the Holy Spirit.
ROMANS 15:13

These words are Scripture. This means that even though they were written by Paul, they are also God's words. They express His heart for each of us: that the source of hope would fill us completely with joy and peace so we could overflow with hope through the power of His Spirit. This is the fertile ground for hearing God's voice, as well as a matchless description of what He sounds like. When our hearts are saturated with hope, joy, and peace, we are primed to hear Him well; and when we hear Him, He will almost always include words of hope, joy, and peace.

That doesn't mean God will never correct us, of course; we've seen too many times in Scripture when He spoke uncomfortable truths to His people. Neither does it mean He will tell us only what we want to hear. It does mean that He will speak the environment of heaven into our earthly context, and this is what heaven is filled with. He will speak words consistent with His character, and this is what His character is like. When we need strength and encouragement, God's words will give them to us.

Whatever hardship you're going through today, God has words of hope for you. He wants to fill you completely with joy and peace because you trust in Him. He wants hope and confidence to come gushing out of you through the power of His Spirit—not because all is well in your life, but because all is subordinate to Him. The power that works within you is greater than any power around you. Let the environment of heaven invade your spirit, and your spirit will overflow into the world around you.

Spirit of God, source of hope, manifest Your power in me. Fill me to overflowing with hope, joy, and peace as I exercise trust in You. Let these attitudes be a magnet for Your voice, and let Your voice speak these attitudes into me even stronger.

SEPTEMBER 11

[The Father] chose to give us birth through the word of truth, that we might be a kind of firstfruits of all he created.
JAMES 1:18, NIV

The words of God—both the written Word and every utterance that comes out of His mouth—are alive. That is the testimony of Scripture as well as every life that has been changed by hearing His truth. Though many dismiss the Bible as primitive speculations, or read it simply as ink on a printed page, those who have embraced its message have found it irresistibly powerful and surprisingly active. So it is with God's messages for any given moment in our current circumstances. They seem to have a life of their own because they come from the mouth of the Living One, the source of all life.

We need life. We are told early in Scripture that we do not live by bread or any other physical sustenance alone, but by every word that comes from God's mouth. We spend much of our lives earning an income, arranging our living conditions, securing our safety, seeking enjoyable experiences, and planning for retirement, yet the truth is that our greatest source of life and all its pleasures and benefits is the voice of God. When we hear Him, we are sustained, secure, and satisfied. When we don't, we aren't.

That's why seeking His voice—and the fruit of His voice, like being drawn into a relationship with Him and fully experiencing His Kingdom—should be the number one preoccupation of our daily lives. It should be the backdrop for all our other endeavors, the context for even the mundane details of our lives. His words are the source of our existence. We need to hear Him more than we need to eat, sleep, or breathe.

Determine to live as one born of the words of God. Let His voice become your heartbeat. Look at your schedule often and make whatever adjustments you need to make. Put the pursuit of God and His Kingdom at the center of your life.

Lord, I am born from Your Word and will seek Your words every day, now and forever. Your voice fills me with life.

SEPTEMBER 12

The LORD spoke to you from the heart of the fire. You heard the sound of his words but didn't see his form; there was only a voice.
DEUTERONOMY 4:12

After a generation of wandering in the wilderness, and before they were to begin their entry into the Promised Land, Moses reminded the Hebrews of their history. After being delivered from Egypt, they encountered God at Mount Sinai. Moses was given privileged access to the divine presence, but all the people were aware of God. How could they not be? He came with thunder, lightning, earthquakes, and loud trumpet blasts. There was a cloud of glory. They were awed by His presence.

But they didn't see His form. God shielded even Moses from the fullness of His appearance when He passed by in all His glory. None of the other Israelites could get that close. God was revealing Himself, but in measure. He wanted His people to know His will and be awed by His presence, but not so overwhelmingly that they felt compelled to obey rather than choosing to do so. He showed as much of Himself as they could handle.

In our relationship with God, we'll find a constant interplay between the *hidden* and the *revealed*. God is always making Himself known, yet there are millions of people in this world who insist He doesn't exist because they can't see Him. Some observe a phenomenon and call it a miracle, while others observe the same phenomenon and call it a coincidence. God doesn't compel our faith; He invites it. In this world, much of God's presence will always be mysterious and obscure. We will always have to choose to see what He is revealing.

That also applies to His voice. He is always speaking, but we will always have to trust what we don't see. The hidden is always being unveiled, but not fully. And we are given an invitation to accept as much of it as we will.

Lord, I hear Your voice, but I don't see Your form. But You allow me to accept as much as I can of what You reveal. Help me accept Your revelation and trust whatever I don't see beyond it.

*You must not turn away from any of the commands I am giving you today,
nor follow after other gods and worship them.*
DEUTERONOMY 28:14

Many religions seek to shape behavior. They emphasize the outward result.
In our relationship with God, motives matter—even more than our outward
actions do. It's true that much of Scripture gives instructions about what to do,
but never apart from the context of our loving God and being loved by Him.
The relationship, not the behavior, is the priority. All of our actions should flow
out of that relationship.

In Deuteronomy, God's people are told repeatedly to stay close to God's
commands and refuse to turn away from them. But some verses don't leave
it at that; they give us glimpses into God's deeper desire. He isn't seeking a
people who will simply follow orders. He's seeking people who will love Him
and respond to Him by becoming like Him in nature. Both obedience and
disobedience are seen as matters of the heart, not of self-discipline. Again and
again, heeding His instructions is juxtaposed with the alternative of following
after other gods and worshiping them. We don't just follow His words; we follow *Him.* We aren't just committed; we give Him our love. He isn't just our
God; He's our *only* God. This is the only context in which hearing God's voice
will be fruitful or satisfying. Anything less is just stale religion.

That's why it's vital to respond with diligence to the words God has spoken. It's all about relationship and His jealous desire for our love. There are
consequences—it's no accident that instructions like these are emphasized
in Deuteronomy 28–29, where the blessings of obedience and curses of disobedience are graphically laid out—so it's in our best interests to listen closely.
But our deeper motive is to love God with all our hearts. With God, motives
always matter.

Father, I do love You; help me love You more. Following Your words works
out well for me, but may I always do it to please You. May my heart always
be motivated by passion for You.

Be strong and very courageous. Be careful to obey all the instructions Moses gave you. Do not deviate from them, turning either to the right or to the left. Then you will be successful in everything you do.

JOSHUA 1:7

God told Joshua to adhere strictly to the instructions He had given through Moses. He should turn neither to the right nor the left. In being strong and courageous, Joshua was never to cut corners in his obedience. This would be the key to his success.

Most Christians don't necessarily have the same mind-set as Joshua, and it's true that the gospel of grace gives us a different approach to God's instructions. When we accept Christ by faith, we accept His death in place of our own, His resurrected life for our own, and His righteousness for our own. That means His obedience is credited to us, and we no longer strive for righteousness by keeping laws that tell us what to do or not do. Yet the New Testament is clear that God loathes lawlessness. Our response to God's words is important. We don't earn righteousness with our works, but our heart-connection with God should produce certain changes in our lives.

So does obedience to God's instructions still matter? That depends on our motives. If our obedience is a response of love toward God, then it brings tremendous blessing. If it's a response of obligation or an attempt to earn His favor, then it doesn't really accomplish anything. In fact, it gets in the way of His relational pattern of dealing with us by His grace through our faith. When we hear Him, we are to respond by following. But how we follow will lead us either deeper into the relationship or deeper into self-effort and fruitless legalism. If we really want to reap the benefit of hearing God's voice, we will cling relentlessly to His words for no other reason than that we love Him.

Lord, my response matters to You. You give me the paths to Your blessings, and I want to follow them tenaciously. You have declared me righteous; now help me live out that truth in practice.

SEPTEMBER 15

Go and make disciples of all the nations, baptizing them in the name of the Father and the Son and the Holy Spirit.
MATTHEW 28:19

When William Carey was called to missions, hardly anyone thought it was a good idea. His work would spark the modern missions movement, but like most trailblazers, he faced a lot of opposition. Few within the church thought it necessary for Christians to take the gospel to distant lands. One church leader even rebuked Carey, suggesting that if God wanted to save "the heathen," He could do it without Carey's help. Yet Carey persisted because he was convinced he had heard God's call.

How did that call come to Carey? By his own account, his heart was awakened to missions by reading *The Last Voyage of Captain Cook*. Most people saw nothing but fascinating adventures in the book. Carey, however, was moved by its depiction of human needs. He felt God's compassion, and he took that—later reinforced by scriptural instruction—to be God's voice to him.

Is it really possible that the modern missions movement, which has taken the gospel to the ends of the earth, was initially prompted in a young man's heart by an adventurous explorer's journal? Apparently so. It wasn't the sole source of God's voice to Carey—God spoke to him through the needs of people and the great commission—but it was a vehicle that began to lead Carey in search of God's will. While some people dismiss the idea that God speaks through nonbiblical sources, God isn't limited to chapters and verses. He can spark our true, divinely ordained passions through art, music, science, adventure, and all other human endeavors. He knows how to capture our hearts, and He uses a multitude of means to do so. He speaks by stirring and cultivating our interests.

Lord, like William Carey, I want to "expect great things" from You and "attempt great things" for You. Toward that end, spark my heart however You choose. There is no division between sacred and secular in Your Kingdom. I embrace everything You use, every hint of Your voice, as sacred to me.

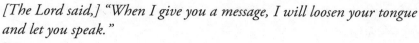

SEPTEMBER 16

[The Lord said,] "When I give you a message, I will loosen your tongue and let you speak."
EZEKIEL 3:27

FROM THE HEART OF GOD

"My Son told His followers not to worry about what they would say in crucial moments. My Spirit would give them the words. That has always been true of those who are close to My heart, and it always will be. Like the prophets and the disciples, you will find yourself in strategic circumstances and realize words are flowing easily. They will sound like your words because they are coming out of your mouth, but they will be words I have given you. When you need to express My truth, I will loosen your tongue to speak it.

"Don't be surprised that your personality and Mine are growing closer together. Don't be alarmed if you have difficulty figuring out which thoughts are yours and which are Mine. You don't always have to know the difference. Ask for discernment, but expect Me to fill your heart and mind with Myself. You've asked that your mind would be renewed, your character would be conformed to the image of Christ, and your actions would be consistent with Mine. Why wouldn't your speech be transformed too? I will use you as My mouthpiece and fill you with My truth.

"For this to happen, you will need to cooperate with the process. Ask Me to fill your mouth with My words and then expect Me to do so. Rest in faith and trust that I am working within you to express My voice. You won't become infallible, but you will be inspired. Believe that I will give you messages to share with those around you. They will feel the weight of My words even when they don't recognize My voice. And you will experience the power of My purposes and the joy of being My messenger."

Lord, use my words to impact others. Loosen my tongue to express Your messages. May I never dismiss my words as insignificant. They always have the potential to reveal Your heart.

259

O our God, . . . we do not know what to do, but we are looking to you for help.

2 CHRONICLES 20:12

Jehoshaphat's most famous battle began in desperation and ended without anyone in Israel actually having to fight. Surrounded by a hostile coalition, Jehoshaphat did what we all do in hopeless situations: He cried out to God. And with refreshing honesty for a king standing before his people, he declared his country's weakness and his own helplessness, and he appealed to God for help. And that's when he heard from God.

Honesty, humility, and faith are the right posture for hearing from God about anything. Most of us cry out to God in desperate situations, but often with a sense of hopelessness and no real expectation that He will answer. But Jehoshaphat began his appeal differently. He worshiped God, declared God's power and might, reminded God of His friendship with Abraham and His stake in the nation of Israel and the land, and emphatically stated his expectation that God would answer their pleas (2 Chronicles 20:6-9). This was no shot-in-the-dark prayer that had little chance of hitting the target. It was an urgent but confident plea for God to intervene. It wasn't just desperation. It was desperation plus faith. That's a powerful combination.

We often ask God to speak, but with a sense of hopelessness embedded in our request. That isn't the best posture for hearing Him. But asking in faith, no matter how overwhelming or urgent the situation seems to be, draws His attention when other attitudes won't. Hebrews 11:6 tells us it's impossible to please God without faith, but the obvious implication is that faith will certainly please Him. It's His nature to respond to those who believe.

When you need God to speak, ask Him with a great sense of expectation. Be confident that He will answer, even if that answer takes time. Look to Him in every desperate situation. But look knowing that He will step in with His wisdom, power, and love.

Lord, I don't know what to do, but my eyes are on You. You have invested a lot in me, and I know You will continue Your work. Let me know what You want me to do.

SEPTEMBER 18

Those who obey God's word truly show how completely they love him. That is how we know we are living in him. Those who say they live in God should live their lives as Jesus did.

1 JOHN 2:5-6

Jesus asked His followers a penetrating question: "Why do you keep calling me 'Lord, Lord!' when you don't do what I say?" (Luke 6:46). It seems obvious that calling Him *Lord* would necessitate following Him as Lord, but most of us aren't nearly so consistent. And though Jesus certainly understands our imperfections, there's a difference between falling short and not even trying. To hear God's voice without doing what He says is at best negligent and at worst hypocritical.

John had harsh words to say about this phenomenon. If someone claims to know God but doesn't heed God's words, he writes, "that person is a liar and is not living in the truth" (1 John 2:4). But if we saturate ourselves in His words—both written and spoken—and make it our zealous mission to carry them out, we demonstrate our love. This cultivates the kind of relationship in which communication flourishes. Any expression of good faith in friendship makes the friendship stronger. And when we declare with our actions that we are serious about doing what God says, what He says becomes a lot easier to hear.

That doesn't mean God only wants to tell us what to do. Life with Him is not all about commands. Far from it, in fact. His greater desire is to share His heart with us. But we can't listen to Him selectively, as if His words were a shopping list from which to pick and choose. When we listen for God's promises and encouragement without heeding His instructions, we generally hear nothing at all. But when we accept the whole package of what His voice brings us, we get the whole package. We tend to approach Him to hear what we want to hear. He approaches us with an all-or-nothing proposition. To hear Him, we need to hear on His terms.

Lord, I want it all—everything You say. I'll take the difficult with the easy because it's all from You. Tell me Your joys, Your secrets, and Your commands.

It happened just as the Scriptures say: "Abraham believed God, and God counted him as righteous because of his faith." He was even called the friend of God.

JAMES 2:23

The Old Testament twice refers to Abraham as God's friend—2 Chronicles 20:7 and Isaiah 41:8—and it's an unusual designation. Not many people in Scripture are said to be friends with God. But James points to Abraham's relationship with God as an example for us. The invitation into friendship with God is open to anyone. We can enter into that friendship by doing what Abraham did.

What did Abraham do? He believed God, and he acted on his belief. Those who emphasize obedience live as if God wants an army of robotic servants around Him. But that isn't a scriptural message. It's possible to go so far in the other direction that we live as if God only wants us to mentally acknowledge Him, but that isn't a scriptural message either. What does God really want in our relationship with Him? Faith that works its way outward in our lives. Faith that results in fruit. Believers who believe so thoroughly that they do something about what they believe. That's what cultivates friendship with God.

When we become friends with God, we grow to be like Him. That means not only that we hear His words and do them, but also that our hearts and minds learn to think, feel, and act like Him. We develop a bond that goes well beyond simply following instructions. We become united with Him in purpose and mission and methods.

When you have that kind of friendship, your heart will become something like a garden in which His best seeds are planted, or a stew in which His most savory flavors come to the forefront. There will be times when you know what He is saying without knowing how you know. Friends not only share thoughts, they influence each other's hearts.

Lord, I want to be Your friend. I want to know Your heart so well that Your words are often unnecessary. Let my faith and my actions draw me closer to You.

The secret things belong to the LORD our God, but the things revealed belong to us and to our children forever, that we may follow all the words of this law.

DEUTERONOMY 29:29, NIV

God has His secrets. He also offers us layers of revelation. There are aspects of Himself that He reveals to everyone, such as His artistry in creation and the common graces He shows to everyone, whether or not they believe in Him. Then there are aspects of His nature and His will that He reveals only to those who have entered into a relationship with Him. The more we get to know Him, the more revelation we can embrace. The more we seek His face, the more of His face we see. Those who keep on asking, seeking, and knocking will find answers and paths and doors opened to them. God's secrets become fewer as our hunger to know Him increases. He satisfies us with more and more truth.

Yet secrets remain. God is infinite, after all, and no human being knows Him fully. We will spend eternity discovering more of Him, yet never discovering enough of Him. His ways are inexhaustible. But even the placement within Scripture of Moses' statement about things secret and things revealed makes a theological statement. Moses spoke of "the things revealed" and how they belong to God's people at a time when there was much more revelation to come. Deuteronomy may be the end of the Torah, but it isn't the end of Scripture. "The things revealed" weren't done yet. There would be history and prophets and wisdom and a Messiah to come. That means God hadn't finished unveiling His secrets. He was still in the process.

That's really true for all of us. No one knows everything that God wants us to know, or has arrived at a place of seeing Him as fully as we ever will. There will always and forever be more. And He will always be inviting us into it.

Lord, let the "always more" shape my heart and drive me toward You daily. Show me something new every day. Take me from glory to glory in the pursuit of hearing and knowing You.

In his grace, God has given us different gifts for doing certain things well.
So if God has given you the ability to prophesy, speak out with as much
faith as God has given you.
ROMANS 12:6

It is astonishing that so many church traditions rule out the prophetic gift as an appropriate practice for today when the New Testament is so open about it. Or that some have redefined it to apply only to preachers in the pulpit. But Paul wrote to the entire congregation at Corinth—young and old, leaders and followers, men and women, high status and low—urging them to pursue the prophetic gift (1 Corinthians 14:1), and here he promotes it to the Romans, too. It's true that there were abuses in how some of the spiritual gifts were being used, but Paul addresses the abuses without ever denying the gifts. In fact, he seeks to cultivate the gifts as necessary aspects of Christian fellowship and experience. And he couples them, especially prophecy, with faith.

Hearing God's voice and speaking it to others always goes hand in hand with faith. The assumption that a prophetic word must not be spoken unless the speaker is one hundred percent certain about it is not a New Testament concept. Even Paul sometimes writes, "I say, not the Lord," as if he wasn't sure that his words were authorized by God (see 1 Corinthians 7:12, for example). Inspiration is much easier to recognize in retrospect than it is in the moment, both to the speaker and the hearer. Yet the Spirit urges us to speak and hear anyway, exercising faith that God's voice will be understood in the process. When we think we've heard God say something that will be beneficial to someone else, we can say so with appropriate caution—not with "Thus saith the Lord . . ." but with "I sense God saying . . ."

God gives us faith, words, and discernment. We can trust the Holy Spirit who is moving among us.

Holy Spirit, give me faith to speak the words You give me—humbly, yet earnestly. And give all of us among the fellowship of believers discernment to recognize Your words. Prophesy through Your people.

My heart is filled with bitter sorrow and unending grief for my people, my Jewish brothers and sisters. I would be willing to be forever cursed—cut off from Christ!—if that would save them.

ROMANS 9:2-3

The student lived in a culture that was hostile to the truth of God, yet she burned with passion for her people. As she spoke of those who were longing for fulfillment yet still rejecting Christ, she overflowed with zeal. "God puts His jealousy in your heart for others," she said, perhaps not realizing that some people don't experience that sort of harmony with God's heart. "I want to go to heaven, but not without these people. God keeps telling me, 'They are yours, and one day they will accept Me.'"

That's essentially the same message God gave Paul about his Jewish brothers and sisters. Centuries earlier, God had told Moses that His name was Jealous (Exodus 34:14), and He inspired Zechariah to convey how intensely He burned with jealousy for His people (Zechariah 1:14; 8:2). The language is strong, fierce, passionate. God has fiery emotions for those He loves, and He plants that fire within those who love Him in return. This "voice" goes beyond words. He is a zealous and jealous lover of human hearts, and He is relentless in His pursuit of their love. The hearts of those who know Him well begin to beat with His, synchronizing with His passions. No words are necessary for such love. The message smolders deep within the spirit.

Listen intently for those messages. Deep passions that connect with God's purposes—not necessarily with sterile theological descriptions of Him, but with His nature as described in His Word—are certainly from Him. He has spoken to His people most deeply by giving them powerful desires that line up with His will. Like Jeremiah and the fire in his bones, people with God's passions are driven by a powerful but inaudible voice that can't be ignored. They have heard a heartbeat that words can never describe.

Lord, give me Your passions. Fill me with Your desires. Let me overflow with Your most intense, relentless dreams for Your people. Drive me with Your heartbeat.

The LORD answered Job from the whirlwind.
JOB 38:1

FROM THE HEART OF GOD

"Job knew only destruction from the whirlwind. To him, it was the force that spun his life into a lengthy, dark confusion. For a time, I did not speak to him at all, but when I did, he needed to hear Me from the center of that force. He had to perceive My voice in the midst of his worst fears and most painful wounds. He needed Me to speak from the very source of His trials into the very wounds they created. He had to experience Me in the depths.

"This is often where you will hear Me clearest. I rarely provide answers and solutions that skirt the issues of your life. I much prefer to step into the midst of them and speak to you there. Wherever your pain is more raw and real than you ever thought it would be, that's where I need to heal. It's a deep healing, and not a comfortable one. You would prefer never to have felt the pain to begin with. But in the end, you will find that the benefit of experiencing Me there is greater than the cost. Only those who meet Me in the depths can know Me deeply. But you can't meet Me there unless something took you there.

"A superficial life can know Me only superficially. A life devoid of whirlwinds can never overcome them. You can't experience the peace and joy of My throne room unless you've passed through the lightning and thunder and clouds that surround it. So know this: If you have experienced deep pain yet found yourself inexplicably clinging to your trust in Me, you have been specially chosen. You have been called to a deeper knowledge. You may not like that, but you will benefit from it. You will encounter Me in the winds that shake your life."

Lord, the process of knowing You can be so painful. I know it's worth it, but part of me wishes I could remain on the surface of life. So make the most of my pain. Don't waste any of it. Use it to unveil deep mysteries about You that I never would have known.

SEPTEMBER 24

> *[Jesus said,] "Pay attention to how you hear. To those who listen to my teaching, more understanding will be given. But for those who are not listening, even what they think they understand will be taken away from them."*
>
> LUKE 8:18

Many Christians are frustrated with how difficult it is for them to hear God's voice. Perhaps this is one of the reasons why. Jesus promised that if we listen well—meaning not only to hear the words but also respond to them faithfully—we will hear more. If we don't, we'll end up confused and directionless, wandering in the aftermath of having neglected God's previous instructions.

That may seem harsh, but when we realize how much revelation it will open up before us, it's liberating. Jesus doesn't mean, of course, that we have to go back and figure out every time we neglected a word from God, or that we must obey every instruction in the Bible perfectly before God will speak to us again. If that were the case, no one would ever hear Him. But we should look for major choices we have made in the past in which we ignored His counsel, as well as any patterns of neglect in the things He has taught. It makes no sense to treat biblical teaching casually while pleading with Him to give us personal direction. He wants us to be fully engaged in His Word before we ask Him for specific words for today.

If you want a greater capacity to recognize God's voice, this is the best place to start. Pay attention to how you hear. Make sure you are pursuing the instructions in His Word to the best of your knowledge and ability while you seek direction for specific situations. If you listen to His teaching, He will give you more understanding. That's a promise.

Jesus, You know how much I want more understanding. If I have neglected Your teaching in any way, I turn back toward You and ask You to restore my spirit to a position of understanding and growth. Open my heart to hear—and follow—everything You say.

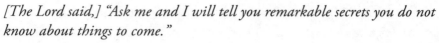

SEPTEMBER 25

[The Lord said,] "Ask me and I will tell you remarkable secrets you do not know about things to come."
JEREMIAH 33:3

"Ask me." That's the only prerequisite God gave Jeremiah for hearing His voice. Granted, Jeremiah had been chosen for a specific purpose at a particular time in history to deliver vital messages for His people, but Jesus essentially gave hearing ears to all His people when He filled us with His Spirit. The prophets were exceptions in the Old Testament; in the New Testament era, they are examples. God pours out His Spirit on all who believe, and we all receive some level of prophetic potential (Acts 2:17-18).

"I will tell you remarkable secrets you do not know." This is the voice of a God who is eager to share His heart. He isn't withholding His mysteries. He is looking for people He can trust with them. He seeks sensitive spirits, faithful messengers, hungry souls who will pursue Him as their heart's desire. When He finds them, He unveils depths of truth we have never before seen. He gives insights and inspiration that draw us closer into His heartbeat than we ever imagined possible. And He leads us into world-changing encounters with the people and culture and institutions around us. His secrets are meant to make waves in our world.

"About things to come." We long for glimpses into the future. Sometimes God gives them to us. He usually doesn't spell out the path in front of us, but He guides our steps, informs us of His greater purposes, plants desires and vision and direction within us, and prepares us for the destiny He has set before us. When we ask and draw close, He whispers the future to us.

God is excited about the future. He isn't dreading it. In Jeremiah's case, the future held correction for God's people, but it was also filled with hope. Ours is too. God longs to share His secrets with us—if we ask.

Lord, I'm asking. Whisper Your secrets to me. Prepare me for what You have planned. Draw me close to Your heart and let me hear the deep longings within it.

The voice said, "Come up here, and I will show you what must happen after this."

REVELATION 4:1

"He's so heavenly minded he's no earthly good." That common expression describes someone who is fully preoccupied with spiritual truth and may seem to others to be out of touch with real life. But real life *is* all about God and His Kingdom, and what many people call "real" life isn't very real in the eternal scheme of things. The fact is that we are only good to worldly realms if we have something of heaven's truth to impart. The fuller we are of that truth, the stronger our impact can be. We best serve "down here" by going "up there" to fill ourselves with revelation from God.

John was given a startling invitation by a loud voice from heaven: "Come up here, and I will show you." It's also an unanswerable invitation from a human point of view. We have no ability to enter heaven through an open door standing above us without divine intervention to enable us. John would have surely gazed at that open door and wondered how to get to it if not for a sudden shift in his perspective. At once he was "in the Spirit" and viewing the panorama of heaven's throne room. There he received visions that still inspire and amaze us today.

That's a graphic picture of how we hear God's voice. There is an open door standing above us, and we have no ability to enter it. Yet somehow, by being "in the Spirit," we do. In that place of communion with the God who is on His throne, we perceive pictures and sounds and words that fill our hearts with the wisdom and purposes of God. Like John, we may not know how to interpret them at first, but we are somehow changed simply by the experience. And we become heavenly minded enough to offer exactly what earth needs.

Lord, I would love to come up there, but I can't unless You take me. Fill me with Your Spirit, take the blinders off my eyes, show me the realities of heaven. Let Your Kingdom come on earth, in my life, as it is in heaven.

While his brothers were jealous of Joseph, his father wondered what the dreams meant.

GENESIS 37:11

Joseph had been roundly rebuked for his dreams, both by his brothers and by his father. The dreams were culturally and socially inappropriate. Fathers and older brothers don't bow down to sons and younger brothers. Surely God would never speak such an offensive picture of the future. That couldn't be His voice. But it was, and Joseph paid a heavy price for sharing what he had seen.

Though everyone around Joseph was offended by his God-given dreams, and though Joseph himself surely didn't understand their purpose, God was busy preparing for a future day when Joseph's presence in Egypt would be needed. God was providing for His people far in advance of their need. He knew they would one day be in a desperate situation, and only a sympathetic government in Egypt would be able to provide for them. God began setting up that sympathetic government years ahead of time.

But God also was providing for Egypt. He knew the Egyptians would one day need a ruling official with divine wisdom, and the Egyptian religious system wasn't going to equip a man with that kind of insight. God placed someone who could dream and interpret dreams in a foreign society long in advance of that society's crisis. He had a solution before the problem ever arose.

That's often the purpose of God's voice. He doesn't just speak into our individual lives or the immediate future. His agenda is bigger than individuals, families, churches, and communities. He is drawing entire nations into His purposes, building His Kingdom at every level of society. When we listen for His voice, we need to listen with grand purposes and long time frames in mind. We serve a big-picture God, and He wants to give us a big-picture vision. He is looking for people who can hear His heartbeat for the world.

✧ ✧ ✧

Lord, raise my vision to look beyond myself, my immediate needs, and my near future. Show me more than I can imagine. Draw me into Your greatest purposes for this world.

Pharaoh said to Joseph, "I had a dream last night, and no one here can tell me what it means. But I have heard that when you hear about a dream you can interpret it."

"It is beyond my power to do this," Joseph replied. "But God can tell you what it means and set you at ease."

GENESIS 41:15-16

God put Joseph in a unique position to bless Egypt's people and prepare the way for Israel's people to be blessed too. If Joseph had not received insight from God on how to interpret Pharaoh's dreams and to deal with their implications, the entire region would have suffered severely from the drought. But God cared deeply for both nations, so He raised His faithful servant into a place of influence.

How did Joseph rise to prominence? Not by rebuking Egypt for its idolatry or its harsh treatment of him. No, it was through his patient endurance in all the suffering he faced and by being open to God's wisdom and revelation. He had experienced his own dreams years before—the dreams that offended his brothers and resulted in his painful exile in Egypt; he had interpreted the dreams of two of his prison mates, which earned him the reputation that would take him into Pharaoh's court; and he was now interpreting dreams of national significance by simply declaring that God would give him insight. Not only that, he followed it with divine wisdom on how to deal with the problem. He knew how to interpret and speak the language of God.

God invites us to ask Him for His solutions not only for our lives but also for our society. He has given many people divine ideas through history and raised them to places of influence. This is how He blesses the world and draws people to Himself. And He will do so with us if we will begin to listen for His answers.

Lord, You have a solution for every problem in the world today and every problem I face. If You will share Your ideas with me, I will commit to ask for them and act on them so I can be a blessing to the world and Your Kingdom.

Pharaoh said to Joseph, "Since God has revealed the meaning of the dreams to you, clearly no one else is as intelligent or wise as you are. You will be in charge of my court, and all my people will take orders from you."
GENESIS 41:39-40

George Washington Carver began each day with an earnest prayer that God would reveal to him the secrets of the peanut—as well as many other flowers, plants, soils, and weeds. Why? So he might help "put more food in the bellies of the hungry, more clothing on the backs of the naked, and better shelter over the heads of the homeless." He believed that unless God drew back the curtain on the mysteries of His creation, these things would never be seen.

God honored Carver's request by showing him more than three hundred uses for the peanut; more than a hundred uses for soybeans, sweet potatoes, and pecans; and many more ideas that changed the face of agriculture in the southern United States. Carver wanted to find alternatives to cotton crops, which were being destroyed by insects and leaving sharecroppers destitute. Apparently the plight of the sharecroppers was on God's heart too, and He used Carver's prayers, as well as his education and dedication, to bless His people. Just as God gave Joseph insight on Egypt's drought, He also gives His people keys to solve pressing problems in the world. It's one example of how He draws people to Himself through His kindness rather than His judgments (Romans 2:4). He longs to show the world the goodness of His heart.

That's one of the most important reasons to listen to Him—so we can show the world His goodness. His plans are better than the enemy's and better than those of human ingenuity. He will lift His people into positions to bless if we will ask Him what's on His heart.

Lord, Your desire is to use me as a conduit of revelation and blessing to the world around me. In order to do that, I need Joseph-like insight into Your mysteries. I will bring problems from my workplace and community to you. Please open my mind to Your divine creativity to solve them.

SEPTEMBER 30

[The Lord said,] "Who is this that questions my wisdom with such ignorant words?"
JOB 38:2

FROM THE HEART OF GOD

"Perhaps I sounded angry at Job, but I wasn't. As you may recall, I vindicated him in the end and punished his friends. I was pleased with him and said so. But before I could lift him up, I had to remind him of his limited perspective. His deepest questions only scratched the surface. His most painful laments only represented a moment. His complaints against Me took into account only a cursory glimpse of My nature. He saw much less than he thought he saw.

"Go ahead. I invite you to pour out your heart to Me. Tell me all your frustrations. Question My work in your life. I welcome your honesty, even when it hurts. But don't be surprised when I remind you of the big picture, when I raise your perspective to see beyond your immediate surroundings into the vast depths of My being. And even in your most pointed questions, remember this: Any doubts about My goodness are wrong. Any complaints about how I have treated you are unfounded. Any agreement with the one who slanders My character is evidence that you have been duped. I have repeatedly said in My Word and in My relationship with you that appearances can be deceiving. There is an unseen world behind the veil of your surroundings, and your life makes sense only in the context of the whole. Don't base any conclusions on the visible. Learn to hear Me and know Me apart from what you see.

"You will see My goodness in your life, and treasure those times. But know that My goodness will also be obscured at times. Understand that you have a limited view, and learn to see beyond it. Don't question My wisdom with ignorance. Wrestle with Me on matters of truth. Your drive and your passion to know My ways will be rewarded."

Lord, help me learn to question Your works without criticizing Your wisdom. Anchor me in the knowledge that You are always good, no matter how things appear. Let me hear the truth behind the scenes.

OCTOBER 1

I will bless the LORD who guides me; even at night my heart instructs me.
PSALM 16:7

In the pattern of Hebrew parallelism, these companion statements are meant to reflect the same idea. "The LORD . . . guides me" and "at night my heart instructs me" are two angles on the same truth. God speaks to us even while we sleep. In fact, He sometimes speaks to us more easily while we sleep, especially during those moments right before falling asleep and right after waking up, when our minds aren't such vigilant watchdogs and allow the deep thoughts of the spirit and heart to come to the surface. When our own thoughts aren't in control, God's thoughts can flourish in us.

Some Christians see the mind as the rightful guardian of the spirit within us, but our minds can be as fallen as any other aspect of our selves. For the Holy Spirit to speak, the mind must let Him, and that happens often in the night. Inspiration comes to us in the very late and very early hours when we're relaxed. Like computer software that downloads while the computer sits inactive, the Spirit pours truth into our inner being. God gets an inroad directly into the heart.

Pray as you lie down to sleep at night. Ask for revelations from the Spirit, inspired ideas that provide solutions to the situations in your life and those around you. Ask for dreams that give you insights into relational dynamics or pictures of God's heart toward you and others. Let your imagination go to un-expected places and see what He shows you there. Take your night guidance seriously and listen to the instruction of the heart. Ask questions when you wake up—about discernment, about interpretation, about how God wants you to respond. Your Father has been speaking to you, even at night.

Lord, as I lie down to sleep, let Your Spirit guide my heart. Download truth into me, sing songs of deliverance over me, show me solutions to problems, open my mind to Your ideas. Give me spiritual breakthroughs, even as I sleep.

[Jesus said,] "I am leaving you with a gift—peace of mind and heart. And the peace I give is a gift the world cannot give. So don't be troubled or afraid."

JOHN 14:27

Christians give a lot of attention to hearing what God says, but much less to recognizing His tone of voice. But the two are linked, and we will scarcely be able to understand what the Lord says if we aren't listening to how He says it. In human relationships, the same words can mean entirely different things if they are spoken in anger rather than with a sense of humor, or with disdain rather than gentle encouragement. As one social commentator suggested, the medium is the message. *How* something is said is often more significant than the words themselves.

So when we hear God's voice, we need to know the tone of voice it carries. In other words, we need to be able to "see" the expression on His face. He gives us plenty of clues for that throughout His Word, and this verse is one of them. Jesus said He was leaving His followers with peace of mind and heart. He didn't want them to be troubled or afraid. We can reasonably conclude, then, that His voice is not going to produce turmoil or anxiety in us. It isn't going to be caustic or critical. He isn't an alarmist who spins us into a panic when something goes wrong. He will calm our fears and soothe our turbulent spirits. His words will sound like they come from the mouth of the Mighty Savior who rejoices over us with singing and quiets us with His love (Zephaniah 3:17).

Refuse to listen to the alarmists of our day who urge God's people to panic over elections, antichrists, or social decay. If there are trials, God will be with us in them. If there are battles, they will end in victory. He will not spare us from trouble, but He will certainly help us overcome it. And He will speak peace to our hearts.

Yes, Jesus, I need Your peace. I cast aside all false voices—words of panic, turmoil, and condemnation. I love the sound of Your true voice.

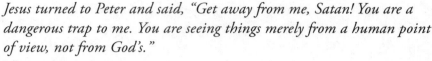

Jesus turned to Peter and said, "Get away from me, Satan! You are a dangerous trap to me. You are seeing things merely from a human point of view, not from God's."
MATTHEW 16:23

Peter was not Satan. In fact, just a few moments before, he had spoken words that could only have come from God, declaring Jesus to be the Christ. On such the Kingdom would be built, Jesus said. But now Peter was expressing words that didn't come from God. He wanted to protect Jesus from execution. If heeded, his words would have prevented the Cross, which paid for the sins of the world and saved all who believe.

Words of concern are not always words from God. We may receive all kinds of counsel from people who care about us, but it may prove to be unwise or wrong. It may appear true because of the trust we have established in our relationships, but it's coming from the person's own desires, not God's Spirit. The human point of view isn't always wrong, but God's point of view is always true, and it's often surprising. He has led people to do "dangerous" things or make "foolish" decisions that few others understand. When we know He has spoken, the approval of others becomes a nonissue. His is the only voice we need to hear.

Develop tunnel vision when it comes to doing what God has said. That's what Jesus did; He set His face resolutely toward Jerusalem (Luke 9:51). He knew His assignment, and no advice, no matter how well intentioned, would cause Him to deviate from it. We must have a singular focus if we are going to hear God and fulfill what He says. When we do, He rewards us with the fruit of faith and obedience and accomplishes His will through us.

Lord, refine my focus. No one's opinion matters to me as much as Yours does. No loving, compassionate counsel can sway me if it deviates from Your words. Give me the strength to commit to only what You say, and honor my resolve to do it.

OCTOBER 4

God works in different ways, but it is the same God who does the work in all of us.
1 Corinthians 12:6

God once spoke to Moses through a burning bush. He once spoke to Balaam through a donkey. He gave a sign of dew on fleece to Gideon, a sign of a child to Ahaz, and a sign of a reversing shadow on a sundial to Hezekiah. But He never repeated any of these forms or signs. Why? Because He is an enormously creative God, and He has no need to duplicate His works. His nature never changes, but His methods are infinitely varied. He knows how to reach each person's heart—individually.

That's why we can never definitively say, "This is how God speaks." We can discern patterns and processes, but only generally. He will not allow us to put Him in a box. He gives a variety of gifts to His people, and even the same gifts will look different depending on the people expressing them. God speaks in a variety of ways because He created a variety of personalities and life experiences through which His words are filtered. He has never been a God of formulas in the way He interacts with us. We are all drawn to Him differently and respond to Him differently.

Honor the ways God speaks to you and to others. When you hear of how others have heard His voice, refuse to measure their experience against yours or yours against theirs. Acknowledge God's creativity and our human diversity. And expect God to speak to you differently next time than the way He spoke to you last time. Allow Him the flexibility to approach you however He chooses. Reject any rigid principles about what His voice will sound like. He loves to surprise us with His range of creativity.

Lord, I worship You for Your creativity and welcome it in my life and the lives of others. May I never place limits on what I expect You to say or how I expect You to say it. Open my mind to anything that's on Your heart.

Do not bring sorrow to God's Holy Spirit by the way you live. . . . Get rid of all bitterness, rage, anger, harsh words, and slander, as well as all types of evil behavior.
EPHESIANS 4:30-31

The Holy Spirit is our means of hearing God. He opens our hearts and speaks God's words into them. He resides within those who believe, and makes His will known to us. Our relationship with the Spirit is the essence of our practical, day-by-day experience of God. So it only makes sense that grieving the Holy Spirit can't be very good for our hearing. If we are out of sorts with Him, we can't expect communication to be very clear.

In Ephesians, Paul gives a partial list of attitudes and actions that grieve the Spirit, and we could probably add quite a few more from what we know of God's nature from the rest of Scripture. We are told to get rid of all bitterness, rage, anger, harsh and critical words, and anything else that doesn't align with God's nature; these are likely to interfere with our hearing as well. If we engage in these things, we have already been unresponsive to the voice that calls us away from them. Continuing in them tends to harden our hearts and make us even less sensitive to God. And if our spiritual sensitivity determines our hearing, we begin to miss a lot.

Nothing can separate us from God's love, of course, but that isn't the issue. Our position in Christ doesn't change according to our behavior or our attitudes. But the depth and closeness of our fellowship with God's Spirit certainly does. When we are apathetic or unresponsive to what He has already said, we are hardly likely to hear more. But when we forsake whatever grieves Him and turn back with open hearts, His voice becomes much easier to distinguish.

✧ ✧ ✧

Spirit of God, it grieves me to think I might have grieved You. I release the junk and clutter in my spirit. Please restore anything in our relationship that needs to be restored and sensitize my heart again to Your voice.

OCTOBER 6

Don't be afraid; just believe.
MARK 5:36, NIV

It seemed like the death of a dream. I had been filled with hope about a certain situation, trusting God to work it out according to His purpose and my desire. But a shift in circumstances turned the situation in the opposite, and seemingly tragic, direction. How could this possibly be God's will? Should I give up hope? Was I still supposed to believe the things I thought God had said, even though they now seemed impossible?

The next day, I went to see a movie with my family. I was hurting inside, begging God to give me direction. When a character in the movie lost something that was precious to him, I heard in my spirit, *Watch what happens now; this is for you.* And when the lost item was soon miraculously restored, I took heart. Later, the same character faced an impossible situation, and once again, my spirit heard the words, *This is for you.* In the next few seconds, that character was told by another, "Only believe." I knew God was speaking.

Even though movies—or books or TV shows or any other form of entertainment—aren't inspired like Scripture is, they can contain biblical themes or even seemingly random words that God applies to specific situations. He makes words and scenes come alive in a deeply personal way to the reader or viewer who needs to hear Him. And when we are questioning faith we once held, whether it's in a promise that God gave or a truth of His Kingdom, He encourages us to hang on. In our weakest moments, when doubts seem to overwhelm us or circumstances seem to challenge our trust in Him, He whispers, "Don't be afraid; just believe." If the dream is given by Him, He will do everything necessary to keep it alive in our hearts—including speaking through the stories in our lives.

Lord, You are a God of stories. You write stories with the lives of Your people, You tell them to teach us deep truths, and You speak to us through them when we listen carefully. Fill my life with stories that impart Your words.

[The Lord told Job,] "I have some questions for you, and you must answer them."
JOB 38:3

FROM THE HEART OF GOD

"Let Me turn the tables on you for a while. Your heart is full of questions, and you've pleaded with Me to answer them. Eventually, you've resigned yourself to not knowing, to believing that your quest for understanding will remain largely unfulfilled in this age. But you will learn more about Me from the questions I ask than you will from the answers I give.

"Answer this, for example: What is your true motivation for knowing Me? Be honest. Is it to master My 'system' for prayer or miracles or success? Is it to make sense of your life and ensure that you have a purpose? Is it to gain My approval so you can eliminate those insecurities you haven't been able to shake? Are you more interested in the gifts or the one who gives? The healing or the love that heals? The provision or the generous heart behind it? In other words, is it all about you? I understand all those longings and desires and insecurities, and I won't rebuke you for them. In fact, you will find those answers in Me, and I am glad to give them. But I want to know if you really care about Me. Am I your passion? Do you want to connect with My heart not only because it's good for you but because it's Mine?

"Get to the bottom of those questions and you will be lifted to a new level of knowing Me and hearing My voice. Even if your answer isn't what you hoped it would be, I will still take you from that honest place and raise you higher. I have always loved you with an everlasting love, but when you open your heart to Me, My heart opens to you in new ways. And you will experience answers to questions you never thought to ask."

Father, You and I both know I have mixed motives, but thank You for welcoming me anyway. Purify my love for You. Fill me with holy passion. Draw me closer than I've ever had the nerve to come. Give us a stronger, deeper, heart-to-heart connection.

OCTOBER 8

You are permitted to understand the secrets of the Kingdom of Heaven, but others are not.
MATTHEW 13:11

The disciples asked Jesus why He so often taught in parables, but His response may have raised more questions than it answered. Why would He permit some people to understand the secrets of the Kingdom but not others? Why wouldn't He speak in a way that everyone could easily understand? Isn't the gospel of salvation for everyone who believes? Why not, then, make it easier for everyone to believe? For some reason, Jesus spoke in a way that created a dividing line between faith and unbelief. Only some could grasp His teaching.

Even those who could grasp His words still had questions. The disciples didn't understand some parables at first, like that of the sower, until Jesus explained them. But at least they could accept His explanations. They received the truth of His teaching, which is more than could be said of the skeptics and legal experts listening to Jesus. Some members of His audiences were listening in order to find fault or disprove Him as a legitimate teacher from God. They did not have "ears to hear," as Jesus often put it. But those who were listening in order to learn—who genuinely believed that Jesus was speaking truth, or at least were open to the possibility that He might be—found themselves in a privileged position. They learned the secrets of the Kingdom.

You can learn the secrets of the Kingdom too. The dynamic is the same when you read Scripture and listen for God's voice. If you come as a true seeker, you will hear Him. If you come as a skeptic, you won't. Or to put it another way, whatever agenda you have as you listen—whether to discover eternal truth or deny it—it will be satisfied. The secrets of the Kingdom are open to you if you are open to them.

✧ ✧ ✧

Jesus, give me the kind of heart that can hear Your mysteries and understand them. Make me a sponge that absorbs eternal truth. Help me root out any attitude that might block my hearing.

[Jesus said,] "That is why I use these parables, for they look, but they don't really see. They hear, but they don't really listen or understand."
MATTHEW 13:13

Jesus' words are deep and insightful, but it doesn't take an advanced degree to understand them. The key issue is not intellectual; it's spiritual. Some analytical minds may not be able to decipher the true meaning of Christ's teaching, but that really isn't the point. Christianity is not a mental exercise. Following Jesus is a matter of the heart.

Jesus' teaching—and the voice of God in general—always comes to us with a context and a choice. It's no coincidence that Jesus' explanation of why He spoke in parables came right after the parable of the sower. It's a story about the condition of the hearer's heart, and Jesus' explanation about the purpose of parables picks up the same theme. Some people have hearts to hear; others don't. Some are looking for a reason to believe; others are looking for a reason not to. The Lord's words are always clear enough for those with open hearts to understand, and always obscure enough that those with closed minds will not be able to understand them. Truth always requires some level of faith and humility in order to receive it.

That's true of anything God says, not just the teachings of Jesus in Scripture. If you are looking for purely objective, rational, analytical, unquestionable words from God, you will be disappointed because you are actually looking for a way to hear that requires no faith. If, however, you are willing to go with the flow of the Spirit and trust yourself to His leading, even when it seems subjective, you have opened your heart to hear. His words aren't illogical, but they are certainly extralogical—above our ability to reason. If we can accept that, we can embrace the deep truths of His Kingdom.

Lord, You don't want me to turn off my brain. But neither do You want me to reject any word from You that doesn't fit my logic. I give You permission to blow my mind with the things You want to tell me.

OCTOBER 10

[Jesus said,] "The hearts of these people are hardened, and their ears cannot hear, and they have closed their eyes—so their eyes cannot see, and their ears cannot hear, and their hearts cannot understand, and they cannot turn to me and let me heal them."
MATTHEW 13:15

A hardened heart is the enemy of God's voice and a frightening spiritual danger. God is perfectly willing to correct a mistaken heart, give wisdom to a simple heart, sway a reluctant heart, and awaken a sleeping heart. But a hardened heart requires softening, and that usually takes time. God doesn't force His way into the spirit of a calloused soul. He woos and pursues, often very persuasively and even irresistibly, but He doesn't demand. He is looking for a loving response, not an obligatory one. Hearts that have grown cold and calloused effectively keep Him out, and He lets them.

That hardening isn't always a conscious choice. In fact, it usually isn't. Little by little, we may desensitize ourselves to whatever God is doing in our lives, slowly and imperceptibly growing cold to His overtures. We justify and rationalize and come up with lots of explanations—many of which may even sound spiritual—for relying on our own wisdom and making our own decisions, but they all create distance between us and God. Over time, our hearts harden and our ears forget how to hear. We become spiritually dull.

Whatever it takes, develop your sensitivity to God and His whispers in your life. Ask Him to tune you in to the sound of His voice. Don't wait for Him to shake the foundations of your life to get your attention. Give Him your full attention every day. Devour Scripture, watch for His words, and look for ways to apply them. Let the softening of your heart draw you into God's nourishing, healing, strengthening presence.

Lord, is my heart calloused? Have I tuned You out? It's difficult to recognize hardness in myself, and I need to know. In any areas of insensitivity in my life, soften me up. Draw me close. Get my attention and hold it. Heighten my spiritual senses to pick up on even the slightest whisper from You.

OCTOBER 11

[The shepherd] walks ahead of [his flock].
JOHN 10:4

Sheep get confused. They don't have a strong sense of where they are going, or at least not an accurate one. They may be stubbornly headed in one direction without really understanding what it takes to get there or why they need to go. Sometimes they think they are headed for green pastures, not realizing they are on a dangerous path. They aren't the most astute animals on the planet.

No wonder Jesus compares us to sheep. He doesn't mean it as an insult—God gave us quite a bit of intelligence, after all—but our sense of direction is just as unreliable. We depend on our senses to get us where we need to go, yet our senses will not tell us how much danger lies ahead or whether the destination will really be as satisfying as we think it is. We don't see the whole landscape and certainly can't account for every "what if" that lies before us. But the Shepherd can. He knows the terrain. Sheep that are independent are destined for danger, but those who trustingly follow Him are destined for safety and pleasant pastures. Like sheep, we need a guide.

When Jesus emphasizes that His sheep can hear His voice, He also gives us this reassuring promise: He goes before us. He is on the path ahead, already aware of what we will encounter tomorrow, next month, next year, and forever. We may listen and wonder if His words will really serve us well, but there's no need to live with that kind of uncertainty. The Shepherd knows exactly where He is taking us—and where we'll end up if we don't follow.

As you tune in to the Shepherd's voice, know that He has gone before you into this day. He knows the terrain. He has good advice for you if you will listen. He can spare you from wrong turns and frightening dangers. His voice will get you where you need to go.

Jesus, what lies before me on this day? What do I need to know as I go forward? Keep my feet safely on Your path. Guide me to fulfill Your will.

[The flock] follow [their shepherd] because they know his voice.
JOHN 10:4

We recognize the voices of politicians, but we don't always follow them. We know the voices of salespeople, and we certainly don't always do what they tell us. We are intimately familiar with the voices of friends and family members, and though we value those voices more, we don't always heed them implicitly. Why? Because all human voices are unreliable. Some are even intentionally deceptive. We have to be careful.

We don't have to be careful with the voice of our Shepherd. With Him, hearing and following should be two sides of the same coin. When He speaks, His words are utterly reliable. And when we follow, we can be certain that we are headed in exactly the right direction. There is no gap between His words and our benefit. We never need fear that He might lead us in a way that we will regret. When we look back on His leading, even through hard trials, we will agree with Him completely. We will be glad He led us where He did.

The relationship between hearing and following also goes the other way. Just as the sheep follow the shepherd because they know his voice, so too do we learn God's voice by following Him. The more we take His words to heart, the more of them He will speak to us. Like a farmer who gives his best and greatest amounts of seed to the most fertile soil, Jesus speaks more abundantly and deeply to those who embrace what He says. He gives special attention to hearts that bear fruit and cultivates them to the fullest.

Treat the words God speaks like precious treasures that will bring enormous benefits to your life. Follow everything He says, and then expect to hear more. To those who have, more will be given. And our relationship with the Shepherd will grow fuller every day.

Jesus, give me more. I'm not reluctant to ask for what You already promised to give. I'll follow every word I hear from You. Please speak to me often.

OCTOBER 13

Is anything too hard for the LORD?
GENESIS 18:14

"Lord, I don't know how to deal with this. Please give me an idea." I've prayed that prayer many times—about a problem I couldn't solve, about writer's block, about anything that needed a creative approach—and He always seems to answer. It isn't an uncommon request for most believers, and nearly all of us could probably point to times when it was answered. And why wouldn't it be? God is the God of answers. No problem exists for which He does not already have a solution. The idea may not come as a concrete message from a divine voice, but when we suddenly have a spark of creativity after praying that prayer, it's from Him. We didn't just suddenly become brilliant. He inspired us.

Think about the implications. In a moment, God could solve any debt crisis or policy issue faced by a government. He could heal any family dysfunction or resolve any conflict. He could overcome the social problems of our cities and our schools. He has all the answers. Perhaps He is simply waiting for His people to ask Him for guidance and direction.

What would happen if every Christian educator, every Christian politician, every Christian voice in media—in other words, every believer in every arena of society—began asking God for divine solutions to human problems? What creativity would fill the body of Christ? What ideas would suddenly come to mind in the middle of the night or to a wandering mind sitting in traffic? Especially if the recipients of divine ideas would give God credit rather than taking the credit for themselves—what blessings would God give us to offer the world? There is no reason not to ask. God's people should be the most creative, ingenious people on the planet—simply because we know the God of all solutions. When we stop struggling and start asking, God will very often give us answers.

✧ ✧ ✧

Lord, I need Your creativity, Your answers, Your ingenuity. Inspire me with Your brilliance, and like Joseph and Daniel, I will gladly tell people of the God who reveals mysteries.

Who gives intuition to the heart and instinct to the mind?
JOB 38:36

FROM THE HEART OF GOD

"You are a sacred work. I carefully crafted all your intricate parts—your mind, your heart, your true interests and deepest desires, your personality with all its qualities and quirks, and every nuance of your being. I knit you together in your mother's womb, and I was pleased with My work. I saw every day of your life before you were born. My thoughts toward you are more personal and more thorough than you have ever imagined.

"Very often when you ask to hear Me, I have already put My truth inside you. I gave you a conscience, and I have urged you to make sure it remains sensitive to Me. I have given you instincts, and I expect you to follow them. You may question your gut reactions, but sometimes they are exactly what I intended. You are suspicious of your own heart, but I have given you a new heart and victory over your fallen nature. Much of what you are searching for outside of yourself, I have already put within you.

"Did you think your thoughts were entirely your own? Did you assume your wisdom and Mine were entirely different entities? Did you expect My voice always to come from outside of yourself? That isn't how I've designed you. You aren't infallible, but neither are you completely distinct from My voice, especially if you've been immersing yourself in My Word and My ways.

"I want you to trust the Holy Spirit that is in you. I didn't send Him to remain outside for you to search for Him there. I sent Him into your heart for you to search for Him within. He makes His home in your body, soul, and spirit because I perfectly crafted you and thoroughly redeemed you to host His presence. Trust My work in you as much as you trust My work outside of you."

Spirit of God, I do trust You, but I don't trust myself. Yet I have been made by the Father and remade by the Son. You have prepared me to know You fully. Anything less is false humility. Give me holy boldness to trust Your work in me.

OCTOBER 15

Once again David asked God what to do. "Do not attack them straight on," God replied. "Instead, circle around behind and attack them near the poplar trees."

1 CHRONICLES 14:14

David had just won a victory over the Philistines by getting permission and direction from God. So when the Philistines attacked again, David could have simply assumed God's previous guidance still applied. But David was wise enough to know that God's direction varies from time to time and situation to situation, so he asked again. This time, God directed him quite specifically to take a different tack. Yesterday's instructions did not suffice for today.

We need to live by that truth. God's nature never changes, so any instructions He gives us based on His character will always apply. But His methods often change, so we need to ask Him repeatedly for specific direction. He won one battle by having His people march around a city, won another by reducing an army to three hundred men, and won this one by signaling His people with the sound of feet marching in the trees. All of these approaches were one-time strategies, never repeated in biblical history, even in similar situations. God refuses to let us live exclusively by principles. We have to stay in close relationship with Him, keeping our ears open, in order to know what to do.

Whatever you are facing today, listen to God for the right approach. Yesterday's methods may or may not be God's desire for you today. You are in unique circumstances, and you need unique guidance. Precepts and principles aren't enough; like daily bread that needs to be eaten fresh each day, the voice of God is your nourishment. Ask Him for a fresh word, listening for His guidance every step of the way. He will speak specifically to your need.

Lord, what should I do? I don't have enough wisdom for the demands of this day, but You do, so my eyes are on You. I desperately need Your guidance. Please make it clear.

OCTOBER 16

The Word became human and made his home among us.
JOHN 1:14

The Gospel of John begins with a startling statement: In the beginning, there was the Word. The Word was with God, but the Word was also God. *With* Him, yet also *Him*. Not another being; the essence of God Himself. We don't understand such mysteries, but that's okay. Finite minds shouldn't be able to understand an infinite being anyway. Still, we wonder. Who is this Word, and why is He called the Word in the first place? What would someone known as "the Word" actually say?

We know from John and the rest of Scripture that the Word is Jesus. He's the wisdom, the *logos* behind creation. When God spoke worlds into being, He spoke through Jesus. Or He spoke Jesus. We aren't sure. However it happened, Jesus was instrumental in creation, and He is one with God. And He is called the Word.

Though that mystery may raise many questions, it also tells us a lot. When Jesus came, He didn't just *speak* the truth. He *was* the truth. And being eternal, He still *is* the truth. That means that when we hear Him, we aren't just receiving words of wisdom or good advice or even eternally significant information. We're receiving *Him*. We can't separate what He *says* from who He *is*. We can't talk about His nature and His voice as if they were two separate entities. Somehow, perhaps mystically, when we receive Jesus by faith and are born of His Spirit, we are born of the Word. Truth is implanted within us. As we grow, we don't just learn His words, we embody them.

Perhaps that's what Jesus meant when He spoke of those who have ears to hear. He wasn't talking about receiving sound waves, but about embodying His nature and His truth. His voice doesn't come to us from outside, but from His Spirit, whom He has put within us. As we embrace the Word, we embody His words.

Lord, You became flesh and lived among us. Enter into my flesh and live through me among Your people. Don't just speak *to* me; speak *through* me. Be the Word in me.

OCTOBER 17

The Word became human and made his home among us.
JOHN 1:14

Throughout Hebrew Scripture, God tells us what He is like. He also shows His nature in His creation and in His dealings with Israel, His chosen people. He reveals His truth and His purposes. He interacts with human beings and teaches us who He is. Then, in Jesus, He came and demonstrated who He is. That's different. The Word living among us in person tells us much more than sporadic encounters with an invisible deity can reveal. If we look at the Word of God as a *person* rather than as verbal communication, we get a dramatic picture of God's heartbeat.

So when the Word embodied in flesh made His home among us, what did He display? First and foremost, He is an expression of love. He was moved with compassion to heal people who were hurting; He cultivated loving relationships among His followers, between one another, and with God; and He made the ultimate sacrifice on behalf of all who would believe, laying down His life to rescue us. The Word embodies love.

If that's what the Word looks like in the flesh, that's also what the Word is going to sound like when He speaks to us today. His words will always be consistent with Scripture, but they will especially be consistent with the personality and presence of Jesus on earth. There is no discord between the Father, Son, and Spirit, nor is there any change in personality among them over time. The communication we receive from God today will have exactly the same flavor as the picture we see of the Word incarnate. God's words to us will look and feel like Jesus.

Never forget that. Many people do, perceiving God through their own wounds and distorted emotional filters. But the Word is still passionately in love with His people, and any words that don't express that love aren't His. He is still pouring out His radical, sacrificial, compassionate love into our lives.

Jesus, I so often assume that You are displeased or demanding, and my ears seem to fill in the blanks with attitudes that aren't Yours. Open my heart—and my ears—to Your relentless love.

OCTOBER 18

The Word became human and made his home among us.
JOHN 1:14

Scout bees looking for a new location for a nest are able to return to the hive and give a detailed map to the rest of the swarm by dancing out the directions. In Southeast Asia, thousands of fireflies light up simultaneously without any apparent prompting from a leader. Spiders weave intricate webs that continue to impress today's most advanced engineers. Birds migrate across thousands of miles to precise locations—and back again—year after year without losing their way.

How? What inaudible voice is guiding these creatures to do marvelous, inexplicable feats? The Word that spoke creation into being wove astonishing detail into its fabric. These marvels are written into creation as its unifying wisdom, speaking without continuing to speak, like a rhythmic echo resounding throughout eons of history. The Word in the flesh is the embodiment of divine wisdom—both in creation and in the direction of its inhabitants. The Word that lived among us is the Word that formed us from the beginning.

What voice is guiding us like that today? Are the bees and birds and other creatures rare exceptions? No, the wisdom of God is embedded in *our* design too. We are governed by the sound of God's voice, guided by an inaudible expression of His will. The intricacies of our makeup work together to form a stunningly complex whole, full of purpose and planning. We are, in essence, an articulation of His voice.

Know that even when you don't hear God's voice, you are being held together by its power and led by His intentions. His wisdom is in every cell of your body and every impulse of your brain. The incarnation of Jesus was the perfect expression of this wisdom, but God continues to express it in you—even when you aren't aware of it.

Jesus, You are the wisdom of God. I don't need information from You nearly as much as I simply need You. Fill me with Yourself, and I will have all the wisdom I need.

OCTOBER 19

The Word became human and made his home among us.
JOHN 1:14

Paul wrote a lot about the power of the Cross, explaining that his message had little to do with human wisdom, but rather was based in the Spirit's power from above. And we see that power clearly in the Incarnation, the Word made flesh, the ministry of Jesus as He made His home among us. His works far surpassed the human efforts of those around Him, demonstrating His authority over storms, diseases, demons, and every other power on earth. The Word-in-the-flesh was and is a greater power. He is an expression of the God who is above all.

What does that mean when God speaks to us? If the Word among us is *power*, then His words to us today will also carry power. He has not changed. He has never spoken impotent messages, and He never will. His words strike at the heart, change lives, turn situations toward His purposes, confound our best logic, and accomplish His purposes. When we are in desperate straits, all we need is one word from God to deliver us. When we are held captive by some condition or attitude or situation, all we need is one word from God to set us free. He is the God who thunders from heaven, even when His thunder is just a whisper. The earth shakes at the sound of His voice.

That's what we really crave when we listen for God. We need His love and His wisdom, but we need them expressed in power. Weak words will not help us; only the strength of His authority can change our lives and our world. When we invite Him to speak to us, we are inviting earthshaking words. And our ears should listen for nothing less.

Jesus, You are the power of God in the flesh. Speak that power into my life. I don't want weak words; I want change. Rattle my world with the thunder of Your voice.

I [Paul] pray that from his glorious, unlimited resources he will empower you with inner strength through his Spirit.

EPHESIANS 3:16

The visiting speaker had a reputation for insightful prophetic words—expressing God's heart for people in situations that no stranger could have known on his own. And even during this service, he spoke directly into the lives of people with remarkable precision. So a woman who had come with a desperate plea for God to give her specific confirmation about her calling had high expectations. And those expectations were dashed when the speaker finally called her out and simply said, "Trust God."

That wasn't the specific word she was looking for, and she was deeply disappointed. But she went back to the next service with high hopes again. And when she heard the same message to "trust God," she was crushed. Why wouldn't God give her specific confirmation like He was doing for so many around her? Why would He remain silent on matters He had clearly spoken to her about before? After praying through her confusion and pain, she realized the answer. She had already heard God clearly, and asking for another confirmation came from a lack of trust. God was letting her know she could rely on what she had already heard.

Can you trust the Holy Spirit who is in you? That's what many of our questions about His will come down to. We can be so worried about being mistaken that we forget His greater power to keep us in the truth. We're suspicious of anything in our own hearts, even when we've received direct promises and confirmation about God's work in us and His will for our lives. We forget that Jesus is in us and we can trust His Spirit. What He has spoken within our hearts is just as valid as what He speaks to us through others. When He is silent outwardly, we can rest in what He says inwardly.

Holy Spirit, may I never be guilty of downplaying the treasure You've put in me. You are completely trustworthy, and You reside within me. Inspire me with Your desires and direction, and give me the faith to believe.

OCTOBER 21

Do you still want to argue with the Almighty?
JOB 40:2

FROM THE HEART OF GOD

"I have never been one to suppress a good conversation. Abraham tried to persuade Me, Jacob wrestled with Me, Moses argued with Me, David vented at Me, Habakkuk questioned Me. . . . I have a long history of contentious conversations with My people. And I actually enjoy the interactions. I entered into those conversations willingly and allowed Myself to be moved by them. I invite you—even urge you—to be completely, audaciously honest with Me.

"I want you to speak with Me as a friend, but I also want you to know the gap I had to bridge for us to have that kind of relationship. My thoughts are higher than yours by far more than you can imagine, and your brokenness has taken you lower than you could ever fear. I've raised you up to enormous heights, and I've lowered Myself to staggering depths, and there in that middle place we meet. Do you still want to argue with Me? You can, but know what it took to make the conversation even possible. Present your best case to Me. But realize how much higher My wisdom is, and listen to it.

"You can have any conversation you want with Me, as long as you remember the gap I bridged. If you saw Me in My glory, you would fall on your face in awe and even fear. And if you knew the depths of your former fallenness, you would make every effort to hide. Now, knowing that, come boldly into My throne room for our sacred conversations. Know Me as your closest friend. Don't shrink back. But never take this friendship for granted. You are always and forever on holy ground. Assume the infinite wisdom of the one to whom you speak."

Lord, I realize I have no right to argue with You. Yet You have invited so many of Your friends into brutally honest conversations with You. What's the right balance? Do I fall on my face or come boldly to Your throne? Teach me to contend with You with honor.

OCTOBER 22

The laws of the LORD . . . are more desirable than gold, even the finest gold. They are sweeter than honey, even honey dripping from the comb.
PSALM 19:9-10

The Old Testament is filled with eloquent passages about the beauty and benefits of God's commands. The longest chapter in Scripture, Psalm 119, and many other verses and passages are odes to the voice of God in the law given through Moses. Hebrew Scripture, as well as the New Testament, is emphatic about our need to live by God's Word and to embrace whatever He says. But there's a problem with that, and it's pointed out specifically by Paul and hinted at by other writers of Scripture: The laws of God, even though spoken directly by Him, do not give life when we attempt to follow them.

What are we to do with this? How do we embrace His commands as "sweeter than honey" while realizing that obeying them won't give us life? Or to put it another way, how can we follow His instructions without becoming legalistic and depending on our own efforts? We have to understand that following the letter of God's words is nothing more than a religious exercise, but following the heart of them—the spirit behind them—is crucial to our relationship with Him. One approach is sterile self-effort; the other approach brings life-giving sustenance. One leads to death, the other to life. In each approach, God's words remain the same; our response to them, however, is drastically different.

In following God's voice, learn to recognize the desire, the intention, and the nature of His heart behind every instruction He gives. Everything He says reflects something of who He is. But then, instead of adopting His instructions as principles and precepts, follow who He is. See the Spirit behind the words, then passionately follow the Spirit. Learn to love the speaker more than the voice.

Spirit of God, You speak life. But I fail to live up to Your truth, and my own efforts are remarkably adept at turning Your words into death. Teach me to love Your words rather than develop formulas from them. Let them come alive in my heart.

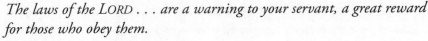

OCTOBER 23

> *The laws of the LORD . . . are a warning to your servant, a great reward for those who obey them.*
> PSALM 19:9, 11

We're uncomfortable with the idea of rewards, but God isn't. He talks about them often. Jesus told His disciples after many of His instructions, "Great is your reward," if they would do what He said. Salvation can't be earned, of course, but there are benefits to hearing and following God's voice, and negative consequences when we don't. That's just the way it is.

That's why God's commands are still intensely relevant for believers today. Those commands are revelations of God's nature and His desires. We know we don't accomplish anything in His Kingdom by our own efforts—we can do nothing without Jesus (John 15:5), and it's actually Christ and not us who lives within us (Galatians 2:20). But we still need to know what He wants from us. If we are being conformed to the image of Christ, we need to know what that image looks like and see if we're on track. And if God is giving out rewards for those who love Him enough to follow Him well, it only makes sense for Him to let us know how to receive them.

In Psalm 19:11, the instructions are rewards in themselves. They are a warning and a reward, a cause that has its inevitable effect, a seed that bears fruit every time. When God tells us what's on His heart and reveals His design for our lives, it isn't because He wants to restrict us; it's because He wants us to experience His fullness. Disobedience may have consequences, but so does living in a way that's consistent with God's nature and character. His words, if followed, become catalysts for abundant blessings in our lives.

Lord, I want Your best for my life. I want to experience Your fullness and joy. My mind realizes that any impulse to step out of Your will might cause me to miss a blessing; let my heart agree. I renounce any attempt to earn Your rewards, but embrace every effort to receive them.

OCTOBER 24

The disciple Jesus loved was sitting next to Jesus at the table. Simon Peter motioned to him to ask, "Who's he talking about?"

JOHN 13:23-24

The disciples were eating their last meal with Jesus, and one of them was leaning against the Lord at the table. John seemed to have that kind of relationship with Jesus; he was one of Jesus' closest friends. And because of that familiarity, he was in a privileged position to hear the Messiah's secrets. He got the inside information on what was about to happen.

God is willing to have that kind of friendship with any of us, of course. He invites us to ask Him questions and listen for the answer. He told Jeremiah to ask Him for His "remarkable secrets," and most of us would welcome that level of communication. We'd even settle for regular, everyday insights about the mundane details of our lives. We just want to hear from Him.

When you need to hear from God—some specific word that isn't already covered in Scripture, like the direction you should take or the decision you should make—ask Him a question. Like John, draw near and listen. Calm your spirit and let Him speak in the silence. If you don't hear anything, ask again and continue to sit in silence, listening for however He stirs your heart. If you still don't hear anything, keep your eyes open for the rest of the day, or even the next few days. The answer to that question will come, whether deep in your soul or through the parables and signs in your life. He will not ignore your question. He will find a way to communicate with you in a way you understand, and you will find a way to hear. He speaks to those who know Him well enough to listen to His whispers.

Jesus, help me silence my soul so the only voice stirring in my depths is Yours. Let me ask You questions, even small ones, as I'm learning to hear. Help me recognize Your answers, however they come. Just as John knew You, let me draw close to You as a friend.

OCTOBER 25

We are not like Moses, who put a veil over his face so the people of Israel would not see the glory, even though it was destined to fade away. But the people's minds were hardened, and to this day whenever the old covenant is being read, the same veil covers their minds so they cannot understand the truth. And this veil can be removed only by believing in Christ.

2 CORINTHIANS 3:13-14

Before Jesus came, fallen human beings had to be shielded from God's glory. The veil that was meant to be temporary became permanent in our thinking. We learned to assume God's distance, except in unusual circumstances, rather than assuming His presence always. In other words, we lowered our expectations. We began basing our faith entirely on experience, which convinced us that there were limits to how closely we could know God and how clearly we could hear Him. Like birds who still haven't realized the cage door is open, we continued to sit in captivity to our tangible surroundings. We stopped pursuing the greater presence because . . . well, we don't really know anyone who has had any success with that.

But actually we do. Scripture is full of testimonies of people who had extraordinary encounters with God. So is church history, and today's testimonies seem to be increasing. We can dismiss them if we want, but we have plenty of genuine opportunities to hear and believe. If we understand that the veil has been taken away, we will.

Deny the veil. Don't be swayed by what you *see*; be convinced of what you *know*. Accept what God has said and press boldly into the depths of your relationship with Him. Because the veil is taken away in Christ, there need never be anything obstructing our hearing, nothing interfering with the signal, no interruption to the connection. The only limits to our hearing are the lack of expectancy in our own prayers and lack of zeal or commitment. Faith and persistence lead to glory.

Lord, may I never impose limits to our relationship that You have already removed. Light a fire in me to press into Your presence beyond the former veil.

OCTOBER 26

[Jesus prayed,] "I am coming to you. I told [my followers] many things while I was with them in this world so they would be filled with my joy."
JOHN 17:13

Jesus had some pretty big requests in His conversation with God the Father the night before the Crucifixion. He asked that His followers be kept safe from the evil one, that they would be one with God and with each other just as the Son and the Father were one, and that God would share His glory with them. Jesus talked about how He had shown Himself to them and had kept them safe in Him. And in mentioning what He had taught them, He made a statement that might defy our religious expectations: He taught them so they would have joy.

It has often been said in our churches and teachings that God's goal is to make us holy, not happy, but the two go hand in hand. Jesus told His disciples that His words and their prayers were designed for the purpose of their joy (John 15:11; 16:24). In other words, the ultimate goal of God's relationship with us is that we would experience fulfillment, satisfaction, and delight. Not necessarily pleasure all the time, though He grants us pleasures forever (Psalm 16:11). Not necessarily an absence of pain, though He is a refuge for us (Psalm 9:9). But in the long run, He wants us to be happy.

God's words will, in general, produce joy in our lives. At times we may be made sorrowful by what He says (2 Corinthians 7:10), and we may need correction (Hebrews 12). But the general direction of His words is for our joy and happiness. He wants us to be fulfilled and satisfied in Him and His will for our lives, with nothing to dread, nothing to fear, nothing to shy away from. That's one way we can know we've heard Him—the fruit of His voice is (or will be) joy. When He speaks, we will be filled.

Jesus, let me feast on Your words and experience the fullness of Your joy. I need satisfaction; I was designed to experience delight. May Your words produce pure, unbridled joy in my heart.

OCTOBER 27

Be eager to prophesy.
1 CORINTHIANS 14:39

When I saw the woman visiting our church, a phrase echoed in my mind: "We don't negotiate with terrorists." It seemed so random. Had I read it in the news recently? Was it a vestige of the incessant sound bites that play in the background of our lives? I didn't know, but I decided to step out on a limb. When the time came for public encouragement of one another, I told the woman, "I hear the Lord saying, 'We do not negotiate with terrorists.'" Her mouth dropped open, and I went on. "I believe He wants you to know that whatever the enemy attempts in your life, you are not to compromise your calling. God wants you to fulfill what He has put in your heart to do. Don't be tempted to make concessions."

The woman later explained that she had been facing a ruthless challenge to her sense of calling, and she was trying to stand firm. She wasn't losing that battle—not yet. But God's encouragement ensured that she would be able to continue to fight the good fight. God let her know that the obstacles against her were not an indication of His will. They were an intrusion, an opposition she was meant to resist and overcome. Knowing that may have made all the difference in how she would respond further along in her journey.

We need to take risks in sharing our impressions and spiritual impulses with others. Scripture gives ominous warnings about prophesying falsely, yet there were schools and companies of prophets in many periods of biblical history— the implication being that the prophetic gift, like all others, involves a learning process. And in the New Testament church, Paul urged everyone to cultivate their prophetic gifts. That can't happen unless we go out on a few limbs. When we take steps of faith to share God's heart, we will find ourselves generously supported by His Spirit and surrounded by plenty of grace in the learning process.

Lord, give me the grace to go for it. I'm willing to try and fail, but expecting to be backed up by Your Spirit. I trust the impulses and impressions You put within me.

OCTOBER 28

[Jesus said,] "I have given you an example to follow. Do as I have done to you."

JOHN 13:15

FROM THE HEART OF GOD

"You want specific direction for your life, and I am glad to give it. My sheep hear My voice—I make sure of it. All they need to do is keep listening and learning. But in all of your attempts to get guidance from Me and to learn about your future, I want you to realize how much I've already told you. Remember that My priority for you is for you to know Me, to be filled with Me, to become like Me. Yes, I want to direct what you do, but I'm more concerned about *who you are*. If I am your source of life—not just by creation, but by your constant dependence on Me—what you do will become clear enough. Your heart is the bigger issue.

"Do you realize how much I've already spoken to you? My example is My word, My illustration for who and what you are to become. In every act, in every word, in every expression of compassion or love or anger, I have demonstrated My will for your life. Just as I looked to the Father and did only what I saw Him doing, I want you to look to Me as your template for life. You can love as I love, feel as I feel, think as I think, and act as I act. Everything I did, I did as a human being depending on the Father and the Spirit. I did not invoke My divine privileges. That would have made Me an exception you could never emulate, not an example you could follow. I intend for you to understand everything you hear Me saying as My words for you. Love what I love, hate what I hate, act as I act, speak as I speak. This is My will for your life."

Jesus, help me to not only listen for the messages You speak, but also to hear the messages You've already given. I can't be like You unless You pour Your life into me. Empower me to do what I see You doing.

OCTOBER 29

Samuel replied, "Speak, your servant is listening."
1 SAMUEL 3:10

Samuel did as Eli the priest had instructed. Upon hearing his name again from the unknown voice, he answered with readiness. The Bible uses various words for "hear" and "listen," and they don't all mean the same thing. When Samuel asked God to speak, he didn't just indicate that his ears were open. He expressed a serious intent to *listen*—to hear with the intent to do what was said. His ears *and* his heart were already committed to the coming word, even before it was uttered.

We have to hear not just with open ears, but with surrendered hearts. We have to be willing to hear whatever God wants to tell us, even if it doesn't fit our expectations or our agenda. We love it when He confirms what is already on our hearts, but we need to listen for the unexpected, too. We almost invariably have a preference of what we want Him to say and which direction we want Him to lead. There's nothing wrong with that, but we need to come to Him saying, "I'll be okay with whatever You tell me. I just want to know Your will. I'll accept it with joy, whatever it is."

When we posture ourselves as the young Samuel did when he was first learning to hear, we need to say, "Speak, your servant is listening"—not just to hear, not just to consider, but to embrace the message. The commitment must come before the information does; that's how God designs it. He speaks loudest to those who already know they are going to act on what He says.

Lord, I've made that commitment. I don't just listen to You in order to consider my options. I'm not just paying attention out of curiosity. I need Your direction. It is life to me. I have already decided I am going to do whatever You say, no matter how much it defies my expectations. Your will is my food, Your wish my command. Speak, Lord, Your servant is listening.

If I say I'll never mention the LORD or speak in his name, his word burns in my heart like a fire. It's like a fire in my bones! I am worn out trying to hold it in! I can't do it!

JEREMIAH 20:9

God's voice can burn. There are times when we are only to hear and respond. But there are also times when He speaks and expects us to be His mouthpiece. Voicing His words becomes something like a pressure-release valve that relieves us from the intensity of the message. But if we hold it in—if we are reluctant to go out on a limb and express what God has told us to speak—the pressure can become exhausting. The word smolders inside of us, growing into bigger flames the longer we hold it in. When God wants to deliver a message through us, it eventually has to come out.

More people are interested in hearing God's voice for themselves than in hearing it on behalf of others. We have all been given an invitation to pursue prophetic gifts (1 Corinthians 14:1), but we are reluctant prophets when we have to handle hard words from God. It's easier not to hear than to hear and try to hold it in. When God's message is unpopular, we don't want to be unpopular by voicing it.

This is why prophetic messengers must find their identity in God alone and not in the approval of others. We can hardly blame Jeremiah for his reluctance to be the messenger; he risked his reputation and his life on many occasions to say what God told him to say. Most of us will never be in that position, but we may get a taste of his dilemma when God entrusts us with His truth. Will we let the fire consume us within? Or let it do its purifying work in the world? Genuine love will compel our hearts to speak hard words when needed.

Lord, I want to be obedient to speak Your word, but I also don't want to miss the timing or speak presumptuously. Fill me with Your fire—and the boldness to spread it wisely.

O LORD, you misled me, and I allowed myself to be misled. You are stronger than I am, and you overpowered me.

JEREMIAH 20:7

Jeremiah was frustrated and humiliated. He felt that God had led him into a ministry that wasn't producing any of the results he might have envisioned. In fact, the only things it seemed to be producing were Jeremiah's frustration and pain. In a moment of pure honesty with God, he blamed God for deceiving him and betraying him. Of course he knew at a theological level that God can't lie, and it isn't His nature to betray. But the prophet felt betrayed, and he said so. God's voice had led him into a seemingly disastrous life's work.

Like most prophets, Jeremiah wasn't called simply to express God's words. He was called to embody them. In this case, his emotions were an embodiment of God's emotions. Jeremiah felt betrayed by God, and God felt betrayed by His people. Those who were meant to adore God and follow His ways were giving their love to idols and ignoring His ways. God's sense of abandonment by those He loved was reflected by the prophet's sense of abandonment by those he loved. The voice of God became a brutal, painful part of Jeremiah's life.

In listening for God's voice, watch your emotions carefully. They may be more than reactions to what you're going through. They may also serve as reflections of how God feels. Delight over a newborn who has done nothing to deserve love may be a picture of God's delight over His children who have done nothing to deserve His love. Grief over a broken relationship may be a picture of God's grief over those who have given their love to other gods. Whatever your situation, your thoughts and emotions can potentially reflect something of God's heart and thereby serve as His voice. Pay attention; He may be speaking not only *to* your heart but also *through* it.

Lord, it's amazing how many times my situations have some divine parallel that give me a glimpse of Your heart. Help me notice the connections. Let me recognize—and even embody—your thoughts and feelings.

This hope will not lead to disappointment.
ROMANS 5:5

It's okay. You can allow yourself to hope. Not many people believe that. Or perhaps it would be more accurate to suggest that not many people believe they can hope for anything other than their ultimate salvation in Christ. But our hope in God is far more comprehensive than "someday in heaven." He has given us everything pertaining to life and godliness and access to His "great and precious promises" (2 Peter 1:3-4). Like David, we can be confident that we will see God's goodness in the land of the living (Psalm 27:13). He fills our lives not only with big-picture hope, but also day-to-day hopes. He is the giver of every good gift.

Many people who listen for God's voice are predisposed to hearing His restrictions, limitations, and corrections. They may expect His encouragement to maintain hope for eternity but not for current situations. Yet God is far more willing to encourage us about today's circumstances than we think He is. He has solutions we haven't yet discovered, promises we haven't yet embraced, and outcomes we haven't yet envisioned. He is the hidden variable in every situation, the trump card yet to be played, the beautiful and satisfying end of the story that looks impossible in the midst of the tortuous, taxing plot. When God is in the mix, no situation is hopeless.

Don't expect disappointment. Don't assume, as so many do, that God will remain distant and not come through in the clutch. Allow your heart to embrace the hope of the whole gospel—not just the Good News of salvation, which is certainly true, but also the good news of His Kingdom, which is coming even now. When God speaks, He is far more interested in filling your heart with expectancy than subduing you with limitations. Embrace the hope that does not disappoint.

Lord, my heart seems so biased toward low expectations. My instinct is to protect myself from disappointment. But Your Kingdom is different; You incline our hearts toward hope. Give me the courage to embrace hope without fear of disappointment. Let me see Your goodness in the land of the living.

NOVEMBER 2

Anyone who believes in me may come and drink! For the Scriptures declare, "Rivers of living water will flow from his heart."
JOHN 7:38

Jesus stood up on the last day of the feast, right at the time when a symbolic act of pouring out water normally took place, and declared Himself to be the source of living water. He not only announced the eternal springs available to all who believe in Him, He located those springs in the heart of the believer. The source of life, of God's truth, of God Himself, would flow from within human beings. If we believe, we can embody the Spirit of God.

This is the primary means of hearing God's voice, even when we're reading Scripture, which we can't understand apart from the Spirit. This internal spring is our access to God's voice. A river is flowing through those who believe—streams of His thoughts and impressions and desires—and all we need to do is get into the current of that river. That doesn't mean that every thought, impression, or desire within us is God-given, but many of them are. We simply need to discern the difference.

That's a pretty big challenge, but not an impossible one. In fact, God would not tell us to rely on His Spirit or listen to His Spirit if He were not going to enable us to do that and teach us how. It's ludicrous to think of God giving us an astounding, costly gift and then leaving us in the dark as to how to access that gift. He doesn't give light for us to fumble around in obscurity trying to figure out how to live in it. He gives us remarkable but simple gifts—if we believe Him. And when we believe, the divine voice resonates inside of us, flowing through us with the thoughts and desires of God Himself.

Holy Spirit, flow through me like a rushing river, filling me with dreams and ideas from Your heart. I want more than trickles; I want torrents. Help me discern the difference between my thoughts and Yours, but let me not get stuck trying to analyze them. Give me faith to believe.

[God said,] "Now I will tell you new things, secrets you have not yet heard."

ISAIAH 48:6

"Lord, teach me something about You that I don't already know." This request of mine was answered when I overheard my wife talking to my son. He had been anxious about a health issue, and he needed reassurance. Lots of it. Again and again. And he kept asking to be reminded that he would be okay. Finally, my wife said, "Saying it again isn't going to make it any more true than it was the first time I told you."

Immediately, I saw myself in that verbal exchange. I had been anxious about a problem and asking God for reassurance. Lots of it. Again and again. And He had given me plenty of encouragement to believe what I already knew to be true. Yet my heart was anxious, and I kept feeling the need to hear His confirmation time after time. He let me know His perspective on my neediness through my wife's words to my son. Hearing it from God again wasn't going to make it any more true than the first time I heard Him. When He says something, it's true—without an expiration date.

Asking God to teach us something we don't already know or that we need to understand better is always a welcome question. He loves to show us new things, and He will open our eyes to illustrations and parables around us to display who He is. When we're focused on learning about God rather than on self-improvement, failures, needs, and desires, we grow in the relationship and are transformed without even being aware of it. As in any relationship, greater intimacy cultivates greater sensitivity and conformity to the other's interests. When we ask God to show us more of Himself, He finds a way to speak to our hearts and draw us closer.

Lord, I long to know who You are—deeply, intimately, and beyond religious explanations. And I know You are zealous to unveil Your nature personally to those who long for You. Give me pictures of Your perspective so I can know Your heart.

[Jesus said,] "I am not saying these things to all of you; I know the ones I have chosen."

JOHN 13:18

FROM THE HEART OF GOD

"The words I spoke to My followers on that night did not apply to the one who betrayed Me, nor to those who did not believe in Me. I have other words to those who are not yet followers. Those who love Me are given inside information in My Kingdom and called to specific works that only those with faith can accomplish. Like a good parent, I know the personality of each of My own, and I deal with everyone differently.

"Many of My words are universal, but many are specifically for you. You may hear of the words I've spoken to another person, but that doesn't mean I've spoken those words to you. Nor do the words I've spoken to you apply to everyone else you know. Don't assume laws or principles or even specific emphases from what I've said to someone else; they may not apply to you at all. And don't try to make your convictions fit everyone else around you. I have given different gifts to different members of the body. Respect the individuality of My people.

"Don't just ask Me to speak. Ask Me to speak specifically to your needs when you need to know My will, and ask Me to speak specifically about My will for others when you want to encourage them with My love. I am not a generic Savior; I know your hearts. Know that I have different seeds for different soils, and I always plant them in the right place.

"Be encouraged by that thought. When you desperately need Me, My words and My touch will be individualized to you. I won't offer you a blanket, one-size-fits-all relationship. I have come to you uniquely and have given you a special calling. You can know Me in ways that no one else can. Don't squander that privilege; enjoy it. I have chosen you to fill a role that no one else can fill."

Jesus, it's hard to imagine that You relate to me in ways that are exclusive to me. Thank You for choosing me specifically to uniquely understand who You are.

NOVEMBER 5

As the deer longs for streams of water, so I long for you, O God. I thirst for God, the living God. When can I go and stand before him?
PSALM 42:1-2

Sometimes we long to be rescued. Or healed. Or provided for. And sometimes we simply long for God. We recognize our need, even when we've been fully satisfied with the best the world has to offer. Money, possessions, status, recognition, accomplishments, and even meaningful human relationships aren't enough. Virtually everyone, no matter how successful, has asked the question, "Is this all there is?" We have deeper needs than we know how to satisfy.

So we thirst. Sometimes we can't put a finger on what we're thirsting for, but we know it's beyond our own resources. If we're spiritually minded, we realize that we're thirsting for God Himself, longing for the one our hearts were designed to connect with. And it's more than just a connection we desire. It's a deep, meaningful, lasting relationship that goes beyond superficial interaction. We need two-way communication, shared thoughts and dreams, a bond that can't be broken. We need to be known at the deepest level and embraced there.

God designed us with this thirst for a reason. It's what drives us closer to Him. Many give up the quest, thinking that if God hasn't shown Himself more fully, He can't be more fully known. But that isn't true. We hear Him by longing for Him. His voice resonates within us when we have decided He is more important to us than anything else.

Never forget: The ability to hear God is not a matter of technique; it's a matter of desire. Yes, there are ways to listen, attitudes that position us to hear, and perspectives that put His words in the right light. But before all that is the thirst. If it's strong enough, we won't stop listening, even if hearing is difficult. We will long for streams of water until we find them.

Lord, satisfy this quest. My relentless thirst is for You. Quench it with gushing streams of Your wisdom and inspiration. Let Your words fulfill my deepest desires.

Why am I discouraged? Why is my heart so sad? I will put my hope in God! I will praise him again—my Savior and my God!
PSALM 42:5-6

The longing heart is, to some degree, a disappointed heart. In our search to know God and hear the sound of His voice, we admit that we aren't satisfied with our current experience. We may be grateful for how He relates to us, but we want more. A taste of God is not enough.

It's one thing to long for God, another to live in discouragement about His seeming absence or unavailability. Longing can be filled either with hope or with doubt, and far too often we settle for low expectations. We may not even know why; we just assume the worst. We've let past disappointments color our outlook.

God has given us the ability to choose our own posture. Like the psalmist, we can speak to our own souls, asking penetrating questions of our emotional tendencies and commanding ourselves to hope in God and praise Him. We aren't victims of our moods; we're their masters. We may submit to them when we don't realize our other options, but we really can make conscious decisions to believe, trust, hope, expect God's goodness, reject doubt, forsake despair, and overcome fears. We don't have to live in the discouragement that so often plagues us. We can take our eyes off of our circumstances and fix them on God's track record. We can choose our internal environment.

Most people would agree with that, but few practice it. Be different. Talk to your heart and tell it what to believe. Don't let visible circumstances or past disappointments negatively shape your faith. Discouragement and dread are negative forms of faith, statements that God might not come through. But He does. Sooner or later, He fulfills hope. He will satisfy your longing heart and meet your pressing needs.

Father, I need You so desperately, yet I expect You to remain distant. Why is my soul so discouraged? Expose my heart for the lies it embraces. I choose to hope in You—in everything, for everything, and for always.

Deep calls to deep in the roar of your waterfalls; all your waves and breakers have swept over me.
PSALM 42:7, NIV

One-way communication with God isn't enough. We need more than prayers that soar upward and may or may not, for all we know, hit an invisible target. This shot-in-the-dark approach to interaction with God may be okay for people who haven't yet recognized their true hunger for Him, but those of us who seek a deeper relationship need more. After all, is it really a relationship if the communication goes only one way? Or if it consists only of the written word apart from living interaction? We can't be content with anything less than a heart-to-heart connection.

God offers us that, and in abundance. But it doesn't happen superficially. The place of real two-way communication with Him is the place in our hearts where we have the deepest issues, scars, and needs. We will tend to hear Him in areas in which we have been most profoundly battered and bruised. When we cry out to Him for guidance or encouragement, He often speaks to us "off topic" before He addresses the deepest need. Perhaps He does so to test our commitment to His voice, even when it isn't scratching our worst itch. But He always comes back to that need. Deep calls to deep, and it's rarely in a comfortable place. Not surprisingly, it's in the depths.

Don't be afraid of the depths—or the waves and breakers of life. Those who have the richest relationship with God have developed it in some pretty painful places. We wish it didn't have to be this way, but usually it does. High callings seem to require some low experiences. Revelations of light seem to come most often in places of mystifying darkness. And life seems to flourish most plentifully out of deathly wounds. Out of the depths, God speaks.

Lord, I want to connect with the deepest parts of Your Spirit in the depths of mine. Is there any other way than in the midst of life's tumultuous seas? Even if not, this is worth it. Let the noise of the breakers give way to the sound of Your voice.

Since we are living by the Spirit, let us follow the Spirit's leading in every part of our lives.
GALATIANS 5:25

In some branches of Christianity, the traditional process of decision making involves praying as a group for guidance and waiting for general consensus on the matter. Hearing the Holy Spirit is a collective listening experience in which unity is a high priority. If the Spirit speaks, after all, it only seems reasonable that He would speak to more than one person. Our God loves unity; it's only right to expect Him to inspire it.

We see this approach in the Jerusalem meeting of church leaders in Acts 15. They wrote that "it seemed good to the Holy Spirit and to us" (Acts 15:28) in communicating their decision to Gentile churches. In keeping with Paul's words in Galatians 5, this pattern of listening should not be unusual. If we are living by the Spirit, we can follow the Spirit's leading—individually or collectively. And if we're following Him in every part of our lives, as Paul says, that will include those parts that depend on and affect other believers. It's important to approach decisions with as many people listening as possible.

God moves not only through the hearts of individual Christians, but also through the collective body of Christ. His Spirit can fill a congregation even more powerfully than He can fill an individual. And the unity that comes from the group experience of God's presence is often visibly supernatural. When He empowers a congregation, permeates a meeting, or sparks a revival, the results can be life changing and even nation changing. He loves the fellowship of many ears listening to Him simultaneously on the same issue and responding with unified hearts.

Spirit of God, forgive me for asking so often that You would speak to me individually without also asking that You would speak to us collectively. Move through us, fill us, empower us, grace us with Your transforming presence. Enable us to move forward in unity.

NOVEMBER 9

This message was kept secret for centuries and generations past, but now it has been revealed to God's people. . . . And this is the secret: Christ lives in you.

COLOSSIANS 1:26-27

Some Christians believe that God doesn't speak today because the Bible is complete. Of course, nearly every believer accepts the authority of God's Word in matters of doctrine, but Scripture itself demonstrates God's desire to converse with His people and guide them. In Paul's words to the Colossians, this kind of relationship is confirmed. The Son of God—elsewhere called "the Word"—is in us. Would the Word be put within us only to remain silent? Of course not. God is a revealer of mysteries, and this one is perhaps most profound. The Word long desired before the coming of the Messiah was planted by faith inside of us after the Resurrection.

A promise is implied in this truth. God has secrets, but He shares them with His people. He is the Word, but He also lets us embody the Word. The much-desired voice of God is no longer "out there," it's "in here." We are carriers of the divine mysteries, and as such, we are now revealers of them too. The secrets of God unfold in His people, especially as we maintain a vibrant, dynamic, intimate relationship with His Spirit. If it is no longer we who live, but Christ who lives within us (Galatians 2:20), then it is also Christ who speaks within us, because He does not live without speaking. The Word is living and breathing in us.

This is not only our hope of glory, as Paul goes on to say, but also the world's hope of glory. God is made manifest in Christ, and Christ is made manifest in us. We may shrink back at such an awesome role, but we do so at great cost. The world needs Jesus and His voice. And it gets them through us.

✧ ✧ ✧

Dare I believe this, Lord? On second thought, dare I not believe it? If it were not Your Word, it would be arrogant and presumptuous. But I don't want to fall short of Your Word. Help me, in every way possible, to be a revelation of Jesus.

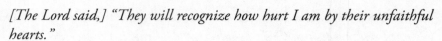

NOVEMBER 10

[The Lord said,] "They will recognize how hurt I am by their unfaithful hearts."
EZEKIEL 6:9

"Lord, teach me something about You that I don't already know." Again, this question was answered when I experienced the pain of rejection from someone I loved deeply. When the object of one's affections gives his or her heart to less worthy loves, it hurts. Unrequited love—whether from a potential romantic partner or a family member or a friend—is one of the worst pains a human being can feel.

I realized in the midst of a season of rejection that God experiences that pain every single day. Millions of beloved people reject His love, sometimes with apathy or ignorance, and sometimes with outright contempt. God is not a human being, but He made us in His image, which means our capacity to feel pain is surely a reflection of His. In fact, He spoke through many prophets about His grief in being rejected by those He loves. When we read the words in Scripture, we understand the theological implications of His love. When we feel rejection ourselves and talk to God about it, we begin to understand the personal pain He feels. In our experiences and our relational dynamics, He gives us a taste of His own emotions and attitudes—not because He wants us to feel pain, but because He wants our hearts to bond with His. He wants us to be able to relate to Him and know Him deeply.

Anytime you experience joy or grief or any other emotion in a relationship, explore how those feelings might connect you with the heart of God. His interactions with human beings are often reflected in our interactions with one another. The things that cause us to feel pain or pleasure often have a parallel in biblical prophecies that describe God's passions for His people. When we are alert to our relational dynamics, we can hear Him portraying His feelings in them.

✧ ✧ ✧

Lord, I don't just want to know about Your heart; I want to experience the things You experience. Share them with me. Alert me to Your feelings. Connect me to Your experiences through my own.

[Jesus said,] "The words I speak are not my own, but my Father who lives in me does his work through me."

JOHN 14:10

FROM THE HEART OF GOD

"I have given you an example to follow. In human flesh, I said and did what I observed from the Father, who was living within Me. You too can do and say what you observe from the Holy Spirit who is living within you. When you are in fellowship with Me, the lines between us begin to blur. You will have difficulty knowing where you end and I begin, or vice versa. That's how it is in intimate relationships. The bond creates a unity that makes distinguishing the source of thoughts and desires extremely difficult—and completely unnecessary. When you live in closeness to Me, you can speak of many thoughts and desires as 'ours'—not yours or Mine, but *ours*. We live and breathe together.

"I have also given you a deep truth in this statement. I've shown you the unbreakable link between words and works. They aren't distinct, as if you can accept the words without living them out. They are two sides of the same coin. To accept them is to live them; to live them is to accept them. Yes, plenty of people have mouthed My words without really embracing them, and as you know, this hypocrisy angers and disappoints Me. But their actions have clearly shown that they did not fully understand or accept the words. Those who truly believe I am Lord will do what I say because My words matter to them. They care for My heart.

"Let unity with Me be your goal. Don't seek to speak or follow either your words or My words as much as you seek to follow *our* words. My Spirit lives in you. Your life is not your own. We function together. I live in you and do My work in you, speaking through you, and to you, and for you. As you draw close to Me, you and I become *we*."

Jesus, I would love to know how You heard the Father and how He did His work in You. Show me how that works. Draw me into that kind of unity.

My ears you have opened.
PSALM 40:6, NIV

In all our searching and listening for God's voice, we need to remember one crucial fact: It's ultimately up to Him to communicate in ways we can understand. There are a number of things we can do to position ourselves to hear, and we can commit to being responsive to whatever God says, but if He doesn't open our ears, we won't hear. For those of us who like to "make things happen," this can be a frustrating process. We want to storm the gates of heaven and have God honor our boldness—an approach that is endorsed and encouraged in several places in Scripture. But even then, the gates of heaven don't open unless God opens them. Our hearing is in His hands.

We can take comfort in that. After all, God is even more interested in our hearing Him than we are. The Shepherd has invested quite a bit in His sheep, and He isn't about to ignore us now. We may go through dry times when we think He's silent, but even in those times, we are very often hearing Him well and simply mistrusting what we hear. In the words of the hymnist Frederick William Faber, "There is hardly ever a complete silence in our soul. God is whispering to us well-nigh incessantly." The problem usually is not that God is silent; it's that we aren't hearing well. We need to listen, but we also need to ask: "Lord, open my ears."

That's a good prayer to pray daily—even several times a day. There's no reason we can't hear as the early Christians heard and know the presence of the Spirit as they did in the outpourings of Pentecost and afterward. In all our praying for revival, this is a good place to start. Those who hear His voice can't help but be changed. Open and willing ears are the key.

Lord, open my ears. Again and again. I'll pray it constantly, relentlessly, until I'm hearing You well. You are the master of my hearing, and I trust You to speak in ways I can perceive and understand.

NOVEMBER 13

You surround me with songs of victory.
PSALM 32:7

It's a beautiful thought. Somewhere beyond our physical senses, we are surrounded with songs of victory. In our most confining captivities, our spirits are hearing words of deliverance. We don't know exactly what that means—Is God Himself singing over us? Are choruses of angels musically declaring the fulfillment of our hopes?—but somehow it's true. Those who have made God their hiding place are, despite what their senses say, being treated to a victory celebration before experiencing the victory.

This is one answer to our periodic lament that God doesn't speak to us. We may not perceive His voice sometimes, but that doesn't mean He isn't being vocal. He speaks in spirit realms even when our spirits aren't tuning in. He whispers to our hearts even when our minds aren't very observant. He blesses us even when we feel that the day's events are cursed. At a spiritual level, we don't have to be conscious of everything that's going on for it to be effective. God can declare victories we don't yet know we even need. And He can surround us with songs of deliverance that no human ear can hear.

Ask Him to let your heart tune in to the songs of deliverance He is singing. If you have made Him your hiding place and are trusting in His shelter, pray from the middle of your battles to hear the news of victory. Pray also that the enemy of your soul would hear the songs of the Warrior who fights on your behalf. Let the adversary tremble while you take courage. These songs carry authority and cause the enemy to flee. They can't be drowned out by the din of the battle. They will accomplish your deliverance and put a melody in your heart.

Mighty God, my Warrior, sing loudly. Let me hear. Direct your angels to join in the chorus. Sing victories and deliverance over me. And encourage me to always remember that when I sing during my battles, I'm not alone. I'm singing along with a powerful, invincible tune.

> *Gideon said to God, "If you are truly going to use me to rescue Israel as you promised, prove it to me in this way. I will put a wool fleece on the threshing floor tonight. If the fleece is wet with dew in the morning but the ground is dry, then I will know that you are going to help me rescue Israel as you promised."*
>
> JUDGES 6:36-37

Gideon had already asked for a sign to make sure God was speaking to him (Judges 6:17). Here he asks for another sign to see if God's promise is true. And when God grants that request, Gideon will again ask for a sign to make sure the last one was accurate. His tentativeness may seem faithless to us, and perhaps it was. But God was patient with him and gave the reassurances he asked for. Gideon's repeated asking wasn't ideal, but neither was it sinful. When God calls people to a big assignment, he makes sure they get the message.

We sometimes hesitate to ask God for multiple confirmations, but then we question the two or three we've already received. We may look down on people who ask for signs, but then we proceed just as tentatively as Gideon would have without them. We need to remember that God is patient with our attempts to hear His voice and follow Him, and He understands our uncertainties. He probably doesn't want us to keep asking after many confirmations—that would be an indication of unbelief—but He will give us enough clarity for us to anchor our faith in what He has said. He wants us to be confident in His words.

Don't be afraid to ask God for something concrete that would confirm His words. Don't depend on outward confirmations; He won't be backed into a corner and compelled to prove Himself. But give Him the opportunity to reassure you. And when He does, believe Him. He wants you to trust the direction He has given you.

Lord, I know we walk by faith and not by sight. But sometimes I need reassurance that my faith is heading in the right direction. Be patient with me. Show me signs, and give me faith to believe them.

The LORD gave [the man of God] this command: "You must not eat or drink anything while you are there, and do not return to Judah by the same way you came."

But the old prophet answered, "I am a prophet, too, just as you are. And an angel gave me this command from the LORD: 'Bring him home with you so he can have something to eat and drink.'" But the old man was lying to him.

1 KINGS 13:17-18

The man of God was told not to eat or drink in Bethel and to return to Judah by another route. And he had already resisted a temptation to disobey this command when the corrupt King Jeroboam tried to get him to come to the palace for a meal. But when an older prophet gave him an alternate word, he thought God might have changed His mind. He fell for the deception. He went home with the older prophet to have a meal in the town he had been told to leave. And he paid for his disobedience with his life.

Why would God put one of His servants in such a predicament? It's a strange passage of Scripture, but one lesson is clear: When God has told us one thing, we are to cling to it relentlessly, no matter who tries to convince us otherwise. When we know He has spoken, not even a bona fide prophet's words should lead us away from the direction He has given.

Stubbornness is generally an unappealing characteristic, but when it comes to faith and obedience, it's necessary. God wants us to measure every word someone tells us and every circumstance we see against the things we already know He has said. If there's a discrepancy, we're to go with the truth He has spoken. By this our faith is proven and God's words are honored.

Lord, I tend to compromise much too often—probably because I'm uncertain about what You've said. Give me confidence to anchor my faith and obedience in Your words and never deviate from them. Cultivate in me a holy tenacity to cling to promises and assignments You've given.

NOVEMBER 16

This is the plan: At the right time he will bring everything together under the authority of Christ—everything in heaven and on earth.
Ephesians 1:10

To understand God's voice, we need to know something about His agenda. His voice informs us of what He's going to do, of course, but sometimes we're listening for an intensely personal word when He gives us a big-picture word, or vice versa. Our expectations may color what we perceive and how we apply it. When we're listening for God's voice, we need to envision both the macro and the micro views.

What is God's big-picture agenda? He plans to bring everything in both heaven and earth together under the authority of Christ. He seeks to bridge the gap between His throne room and His creation—the new Jerusalem coming down out of heaven in Revelation is a dramatic picture of that—and establish His uniform reign in both realms. He wants heaven to come down into our lives, through our prayers, through His work in us, through our actions and words, and into our surroundings. Miracles that are commonplace in heaven are to become commonplace here on earth. Answers to prayer that are clear in heaven are to become clear here. The gap between the realms is to gradually disappear through the ministry of the Holy Spirit within His people. And His voice will very often be directed toward this end.

Listen for the heavenly agenda. Expect directions on how to prepare your world for life under the authority of Christ. Never limit your prayers to what is "feasible" on earth, but include requests that will display the glories of heaven in the here and now. At the right time, Christ will culminate this process, but it doesn't simply begin when He appears. It begins now—in and among His people who are filled with His Spirit. We are citizens of two realms, and we are not called to keep them separate.

Jesus, I long for everything to be under Your authority—everything in heaven and earth and in every corner of my life. Give me clear instructions, revelations, and directions for praying for Your Kingdom to come on earth as it is in heaven.

NOVEMBER 17

The LORD said to Moses, "How long will these people treat me with contempt?"
NUMBERS 14:11

"Lord, teach me something about You that I don't already know." This now-familiar request was answered in a surprising way when I had spent quite enough time hearing people complain about a situation they were going through. They had some basis for their complaints, but they couldn't see that their blessings far outweighed their hardships. Were they going through a difficult time? Sure—but not without God's grace or guidance. They would come through it fully supported.

Parents often hear complaints from children who don't realize how good their situation is. At times, that can be amusing; more often, it's disappointing. Even when we have a lot of grace for their limited perspective, we long for them to see how much they are loved. Clearly, the spirit of complaining and negativity of the Israelites in the wilderness was offensive to both God and Moses, and my prolonged exposure to a group of complainers helped me understand why. In a moment of awareness, I realized how God can take our complaints personally and experience a measure of grief from them. And in that moment, I felt deep sympathy for His heart.

God gives us snapshots of life that make His Word intensely personal for us. It's one thing to read about Him in a particular story, another to find yourself in a somewhat similar situation that brings to life the relational dynamics of that story. If we listen carefully, we will sometimes hear a whisper: "This is how I feel when . . ." That whisper may tell us of joy, delight, compassion, or zeal, or it may tell us of grief, jealousy, or anger—all emotions that Scripture assigns to God frequently. The result is greater sensitivity in our hearts to God's nature and a greater bond of fellowship with His Spirit. When He shows us who He is, we have heard an invitation to draw closer.

Lord, I know from my own experiences how hearts are affected by negativity. May I never grieve Your heart that way, and may I always be sensitive to Your reactions to the words of Your people. Expand my empathy with You.

[Jesus said,] "I will ask the Father, and he will give you another Advocate, who will never leave you. He is the Holy Spirit, who leads into all truth."
JOHN 14:16-17

FROM THE HEART OF GOD

"If you need an example of the simplicity of answered prayer, notice what I promised: *I will ask the Father, and He will give you the Spirit.* If you need a commitment that your relationship with Me isn't an up-and-down ride, notice the Spirit's plan: *He will never leave you.* And if you need assurance that you can hear My voice, notice the Spirit's agenda: *He will lead you into all truth.* Do you see it? I have given you a model of interaction with the Father, an unbreakable vow of presence, and unwavering dedication to reveal everything you need to know and more. The Father *will* give, the Spirit will *never* leave, and He leads into *all* truth. I've left you little room to wonder.

"Why do I speak in extreme terms? Because those terms are true. Casual words would not suffice. I've given you an extreme calling and made extreme commitments to you. You may not experience the reality of these words as tangibly as you would like, but you will if you continue to believe them without compromise. Press Me on them. Push Me to follow through. Persist in your asking. I invite you to be unyielding, to pester Me to do what I've already said I'm going to do. I take no pleasure in those who fall back and think perhaps they have asked too much. Too much for Me? Do you realize how much I have to offer? There's never 'too much' when you're talking to an infinite God.

"Accept the extremes of My promises. Take Me at My word. Trust that I am fulfilling everything I said I would fulfill. I haven't invited you to come tiptoeing up to the throne of grace. I said to come boldly. Ask according to My greatest desires for you."

Jesus, Your dreams for me are even greater than my own, which is saying a lot. Unveil them and fulfill them. Help me to think big. I want everything You promised to the fullest.

NOVEMBER 19

The word of the LORD holds true, and we can trust everything he does.
PSALM 33:4

The world is full of prognosticators. We predict weather, elections, football games, fashion trends, award winners, stock reports, business projects, behavioral tendencies, pregnancy due dates, and so much more. And whenever we hear one of these predictions, we hope it is true, or perhaps false, or maybe even just in the ballpark. Sometimes we turn our hopes into a promise, or at least a firm expectation, forgetting that no human can guarantee the future.

Neither can we fully understand the past or the present. We offer analyses and insights, and sometimes they point us to rock-solid truths, but they are still the products of human perceptions. History is full of experts who were proven wrong about something they were once absolutely sure about. Even once-certain laws of physics are now being questioned because of observations in the quantum world. Why? Because we never see the whole picture, and our reasoning isn't infallible. We don't know everything we think we know, and everything we say is, to one degree or another, suspect.

The Word of God is decidedly different. When He speaks, His words hold true. He has no lack of foresight, nor any limitation on His perspective. He sees all in space and time and declares absolute realities. Whether He is speaking about the past, the present, or the future, He is right. We can count on it.

We have a trust problem with God, and it's a lifelong battle. That's why His Word so often reminds us of who He is and how unfathomable His wisdom is. His words must be handled differently than any other information in our lives. Though we can never be fully confident of our interpretations, we can wholly trust the source. In the words of David Livingstone, God's promises are "the word of a gentleman of the most strict and sacred honor." We can believe them always.

Lord, help me live as someone who is anchored in reality, never moving from Your truth or questioning Your promises. Thank You for the assurance that You will lead me, teach me, promise me, and inform me with rock-solid, absolute, never-wavering truth.

[The Lord] said to me, "Prophesy to these bones and say to them, 'Dry bones, hear the word of the LORD!'"
EZEKIEL 37:4, NIV

God showed Ezekiel a vision of a valley full of bones. Not the bones of the recently deceased, but dry bones. In other words, these bones are far removed from any hint of life. Yet God tells Ezekiel to prophesy to the bones to command them to hear God's word. The prophet speaks life and breath into them.

Why would the living God need a human to command bones to hear His voice? Can't God make His voice heard to anyone or anything He wants? Of course He can, but a lesson is being demonstrated in this vision. God implements His will through partnership with His people. He rarely does anything in human affairs without prompting a human spokesperson to pray for it or speak it. Apparently, God takes seriously the commission He gives in Genesis—the assignment for humanity to govern the earth. And apparently, there's something to Amos's comment that God does nothing without telling His prophets (Amos 3:7). When God wants to intervene on earth, He partners with someone who will hear His words, respond to them, and speak them.

We don't fully understand the role we have in declaring God's will, but we know we're called to do it. Our words have power; God's universe is wired that way. What we say has a practical and spiritual effect on the course of events. Our words shape our lives, the lives of people around us, and the environment we live in. And when our words line up with what God has spoken to us, we can change the course of history. His will is accomplished through them. Even dry bones come to life at the sound of a human voice in tune with God.

Lord, tell me what to say. Inspire my words and give life to the things I declare. Whenever You prompt me, I will speak life into dead situations, truth into deceptive circumstances, and possibility into impossibilities—and then watch Your Spirit work. May my voice line up with Yours and accomplish great things for Your Kingdom.

The person who is joined to the Lord is one spirit with him.
1 CORINTHIANS 6:17

When a husband and wife become "one flesh," they begin a lifelong process of learning each other's personalities, tendencies, habits, and even thought patterns—to the point that they often know what the other is thinking even when those thoughts are not expressed. With no loss of individuality, they become one. And the world begins to see them as a unit, not without distinct personalities, but with a common will and purpose. They are joined to each other in a way that gives them the ability to know and represent each other's voices.

In a much deeper way, we are joined to God's Spirit when we enter a relationship with His Son. We then begin a lifelong process of learning His personality, ways, and thoughts—even to the point of knowing what He is thinking. Paul earlier noted that we have the mind of Christ, and now he writes that our spirits and Christ's have become one. Paul wrote these words in a specific moral context, but the truth, also expressed by Jesus in John 17:21-24, has huge implications. It means, among many other things, that when we are listening for God's voice, we aren't listening at a distance. When the Spirit leads us to speak His words, we aren't being presumptuous. We can hear and express His thoughts, not because we're well educated or superspiritual, but because we're connected. His Spirit and ours are one.

Many of us err by being either overassuming or underassuming about our awareness of God's presence and voice, but humble confidence is always appropriate. He has assured us that we are united with Him, not just theoretically, but practically. We don't know Him perfectly, but we do know Him with certainty. And when we need to hear Him, we need listen no further than our own spirits.

Lord, it's hard to understand how I can be "one" with You, and even harder to know how to hear Your Spirit when it's joined to mine. Yet this is the close relationship I've longed for. Help me know Your thoughts with certainty.

The human spirit is the lamp of the LORD.
PROVERBS 20:27, NIV

"God is light and in Him is no darkness at all" (1 John 1:5, NKJV). That's what the apostle John writes in one of his letters. But centuries earlier, a proverb identified a key medium that makes God's light visible. The human spirit is the place where God intends for His light to shine. He created us for glory.

That's one of the reasons God made us in His image. We were designed to reflect who He is. But in order to do that, we have to connect with Him, live in relationship with Him, and communicate with Him. Every aspect of our being, even our physical senses, was designed to be a contact point between us and Him. We perceive God through the power of His Word, the life of His Spirit, and the experiences we have in the context of our relationship with Him. As A. W. Tozer writes, "God desires and is pleased to communicate with us through the avenues of our minds, our wills, and our emotions." We can receive His truth in every part of us.

Then what? We are to reflect the Lord. He is the light; we are the lamps that draw their light from Him and display it to the world. We are flames of His fire, pictures of His glory, reflections of His nature. He has given us a standing invitation and every opportunity to be living, breathing expressions of the Godhead. That's why we were made.

Don't squander that opportunity. You may not think yourself worthy, but that isn't the issue. God has crafted you for a purpose, and He will shine through you whether you think yourself worthy or not. Remain in vital connection with His voice and His presence, and your role as a lamp will be fulfilled, even without your awareness. Your spirit is where God chooses to shine.

Lord, shine Your light on me, in me, and through me. Let me be an accurate reflection of Your glory. Speak to my spirit and light the fire within. May I glow with Your presence everywhere I go.

*The LORD merely spoke, and the heavens were created. He breathed the
word, and all the stars were born.*
PSALM 33:6

We long to be more than products of our past or victims of our circumstances.
Society offers us little hope of that; it tends to define us by our experiences and
our environment. We live at the mercy of whatever happens to us, as if "fate" or
"chance" were inescapable. We can choose how to respond, we're told, but we
can't choose what life offers us. We have to play the hand we're dealt.

But that isn't what Scripture tells us, is it? We can affect the outcomes of
our situations through prayer, making wise choices, and following God's leading. And even in our strictest limitations, we have the ear of a God who can
turn any circumstance in a moment. We are never helpless victims of life's circumstances; rather, we have been called to shape them. We are sons and daughters of the King, and He has given us spiritual authority in heavenly places to
influence the kingdoms of earth. The question isn't whether we can deal with
what life hands us; it's how God is going to affect the world through our role
as His children.

Ask God to speak into your life—words of change, words of fulfillment,
words of destiny. Ask for His voice to heal your wounds, shift your circumstances, and shape your future. Most of all, ask Him to raise up people and
churches, and even entire societies, that will embody His Kingdom here on
earth as it is in heaven. Regardless of whatever issues are lingering from your
past, whatever situations you're stuck in, and whatever obstacles stand in the
way of your calling, all you need is the sound of God's voice. He merely speaks,
and an entire universe is created by the sound. He can certainly alter anything
in your life with just a word.

❖ ❖ ❖

Lord, You are a world changer and have called me to join You in Your work.
Speak words of power into my life, my family, my city, my country, my world.
Create Your Kingdom everywhere on earth.

[The serpent] asked the woman, "Did God really say . . . ?"
GENESIS 3:1

"Lord, teach me something about You that I don't already know." As is sometimes the case, God's answer came through an unpleasant circumstance. I was being misrepresented by a slanderer, and even some people who once respected me were starting to get a false impression. I was outraged, of course; most of us get pretty offended when our pride is wounded for any reason, especially a false one. I did not respond well. But there was nothing I could do to stop the smears. All I could do was continue to be myself and trust that people who knew me well would know the truth.

During this painful season, I was hit with a disturbing thought: *God is misrepresented millions of times every day.* Even people who should know Him and love Him well are sometimes swayed by the lies. The Accuser whispers slanderous thoughts against God almost constantly. The one whose love is higher, longer, deeper, and wider than we can imagine has His love questioned all the time by millions who think He doesn't care or isn't there. The world lives in suspicion of God's goodness because a con artist has misrepresented Him for thousands of years.

This must grieve God's heart deeply. He created us to know Him and love Him and to pour His love into others. Yet His relationship with us encounters constant interference; and unless we relentlessly cling to what we know to be true, the interference is effective. We spend much of our lives in a battle to trust God's goodness. But if we saw clearly, trust would never be an issue.

God shows us the truth in the words of Scripture, so we already know. But the message sinks into our hearts much deeper when He gives us a taste of what He experiences. He moves our hearts to understand how His heart is moved.

Lord, I invite You to move my heart anytime to synchronize it with Yours. I need to connect with You. Only Your voice, Your expressions, Your revelation can accomplish that. Give me insights into who You are.

[Jesus said,] "I will not abandon you as orphans—I will come to you."
JOHN 14:18

FROM THE HEART OF GOD

"An orphan's natural instinct is to try to become self-sufficient. He has to; he can't depend on a parent to provide, protect, and nurture. This has been the spiritual attitude of the entire human race, including you. It's a deeply ingrained assumption; you don't expect Me to be the parent you need. You expect to have to scratch and fight for everything you get, while I remain distant and detached. Even when you come into My Kingdom, this attitude persists. It sometimes takes years to discard it.

"When you listen for My voice with an orphan mentality, you decide ahead of time that I will tell you what to do or how to change. When I say, 'I love you,' you dismiss the words, assuming that it's only what you wanted to hear, that I would surely say something deeper than that, or that I would never speak such a basic or remedial message to someone who needs harder truths. When I offer to give you what you want rather than what you need, you object and try to rid yourself of whatever pride caused you to hear the wrong thing. When I declare your complete cleansing, you linger in your guilt so you can experience the pain you think you owe Me. When I offer freedom, you make rules just to be safe. Like an orphan who still isn't comfortable in his adoptive father's mansion, you refuse to heed My generosity, My encouragement, and My love.

"Don't live with an orphan mentality or listen with an orphan's ears. You will rarely hear My true voice when you do. You can't hear Me well if I am anything other than your *Abba*, your Father, your Friend. Your perceptions of Me shape what you hear. Always remember—be thoroughly convinced—that I have not abandoned you. I am with you every moment, closer than you realize."

Father God, it's true—I often hear what I expect You to say, and what I expect doesn't reflect Your extravagant blessings and grace. Forgive me, and give me the ears of an adopted, adored child who expects Your warm embrace.

NOVEMBER 26

[The tribal leaders and elders of Israel said,] "If the LORD our God speaks to us again, we will certainly die and be consumed by this awesome fire. Can any living thing hear the voice of the living God from the heart of the fire as we did and yet survive?"
DEUTERONOMY 5:25-26

When God's people had seen the trauma of God's presence on Mount Sinai, they asked Moses to listen to God on their behalf. They feared hearing Him directly. And God said they were right to feel that way. Yet God had already spoken directly to Moses at a burning bush, in Egypt, and on the mountain, and He would speak "face to face" with him in the Tabernacle. This God would also speak directly to Joshua, fill the temple of Solomon with His presence, and show Himself dramatically to many prophets. None of them died. Daniel and John fell at His feet in near paralysis, but a divine touch brought them back to their feet. As fearful and awesome as God's presence and His direct voice are, they are not fatal. God can be heard and understood by those who are bold enough not to run from Him.

That hasn't changed over the centuries. Those who are boldly persistent about hearing God's voice will eventually hear it, and those who are fearful rarely do. That fear wears many masks: apathy, avoidance, a doctrinal belief that God no longer speaks, anxiety about His intentions, and more. But God invites us to come boldly to His throne of grace and urges us to listen for His voice. No matter how fearful that experience may be, God still rewards those who persist through the fear and come anyway. In His Kingdom, spiritual hunger is satisfied.

The answer to the Israelites is a resounding *yes*. Living creatures can hear the voice of the living God from the heart of fire and survive. In fact, we thrive. His voice is bread from heaven and life-giving water. Be bold enough to persist.

Lord, I've resolved to persevere and not lose heart, no matter what obstacles stand in the way or what fears try to hold me back. I'll accept the trauma of hearing You; but please reward me clearly enough and often enough to keep me coming to Your throne boldly.

Simon Peter replied, "Lord, to whom would we go? You have the words that give eternal life."
JOHN 6:68

Jesus has just finished preaching some difficult truths, and crowds of followers have left Him. All that remain are the Twelve, and even they haven't quite understood the teaching. Yet when Jesus asks them if they are about to leave Him too, Peter answers with the only reasonable response: *Where else would we go?* Any alternative would be unsatisfying. Sure, other teachers and other truths might be easier to understand and less controversial, but none would be connected to eternal reality like Jesus. Following Jesus may be difficult and frustrating at times, but there are no better options.

We have to have that attitude toward God's voice. Sometimes His words are obscure; we aren't sure whether we're getting a confirmation or a correction, or apparent guidance seems to lead in a direction that makes no sense, or we don't know whether we heard His voice or simply misread the messages we're hearing. We may get disoriented and have no idea how to respond. But where else are we going to go? To a more understandable but merely human philosophy? To a more convenient religion? To a Scripture that's better organized or less laden with obscure names and places? No, even when we realize how much we don't understand about God and His ways, we know He is truth. And we simply can't settle for anything else.

Even when God's words are hard, we cling to them because we know that every other alternative is unsatisfying. We want reality, even when it hurts. And we will keep pressing into His presence to hear what He says because we need Him, love truth, and know His words are life.

Jesus, there have been times when I would have left if I had somewhere to go. Following You can be hard. But I know You are the Lord of truth and the gateway to eternity. And deep down, I love Your willingness to be known. I want to hear Your voice, whatever the cost.

[Jesus said,] "Look, I have given you authority over all the power of the enemy, and you can walk among snakes and scorpions and crush them."
LUKE 10:19

Our hearts are hungry for truth—so hungry, in fact, that we have to be careful not to consume lies. Our ears are open to God, but they also hear other messages. We perceive words and thoughts that produce fear, discouragement, depression, confusion, doubt, and all sorts of other destructive emotions and attitudes. Those are deceptive enough, but there are subtler counterfeits than that—messages that promise what God hasn't actually promised, that offer us what's good instead of what's best, or that pledge to fulfill God-ordained dreams in corrupt ways. God speaks exclusive truths into our lives, yet the contradictions are almost limitless.

A necessary aspect of hearing truth is refusing to hear lies. To accept God's voice is to reject others. We don't have to be victims of false messages. God has given us authority over the deceptions of the enemy and even the deceptions of our own hearts. When we refuse to fuel them with our own biases and inclinations and become merciless toward any thought that isn't captive to Christ, the deceptions begin to crumble and the truth doesn't. Discernment is much easier when truth is the last word standing.

Pray for discernment with authority. Don't be tentative. From the moment God puts His spotlight on a counterfeit message, refuse to entertain it. Take every thought captive to Christ, pulling down philosophies and agendas, and even subtle attitudes that don't fit His character or His purposes. Trample on any hint of guidance that conflicts with what God has already revealed. Relentlessly pursue the dreams and calling He has put within you. If they are His dreams, they must be accomplished His way. Any tempting words that are inconsistent with His voice are worthy of being crushed.

Lord, if You give me the discernment to recognize counterfeits, I will be ruthless with them. False messages will not take root in my heart. Establish in me only Your words, and let me live them without compromise.

[Jesus said,] "Why do you keep calling me 'Lord, Lord!' when you don't do what I say?"
LUKE 6:46

It's a piercing question that immediately undoes any casual approach to following Jesus. It's one thing to claim to be a Christian and to believe Christian doctrine, but quite another to follow Jesus and live out His teachings. In other words, there's a huge difference between *calling* Jesus Lord and *submitting* to Him as Lord. The former is very common. The latter . . . well, not so much.

Why do we call Him Lord without always following Him as Lord? Maybe we're interested in salvation, but not in investing the time and energy it takes to have a relationship with Jesus. Perhaps we expect His lordship over us to be painful or unfulfilling. Or maybe we just haven't understood who He is—the King of all creation—and as such, His words carry enormous weight. Regardless of the reason, many believers fit easily into cultural Christianity, but are uncomfortable with the radical call of Jesus. That ignores the gravity of His voice.

Imagine God giving you these two options: (1) to live a mediocre existence without too many highs or lows; or (2) to lay it all on the line and experience ultimate joy and rewards along with genuine sacrifices. Which would you choose? Most of us would say we want the second option—to live life to its fullest, in spite of the costs. But that's exactly the choice God gives us, and most of us tend to opt for average on a daily basis. If it were a one-time, big-picture choice, it might be simpler. We can lay down our lives once and for all. But in each moment of each day? Compromise is so much easier in the small choices.

God is calling you higher. Don't ignore the gravity of His voice. There's a great cost to doing what He says, but a greater satisfaction, too. When He speaks, our responses matter.

Lord, You are leading me to lay down my life daily. You say some difficult things, but You also promise unimaginable blessings for doing them. I choose to follow You completely.

[Jesus said,] "I will show you what it's like when someone comes to me, listens to my teaching, and then follows it. It is like a person building a house who digs deep and lays the foundation on solid rock."
LUKE 6:47-48

We say we want the best life possible. We make plans and decisions that will position us for success in relationships, careers, and finances. And though Jesus tells us that the greatest key to a life well lived is to listen to His words and follow them, we are generally reluctant to follow Him fully. Most people heed His words only to the extent that they make sense.

Yet Jesus spoke a lot of words that don't make sense on the surface. He gave us authority over the enemy, but we question it because we don't always seem to experience it. He made extravagant promises about answering our prayers, but we have a hard time believing them and feel compelled to add some fine print that explains them. He gave us difficult commands about turning the other cheek and going the extra mile and avoiding the dangers of wealth. He spoke harshly about our sinful condition and urged us to accept His grace at all costs. He insisted that we love the unlovable and forgive the unforgivable. And He told us to take up a cross and die daily, living sacrificially toward God and others. He urged us to embrace truths that go against our natural inclinations.

Jesus never insisted that His followers understand Him. He insisted that they trust Him. That's God's priority for us. Whether we understand or not, following His Word is like building a house on a rock-solid foundation. We can't lose. There's nothing more rewarding than embracing His teaching—even when His teaching seems difficult.

Jesus, I have to admit that Your words don't always make sense to me. And I have to admit that I'm afraid to follow some of them fully. But I do trust You, and I want my life to weather any storm. Anchor me to the rock as I follow You completely.

DECEMBER 1

God opened her eyes and she saw a well.
GENESIS 21:19, NIV

The couple had walked far across the field and back again, only to find that the keys to their car were missing. They weren't locked in the car, and they weren't in their pockets or purse. Miles away from the nearest town, the couple turned around and looked at the vast field in front of them, knowing that somewhere in the grass lay their only means to get back to civilization before dark. And they didn't know where to begin to look.

They tried to retrace their steps because there was no other choice, but the situation looked hopeless. But they also knew no situation is hopeless with God, so they prayed, "Lord, lead us to the keys. Open our eyes to see them." The woman was even more specific. "Lord, which direction should I go?" She sensed that she should concentrate on the right side of the field, so she headed in that direction. After a few minutes, which seemed more like hours, she stumbled, and in catching herself, her eyes fell on a glimmer in the grass. There were the keys. A skeptic could call it a coincidence, but to a couple who prayed, it was an answer. God had guided their steps and helped them in a time of need.

God is concerned even for the minor details of our lives. A prayer for a lost item in a much less serious situation would still have been answered. God has led people to lost jewelry, glasses, credit cards, and even toys. He doesn't always eliminate the search, but He very often rewards it. He knows how to guide our steps and open our eyes, even when we aren't consciously aware He's doing it. He comes to our aid when we ask.

Lord, thank You for Your attention to detail. You care about the things that are precious to us, and You offer Your help. May I never try to solve a problem without You.

DECEMBER 2

Jesus replied, "All who love me will do what I say. My Father will love them, and we will come and make our home with each of them."
JOHN 14:23

FROM THE HEART OF GOD

"How would you feel if you had a friend who listened to your advice but never really acted on it? How would you feel if your most heartfelt words were neglected or casually dismissed? Would you take it personally? Most people would, and understandably so. Your thoughts and feelings are expressed in words, and when your words are ignored, it hurts. They represent who you are. And when someone takes them seriously enough to act on them, you feel valued.

"Many people say they love Me but don't demonstrate that they value Me by doing what I say. It's possible to do what I say without loving Me, but it isn't possible to love Me without doing what I say. Those who disregard My words don't really value them or understand My heart. Those who want to know Me and love who I am will also embrace wholeheartedly what I say. Your response to My words is a revealing picture of what you think and how you feel about Me.

"My heart warms when you embrace My words. The Father and I love you at all times, regardless of how you respond to us, but our love for you swells with joy when you honor us, want to become like us, and are eager to do what we say. I have drawn you into a relationship not only so you can know My love but also so I can know yours. The substance of My instructions is important—I want you to do what I said—but it is much less important than the love your response reveals. I'm much more interested in your heart than your obedience. But show Me your heart by what you do."

Jesus, forgive me for assuming I can love You in attitude without loving You in action. I love this promise—that You and the Father will come and make Your home with me. Please do so. I want You to feel at home in my heart.

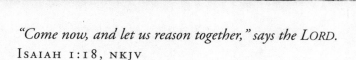

DECEMBER 3

"Come now, and let us reason together," says the LORD.
ISAIAH 1:18, NKJV

God rarely urges human beings to depend on their reason. He doesn't want us to be unreasonable, of course, but He knows the mind's capacity to deceive itself. The religious leaders of Jesus' day were often standing apart and reasoning to themselves, trying to trap Jesus in His own words. Why? Because they had well-constructed theologies in their own minds, and Jesus didn't fit them. So human intelligence has been known to be less than reliable in spiritual matters—perhaps best evidenced by the tens of thousands of Christian denominations that are convinced they have interpreted the Scriptures correctly, even though they have all done so differently. Sadly, the human mind is not a great interpreter of spiritual truth.

But God still wants us to reason if we do it together—with Him. He wants to be an integral part of the logical process, guiding our understanding to be able to grasp things we could never grasp naturally. He gives us revelation to aid our mental processes, leading our thoughts and feelings and spiritual senses to embrace truth and discern error. He speaks into every aspect of our being and awakens us to the realities of His Kingdom. Those who submit their minds to Him will find them filled with thoughts that natural minds can't receive.

Never approach Scripture only as an intellectual exercise. Your mind was created to understand, but not to arrive at knowledge independently of God. Invite Him into your thought processes. Ask Him to enlighten your understanding and give you a spirit of wisdom and revelation. Trust Him to bring your heart and mind into alignment with His truth. And then you can be confident in the knowledge He has given.

Lord, You are the author of reason. Your logic, Your *logos*, is the wisdom behind all creation. Impart that wisdom to me. Enlighten my mind with Your truth. Cut through all the false reasoning of the world and draw me into the realities of Your Kingdom. Let me think clearly and consistently with Your Spirit.

DECEMBER 4

Hear me as I pray, O LORD. Be merciful and answer me!
PSALM 27:7

David wrote this psalm, as well as many others, under duress. Apparently he felt surrounded and besieged, yet the one thing he asked for was not deliverance. He asked to delight in God and meditate on Him in a Temple that didn't exist yet. David was concerned about his situation, but he wasn't obsessed with it. He kept his gaze on God.

Many of the psalms are a field manual in how to get from point A to point B in our emotional lives and in our faith. They begin with stress and end with praise. Psalm 27 is one of those psalms, and it teaches us to seek God first, even in the midst of an unresolved and desperate situation. In fact, that's where we're most likely to encounter God. These times when life seems overwhelming and God seems far off are often a test. Will we keep our focus on Him or on the circumstances? Which looms larger in our hearts? If we're able to be preoccupied with Him, even when all else dictates against our faith, we will experience His presence and hear His voice.

God often shows up when we least expect Him to. That means our worst times are His best opportunities. Romans 4:18 tells us that even when there was no reason for hope, Abraham kept hoping—counting on God's promise in spite of all appearances. That's what God is looking for: those who hope against all hope, who believe regardless of what they see, who look for Him even when there are so many distractions. God rewards those who seek Him, even when contradictions to His blessings are weighing on their hearts, when the walls are closing in on their faith, or battles are raging against them. Those who desire God above all else and call to Him in times of trouble will be answered.

Lord, this has been my prayer so many times. I'm not just calling to You to get out of trouble; I'm calling to connect with You. Please be merciful and answer me.

DECEMBER 5

My heart has heard you say, "Come and talk with me." And my heart responds, "LORD, I am coming."
PSALM 27:8

David's heart heard God invite him to come and talk, and he responded by accepting the invitation. Most people are comfortable with the idea of David having this conversation with God, but far fewer are comfortable with claiming it for themselves. How many people claim, "God told me to come and talk with Him"? It can sound presumptuous, yet this is exactly the invitation He gives us—not just to everyone in Scripture, but to each of us individually in conversation with Him. If our hearts are listening, this is what we'll hear.

We don't normally have any shortage of words for God, but we do think He's short on words for us. And when we listen, we very often expect Him to focus on what's wrong—where we need to be fixed or what He wants us to do that we haven't done yet. But God's invitation is much more relational than that, and He has much more on His mind than "fixing" us. He wants conversation, and He wants us to know that a conversation with Him isn't all about troubleshooting our lives. God knows that any relationship, human or divine, that is always centered on advice and instructions is unappealing and draining. And it isn't satisfying for any party involved—including God.

Conversation with God is life giving. He breathes His love into us and is far more focused on encouraging us than on tearing us down or telling us how to improve. When He says, "Come and talk with Me," He actually wants heart-to-heart interaction. And we have nothing to fear by giving it to Him.

Lord, I admit that I'm sometimes reluctant to have a conversation with You because I assume it will be about my shortcomings. I know this is shortsighted and that it grieves You. As I come to You, give me ears to hear Your life-giving encouragement and blessing. May Your words fill me with hope and joy and peace.

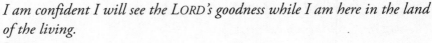
I am confident I will see the LORD's goodness while I am here in the land of the living.
PSALM 27:13

"One day, when the Lord returns . . ." These words have come off the lips of innumerable Christians when life in the present isn't quite working out. We tend to give up on the here and now and focus on the there and then. These words have an uncanny effect of sounding like a lament and a comfort simultaneously, and sometimes we're not sure which it is. But we know they signify some lack of satisfaction now.

These words are true, of course, but we tend to focus on "one day" much more often than Scripture does. Yes, it tells us of the coming Kingdom and describes a glorious end, but it also tells us the Kingdom has already come and that glory can be experienced now. Here, David expresses confidence that he will experience God's goodness in the land of the living—that is, in this age in this earthly realm. Life isn't all hardship, no matter how difficult our momentary circumstances might be. For David, and for us, there are tangible blessings to be discovered and received right now.

Much of the church has spent so much effort combating the health-and-wealth gospel that it has presented an opposite error: the suffering-and-poverty gospel. In truth, neither picture is biblical. We live in two realms simultaneously, and we experience the good and bad in both. And though we will encounter hardships in this world—Jesus assured us of that—we are nowhere told that we will encounter *only* hardships. We can come to God with the confident expectation that we will see His goodness here, now, and forever.

Lord, these are the ears I want to listen with—the attitude that assumes Your goodness will show up in every situation I face in every area of life. Your goodness is not a theory; it's real and tangible and evident. I'm grateful for that and fully expect to see it more.

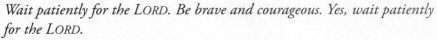

DECEMBER 7

Wait patiently for the LORD. Be brave and courageous. Yes, wait patiently for the LORD.
PSALM 27:14

Ents, the treelike beings of J. R. R. Tolkien's Middle Earth, were known for having meandering conversations with seemingly tangential trails that might or might not come back to the subject at hand. Such conversations would be painfully tedious in a world of e-mails and text messages, but in developing relationships, they might be enlightening.

Our well-conditioned impatience wars against God's Ent-like conversations with us. Microwaves, drive-thru windows, and ATMs have allegedly made life easier, but they have also made a relationship with God much more difficult. We have learned to expect that if things don't work out quickly, they won't work out at all. And in a conversation with God, that simply isn't true. His dealings with us are usually a process. A lengthy one.

It takes courage to remain focused on God when He seems absent or silent. The faith required to take a step forward is usually easier than the faith required to wait when everything in us is itching for a resolution. When we've asked God to speak to us, give us direction, or work out a problem, it's much easier to believe "it just wasn't His will" than to believe He is still planning to accomplish what we asked, though the answer is lagging long after the request. Holding on to faith in a situation that dictates against it requires fortitude, patience, and boldness.

We strive for efficiency in our lives. It's a common cultural value in a postmodern world. But God values drawing out our interaction with Him into a piece of artwork. He's writing an epic poem in our lives, and we'll miss Him if we have a Post-it note mentality. We need to sit. And listen. And listen some more. And be very, very patient. And over time, we will find the conversation entirely satisfying.

Lord, my conversations with You resemble Morse code more than lengthy and winding dialogues. Yet You have so much to say in the process of communication other than the words themselves. Give me patience—and courage—to hear You in the pauses and tangents of our talks.

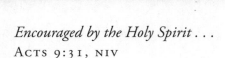

DECEMBER 8

Encouraged by the Holy Spirit . . .
ACTS 9:31, NIV

The battle had been raging for a long time. I was enduring one of the most difficult periods of my life, and I wasn't sure if I could keep going. Was I headed in the right direction? Were my ways pleasing to God? Was my faith going to be rewarded? I was very discouraged, fearing the answers to those questions might be no. I was emotionally at the end of my rope. One morning when I was particularly depressed, I prayed before I got into my car: "Lord, please encourage me today. I just need to know You're with me."

When I got to work, the "verse of the day" on my personalized web browser was Isaiah 43:1-2: "Do not be afraid, for I have ransomed you. I have called you by name; you are mine. When you go through deep waters, I will be with you. When you go through rivers of difficulty, you will not drown. When you walk through the fire of oppression, you will not be burned up; the flames will not consume you." A few minutes later, someone stopped by my office to let me know they had been praying for me. And in the afternoon, I received some encouraging news about the situation. It wasn't a resolution, but it was a promising turn of events. And to top it off, I received a completely unrelated phone call from one of my favorite people. By the end of the day, I felt lighter and my faith felt stronger. The situation hadn't changed, but I knew I wasn't alone in it or on the verge of defeat. God had orchestrated an encouraging day.

It doesn't always happen that way so quickly. Sometimes God lets us experience a little darkness as we reach out for light. But He eventually encourages us because it's His nature to do so. He wants us to know He is on our side, and He will use His entire repertoire of expressions to say so.

Lord, I need Your encouragement today—and every day. Strengthen me with the sound of Your voice and the knowledge of Your presence.

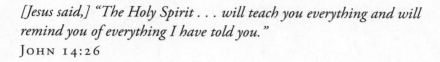
[Jesus said,] "The Holy Spirit . . . will teach you everything and will remind you of everything I have told you."
JOHN 14:26

FROM THE HEART OF GOD

"I created your brain. I know its wonderful abilities as well as its limitations. When I left My Word with you, I never intended to abandon it entirely to the mental capacities of theologians and preachers and your own thinking. I want you to understand what I've said, of course, but I never indicated that understanding My Word was simply a matter of applying your logic and sorting out your best 'system' or summary of truth. Human thinking is finite and flawed. I left My written Word in the hands of My Spirit—your Counselor and Advocate and Friend. You only hear My words in it when you read it and listen to it with Him.

"My followers were guided by My Spirit when they wrote down our conversations. The Law, the Prophets, the histories, the wisdom, the Gospels, the letters—everything you accept as My Word—was breathed by the thoughts of the Spirit. He brought to the writers' minds everything I had said to them and everything I wanted them to teach. But the Spirit didn't leave when these writers died. He remains with you even today. He will bring to mind everything I want you to know and teach you things you have never learned from a human being. If you listen, He will open up insights and remind you of truths that will guide you through life.

"Look to the Spirit as your Teacher. This is a learning process, as it doesn't come naturally. Your habit is to look to your own mind and to the minds of your experts and teachers. Use your mind, yes; but don't depend on it. Depend on the Spirit, who fills you with knowledge of My will and of the realities of My Kingdom. Never interpret My Word without first asking the Holy Spirit what it means. Invite Him to provide the lenses through which you see. He will guide you into all truth."

Yes, Holy Spirit, give me eyes to see. No Scripture is a matter of my own opinion; Yours is the only one that counts. Enlighten me to see heavenly realities behind these very visible words.

343

[Jesus said,] "Anyone who is thirsty may come to me!"
JOHN 7:37

Anyone who is thirsty. That's who is qualified to come to Jesus. Our thirst will drive us to Him for salvation, for deliverance, for provision, for fulfillment, for anything we need. But the promise of Jesus when He shouted these words to the crowd in Jerusalem was that our thirst coupled with our faith would give us access to an ever-gushing river of water, the Spirit Himself. Those who drink of Him will be satisfied.

Isaiah had issued the same invitation centuries earlier (Isaiah 55:1), and God's promise of thirst-quenching provision was provided through His Son. Jesus had echoed the same promise in an earlier sermon: "Blessed are those who hunger and thirst for righteousness, for they will be filled" (Matthew 5:6, NIV). Clearly, God is interested in our desire and uses it to draw us to Him. We long for fulfillment, for the "shalom" of the Kingdom, for the wholeness and peace of knowing everything is just as it should be. His Spirit gives us deep tastes of that fullness now with the promise of its thorough completion at the end of the age. But it all begins with thirst. That's the key to experiencing it.

How relentlessly would you pursue God if He said your relationship with Him hinges on your thirst? Your ability to know Him, experience His presence, and hear His voice will be defined in large part by the intensity of your longing. He rarely speaks to the apathetic, but those who long for Him, who crave Him and seek Him with all their hearts, will be rewarded. If you want to hear Him, keep thirsting. Let your longings drive you toward Him. Never give up your persistent petition for His personal touch and clear response to your cries. He will reveal Himself clearly to those whose thirst settles for nothing less.

Lord, I echo Jacob's words: I will not let You go until You bless me. My thirst will not let me settle for a mediocre spiritual experience. It's too strong for that, and I know You will honor my persistence. May the river of living water flow freely in me.

"Abraham!" God called. "Yes," he replied. "Here I am."
GENESIS 22:1

Abraham's hope in God's promise took a surprising and excruciating turn one day when God told him to take Isaac, the promised son, to a mountain and sacrifice him. God revealed this plan only after calling Abraham's name and hearing his response: "Here I am." It's a simple expression, used only a few times in Scripture. When used in conversation with God, it's an obedient response that always seems to have monumental consequences.

Jacob used this phrase twice: once when an angel spoke to him in a dream, which led to his return to the homeland and his name being changed to Israel; and once when Joseph was rediscovered in Egypt, which led to Israel's four hundred years there. Moses used it at the burning bush, which led to Israel's deliverance from Egypt. Samuel responded to God's call with that phrase and became the priestly prophet who would anoint Israel's first two kings. One of those kings, David, wrote a messianic verse that includes that phrase and declares the speaker to be "the one" written about in the scroll. The writer of Hebrews attributes this phrase prophetically to Jesus, the Messiah who saved humanity. And Isaiah spoke it when he encountered God's glory and heard the Lord ask, "Who will go for us?" In every case, major historical events turned on the response of "Here I am."

How would your life change if you said "here I am" to God? You can't know for sure unless you do, but you wouldn't regret it. It might require laying down a dream or destiny you've long held tightly, but the cost pales in comparison to the blessing. God Himself spoke this phrase once—"When you call, the LORD will answer. 'Yes, I am here,' he will quickly reply"—about our salvation and healing coming quickly like the dawn (Isaiah 58:8-9). When we make ourselves completely available to God, He makes Himself completely available to us.

Lord, I present myself to You as a living sacrifice, whether history hinges on my commitment or not. I make this offering to You: to be moved and activated by Your voice. Here I am.

This man must die! That kind of talk will undermine the morale of the few fighting men we have left, as well as that of all the people. This man is a traitor!
JEREMIAH 38:4

Jeremiah spoke God's words, but very few people believed him. Most were certain that he was simply being negative and speaking from his own fears and biases. So they responded to Jeremiah—and therefore to God—by rejecting his words and making the prophet suffer. They could not discern the words of God in the voice of a man.

When speakers uttered God's words, listeners had to distinguish the difference between the human and divine elements. It wasn't any easier then than it is today. Many rejected God's words because they came through a human voice, sometimes even insulting or persecuting the messenger. Others accepted anyone who claimed to speak in the name of God, naively believing messages that clearly contradicted Scripture and the nature of God. But despite all this, God never stopped speaking through human beings. He didn't decide we were too imperfect to receive His thoughts and express them. He sent us into the world with His message, filled with His Spirit, and capable of communicating His words.

Many people claim to hear God speak. Some actually do. And any of us can. Though God calls us to be discerning, He never tells us to be hypercritical. We are to listen with spiritual ears, Scripture-saturated minds, and receptive hearts. We are also to take what we hear to God Himself and ask Him whether it's true. He will guide us in the listening process, even when He speaks through flawed human beings. When we hear false teachings, we are to reject them. But we can never reject human beings simply for saying they heard God. They might be telling the truth.

Lord, forgive me if I've been too critical of any of Your servants who speak Your words. Give me an open heart with true discernment. Let me hear Your voice, even when it comes through someone just like me.

DECEMBER 13

Saul died for his unfaithfulness which he had committed against the LORD, because he did not keep the word of the LORD, and also because he consulted a medium for guidance. But he did not inquire of the LORD.
1 CHRONICLES 10:13-14, NKJV

God wants us to seek His voice, promises to speak to us, and often uses a variety of ways to express and confirm His message. But that doesn't mean we can hear Him through any means we choose. There are plenty of counterfeits out there, and they can be dangerous. God is not the only spiritual entity who speaks; the kingdom of darkness has voices too. We have to be very prayerful and very careful.

God warns us clearly and emphatically not to consult with "mediums or . . . those who consult the spirits of the dead" (Leviticus 19:31). He calls that "spiritual prostitution" (Leviticus 20:6). Nor are we to give any attention to clairvoyance, astrology, fortune-telling, witchcraft, divination, or any similar attempt to tap into supernatural knowledge from unknown or ungodly sources. No, we are to listen to God alone—His Word, His Spirit, and His people. He may speak through circumstances, events, and ideas that are otherwise spiritually neutral, but whatever we think we hear must be measured by His written Word, taken to Him in prayer, and accompanied by a sincere desire for discernment. Anything else is like drinking mysterious substances indiscriminately and hoping they aren't poisonous.

Don't assume all spiritual voices express spiritual truth. They don't. Many messages in our world are lies from the kingdom of darkness. Ask God about them. We don't just want to hear from spiritual sources; we want to hear from God. In order to open our ears to Him, we have to close our ears to counterfeits. The stakes are high. Whatever you think you've heard, take it to God, to His Word, and to trusted and spiritually mature advisers for discernment.

Lord, I don't want to be so afraid of counterfeits that I also shut my ears to You. But I do want to be discerning. Help me to spot counterfeits quickly and accurately. And silence any voices of darkness in my life.

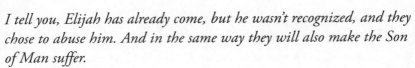

DECEMBER 14

I tell you, Elijah has already come, but he wasn't recognized, and they chose to abuse him. And in the same way they will also make the Son of Man suffer.
Matthew 17:12

Many people believe that the prophetic gift of the Spirit is not at work in the church today. One of the reasons for the skepticism is that most believers look like normal human beings, not superspiritual prophets—as if a prophetic gift would make someone glow or appear extra holy. In the Bible, however, even the greatest prophets were flawed human beings. None was sinless. And most were rejected by plenty of people because they didn't look particularly prophetic.

In Jesus' day, John the Baptist was celebrated as a prophet by many, but he was also rejected by many others—especially the religious experts who were supposed to be close to God. In fact, Jesus criticized the religious leaders for not recognizing John as the "Elijah [who] has already come." And Jesus knew He would suffer at their hands too. A great prophet and the Son of God Himself were rejected as genuine prophets by those whose religious grid didn't allow for the presence of prophets in their midst. And a generation missed the time of its visitation by God.

That's sobering. Multitudes of people filled with the Spirit of God are unrecognized for their gifts because we live in a generation highly skeptical of prophetic insights. We aren't sure what a prophetic voice would sound like; we assume it couldn't be nearly as human sounding as the ones we hear. But our assumptions may be causing us to miss the times of our visitation. God is among us, and we often don't recognize Him. What are we to do? Open ourselves up to the possibilities. Allow the Spirit to speak through His people. And listen as if we may be hearing the very words of God.

Lord, what does a prophetic word sound like? How can I know it's You? Teach me to be discerning without being skeptical, to be open without being gullible, and to listen to anyone through whom You might be speaking. Open my ears to Your voice—whatever it sounds like.

Ask the Lord your God for a sign of confirmation.
ISAIAH 7:11

A situation I had been praying about took a sudden turn for the worse. I was confused and more than a little distressed. Why was God not answering my prayers? Why would He allow this problem to come up? Didn't He care about the situation? I got in my car to drive home, pleading with Him—even arguing with Him—about the injustice of the situation. And when I pulled into the garage and stopped, I looked down at the mileage marker above my odometer—the four-digit counter for tracking trips. It stood at a number that had already been very significant in the situation, a number that had been tied to the victim of the injustice in several ways. God was reminding me that He was still on top of the situation, no matter how it looked.

Many would regard my seeing that number as a coincidence, but in context, it wasn't. The odds of seeing that four-digit number at any given moment were one in ten thousand, and it happened to be at an exact moment when I was distraught and praying about the situation. To a casual observer, it's random. To someone crying out to God, it's His voice.

God is the master of all circumstances, and there are no real coincidences in His Kingdom. Yes, life functions by the laws of physics that God has put in place, but He has a way of timing occurrences to speak through them, especially to those who are carrying on a conversation with Him. When we ask Him for encouragement or confirmation, we are negligent not to receive it when He gives it. And giving it through an outward sign has significant biblical precedents. God doesn't want us to depend on outward signs, but He certainly allows us to receive confirmation through them. He speaks through the events He orchestrates—even the seemingly random ones.

Lord, make me attentive to the signs and symbols around me. Draw my eyes to what I need to see. Let the world around me—and the events You orchestrate—become an integral part of our conversations.

DECEMBER 16

[Jesus said,] "If you remain in me and my words remain in you, you may ask for anything you want, and it will be granted!"
JOHN 15:7

FROM THE HEART OF GOD

"*In Me and My words in you.* You struggle to understand this, but it isn't complicated. I graft My life into yours and yours into Mine; we become one. And I plant My words in you for them to grow up and bear fruit. This is why you are able to relate to Me and pray in complete faith.

"Maybe it will help if you understand what this does *not* mean. When I give you an instruction, I want you to consume it, not weigh it as an option. When I give you a promise, I want you to cling to it regardless of what you see or what anyone else says about it. When I give you encouragement, I expect you not to dismiss it as 'fluff' or underestimate its power but to be nourished by it as life-giving truth. To have My words 'abiding' or 'remaining' in you means not only to nod your head in agreement but to let them shape your identity. I speak My Father's spiritual DNA into your spirit with My voice. On that basis, I give you this promise of answered prayer.

"Hold on to My words. They are more than encouragement, instruction, and promise. They are your life. They shape you. They plant seeds in your heart that will grow up and produce a harvest. They are promises that come true only when you can hold on to them without letting go, even when wind and waves try to shake you off of them. I honor the holy stubbornness of those who have so thoroughly embraced My words that they could not possibly give up on them without abandoning a part of themselves. Don't just hear them. Let them become unquenchably alive within you."

Jesus, I have longed for the fulfillment of this promise; let the condition become my reality, my experience in every area of my life. Let me find my identity—every impulse, every breath, every heartbeat—in Your words. And may the Father answer my prayers as though they come directly from You.

You have tested us, O God; you have purified us like silver.
PSALM 66:10

Psalm 66 is like a sandwich, and the substance between the slices isn't very pleasant. It begins and ends with praise, recounting God's great works in the past and trusting Him for answered prayer in the present. But in the meantime, He has allowed the people to be oppressed and taken captive. In other words, He has given them enormous contradictions to His goodness and His ultimate purpose for them.

Why would God do such a thing? Why would He save us and then allow disaster, promise us good things and then allow evil, promise to answer our prayers and then seem silent? What kind of God is this who puts contradictions right in front of our faces? He is a God who insists that we live by faith and not by sight, that we invest all of our affections and hopes in the unseen world and not the seen. Only when we do that are we ready for the manifestation of what was spoken.

This relational dynamic with God is like an obstacle course. It gives us every reason to question His goodness and faithfulness. But this is by design. Our capacity for faith grows only by stretching, and if God has called us to great things, He stretches our faith a lot. He wants us to believe despite the contradictions, to not be swayed by paradoxes. Those who trust His voice must learn to hear it above all other voices out there. And the only way to do that is to hear the other voices and still choose His.

When we can do that, we begin to hear God more often. He trusts us with His secrets and reveals His plans. He never removes the need for faith—we will always see and hear in part, not in full—but we see and hear more than before. Why? Because He has tested us, and we have passed.

Father, please help me understand Your ways and not mistrust You when circumstances seem to contradict You. You are always working out Your best purposes for me.

DECEMBER 18

The voice of the LORD echoes above the sea. The God of glory thunders. The LORD thunders over the mighty sea. The voice of the LORD is powerful; the voice of the LORD is majestic. . . . In his Temple everyone shouts, "Glory!"
PSALM 29:3-4, 9

The more we grow accustomed to God's voice, the louder it sounds. What used to be a faint whisper—and dare we even follow such a subtle and tenuous word?—is now a lightning bolt in our souls. "The voice of God," said Ignatius of Loyola, "having once penetrated the heart, becomes strong as the tempest and loud as the thunder." Our sensitivities have increased, even though we think we're still as hard of hearing as ever. How could we *not* heed what we're hearing? It's God. We recognize the sound.

We may not recognize His voice infallibly, and we certainly have questions sometimes about whether we're hearing correctly or not. But when we know it's God, we can hardly escape the implications. We simply have to respond or else rebel in disobedience. The more we learn to recognize His words, the less middle ground we find in our relationship with Him. Something in us compels us to align ourselves with His perspective. We sense the connection with His Spirit and cannot ignore it.

Not that we would ignore it anyway. Sometimes He asks hard things of us, but that's much better than not hearing Him at all. Other people may be satisfied with a casual or distant relationship with God, but we asked at the beginning to know Him at all costs. When a heart loves the Lord deeply, it can't be content with long silences or unexplained gaps. We have to pursue Him until His voice resonates within us again. That's what we were designed for. And in His temple—even the temple we have become—we shout, "Glory!"

Lord, it often seems that I've made no progress at all. Yet when I recognize Your whispers within me, they sound more compelling than ever. Echo them loudly and clearly. Let me not escape them. Deep in my spirit, turn up the volume of Your words.

DECEMBER 19

We [run our race] by keeping our eyes on Jesus, the champion who initiates and perfects our faith.
HEBREWS 12:2

At some level, this is the answer to every question in the Christian life: Keep your eyes on Jesus. Need a picture of God's nature? It's Jesus. Need words that come straight from God's mouth? Jesus speaks them. Need your prayers answered? Abide in Jesus, as He promised, and then ask whatever is on your heart. Need to know the lifestyle of someone who does what the Father does, hears what the Father says, and accomplishes miracles in the power of the Spirit? Jesus gives us ample cues about how to stay connected with God and bring the climate of heaven to earth. Whatever growth we desire, whatever promises we've been given, whatever calling and destiny we step into, it's all through our life in Him.

That means we don't have to figure out our priorities every day. Jesus is at the top of the list all the time. If we lose our focus at any given moment, we must do whatever we can to regain it. Somehow, amid all the distractions and responsibilities of life, we're to keep Jesus front and center. When we are fully living "in Him," not just as our God-given position but in our practical awareness, we don't just "get by." We are more alive than we have ever been.

This life in Jesus is our connection with the Father's voice. Cultivating that connection is essential. This comes before all techniques, principles, advice, and anything else we try to figure out. Anyone can hear God if he or she is aware of being deeply connected with Jesus moment by moment. He is in us. We are in Him. And all of life—every aspect of it—is based on that relationship.

Jesus, it's so easy to forget that it's all about You. My life, my desire to follow God, my longing to hear His voice—it's still all about You. As You live Your life within me, my heart softens toward God and my spiritual ears open up. So live fully, deeply, boldly in every inch of my being.

> *The LORD gave the donkey the ability to speak. "What have I done to you that deserves your beating me three times?" it asked Balaam. . . . Then the LORD opened Balaam's eyes, and he saw the angel of the LORD standing in the roadway with a drawn sword in his hand.*
>
> NUMBERS 22:28, 31

Balaam knew that God was not going to let him prophesy a curse against Israel, as the Moabite king had hired him to do, but he went out to Israel anyway. The donkey he rode could see an angel blocking the roadway, so it stopped, only to suffer the wrath of the misguided prophet. Finally, after the donkey had endured several beatings, God opened the animal's mouth. And after a brief and strange conversation between man and beast, God opened Balaam's eyes to see the angel too. God went to extreme measures to get the attention of the stubborn prophet.

Yes, God can speak through anything, even a donkey. It's easy to view this story as a myth or fable, but only when we forget that the infinite God who created the universe can do anything He wants at any time through any means. If He can speak the world into being by the sound of His voice, everything else is simple. A donkey talking for a few seconds? Not a problem. And more than a little humorous.

Never have contempt for the crude messengers in your life. We strain to hear God's voice through a high-profile speaker or a powerful and popular book, but He often tests us to see if we will also hear Him through that awkward misfit in the congregation or a grossly misspelled quote on Facebook. If we tune out the unlikely, we are unlikely to hear Him even in the obvious—as quite a few people in and around Bethlehem and Galilee found out during the time of Christ. The medium isn't the issue; the voice is. Listen *everywhere.*

Lord, there is no such thing as "unlikely" with You. I don't care to be impressed by the medium. I simply need You. Test my hearing however You choose—even if You have to open the mouth of a beast.

Mary responded, "I am the Lord's servant. May everything you have said about me come true." And then the angel left her.
Luke 1:38

This couldn't have been easy news for Mary to hear. Like most girls, she surely had dreams about marriage and family, and they probably didn't include a scandalous pregnancy that would appear immoral to everyone around her. What was she thinking when the angel told her she would conceive God's Son by His Spirit? The honor and privilege could not have escaped her, but neither could the potential shame in the eyes of her family and community. How could she explain a once-in-forever phenomenon and expect people to believe her? Most wouldn't. She would begin her marriage to Joseph with a child on the way. And she wouldn't be publicly vindicated until several decades had passed and it became clear who Jesus was.

Nevertheless, Mary accepted the awesome, traumatic words without complaint. She affirmed them as true. She didn't hesitate at the enormous cost to herself; she simply complied with God's stated will. Being chosen by God usually involves both an immense privilege and a great sacrifice, and many of us focus on the latter rather than the former. But Mary embraced the news that this assignment was given to her because she was highly favored. And this response gives us a glimpse into why she was chosen. She was ready to serve God in whatever instructions He gave.

There is no better illustration of how to listen to God than this. He loves to hear a heart say "yes" before it understands the details, even when He upsets our plans with something bigger and stranger than we can grasp. Mary could not possibly have envisioned all that the rest of her life would entail, but she didn't need to. God favored her with His plan, and her answer demonstrates why. She accepted the impossible simply because it was God's word.

Father, may everything You've said about me and to me, from all eternity past until now, come to pass exactly as You have said. I accept it—even before I know it and understand it.

Daniel had a dream, and visions passed through his mind as he was lying in bed. . . . "I, Daniel, was troubled in spirit, and the visions that passed through my mind disturbed me."
DANIEL 7:1, 15, NIV

The mother sat at her son's bedside. In her mind's eye—that movie screen of the imagination that plays inside our heads—she saw Jesus walk into the hospital room, lay His hands on the child's head, and mouth the words, "Be healed." That had been her prayer, but she hadn't "seen" it until now. Was it just her wishful thinking? Was she forcing her own desires on her imagination? Possibly. But from that day forward, the child began to improve. He was given a good report, his hair began to grow back after the chemo, and he was soon discharged to go home and live a normal life.

Where were Daniel's visions? In his mind. If Daniel lived today, most of us would tell him not to trust what goes through his mind. If God wanted to give him a vision, He would do it openly, not in the context of human thought processes. We know our condition; our thinking gets distorted and we see through lenses colored with all sorts of biases and agendas. "No, Daniel," we might tell him. "You can't trust your imagination."

But you *can* trust your imagination if the Spirit of God is guiding it, and He often does when we yield it to Him. All of our faculties can be distorted and deceptive, but they can also be used by God. In fact, He gave them to us for that purpose. If we ask Him to write on the screen of our imagination, we can expect Him to do so. That's where life's parables play out, where the Spirit draws profound images of redemption and restoration, and where our prayers and dreams are envisioned. God speaks even in our own minds.

Lord, I present my imagination to You for holy purposes. Fill it with pictures of Your purposes. Let me see the calling You have placed before me. Show me what You're doing. And inspire me with my prayers or actions to step into the stories You present to me.

DECEMBER 23

The world would love you as one of its own if you belonged to it, but you are no longer part of the world.

JOHN 15:19

FROM THE HEART OF GOD

"The world does not naturally accept Me. Only by My Spirit can I be welcomed into the world and into your life. Why? Because My ways and the world's ways are at odds with one another. Remember the counterfeit kingdom that wages war against My true Kingdom. This false system is based on independence and pride, not on dependence and worship. All of its ways are strategically calculated to shut Me out. Friendship with the world and its self-sufficient ways is tantamount to hostility toward Me and My life-giving Kingdom.

"This is why you can never expect to reconcile My voice with the other voices around you, especially those voices that reflect the thinking of the world rather than the heart of My Kingdom. There will be tension between what you hear from Me and what you hear elsewhere. Even the wise and godly around you are still emerging from the web of deception in the world, and their counsel may sometimes contradict My voice. Hear them, weigh what they say, but defer always to My voice. When I speak directly to your heart, My words may not fit the understanding or the assumptions of the people you know.

"For this reason, be careful with the pearls of revelation I have given you. Don't share them indiscriminately. When you tell someone what I have told you personally, you may be submitting it to false judgment. Don't keep everything private—you do need counsel—but learn to discern the wisdom of the world. Let your faith be stirred by My voice and not by the opinions of human beings. Be firm against every thought derived from the world's wisdom and submissive to every thought that comes from the wisdom of My Spirit. I will lead you in much higher ways."

Holy Spirit, I need discernment. It's scary how much we are steeped in the wisdom of the world. Help me sort out all the voices I hear. Tune my ears to Your counsel and the counsel of those who know Your voice.

You are blessed because you believed that the Lord would do what he said.
LUKE 1:45

Nearly every Christian affirms a strong belief that God will do what He said He will do—that He will keep His promises, fulfill the blessings described in His Word, and prove Himself faithful and true in our lives. Yet if we're honest, in the back of our minds is a very subtle doubt, an "I hope so" or a "we'll see" that undermines the fullness of our faith. That's okay; God understands. When a man told Jesus he believed while also asking Jesus to help his unbelief (Mark 9:24), Jesus followed through with a miracle. But that isn't ideal. Jesus also gave promises about prayer that were conditioned on not doubting (Matthew 21:21), and marveled at His disciples' unbelief in the midst of storms (Mark 4:40). His desire is for us to believe He will do what He said. And His blessing is often reserved only for those who believe.

That's hard for us to swallow. We don't want God's blessings to depend on the purity of our faith, but some of them are. The size of our faith doesn't seem to be an issue; all we need is faith the size of a mustard seed (Matthew 17:20). But the quality of our faith may certainly have an effect on what we receive from God. Several passages of Scripture urge that our faith should not be mixed with doubt. He saves some of His most precious blessings for those who believe He will give them.

Elizabeth blessed Mary because Mary believed God would do what He said. Many people wouldn't have believed, finding the angel's words too bizarre to be literally true. But Mary accepted them, and Elizabeth expressed a profound biblical principle when she saw her. Just as Abraham was declared righteous because He believed God's impossible words, Mary was declared blessed because she believed Him too. Those who trust God's extraordinary words will find Him extraordinarily faithful.

Lord, I believe. If You said it, it's always true, no matter how strange or unlikely it seems. I accept Your ability to do the impossible, and I gratefully receive the blessing that comes through believing.

Mary kept all these things in her heart and thought about them often.
LUKE 2:19

God was clearly doing a marvelous work in the birth of His Son, and He had chosen to do it through a normal, humble family. Mary could not look to any precedent for understanding these events. She could not find a template for God's new work in Abraham, Moses, Joseph, David, or any prophet in the Scriptures. At this point in history, she could not unfold all the messianic prophecies and see how they applied to her current situation. This work was—and still is—unique to human history.

It's wonderful when God does something in our lives and we are immediately able to relate it to some story or character in His Word. That makes it easier to see how we are fitting in with His overall work and His ways. But when He does something unusual in our lives, we walk through our circumstances with both caution and awe. We ask lots of questions. We wonder how things will turn out. We treasure the possibility that we have been chosen to do something specific for God's purposes.

Mary miraculously conceived and gave birth to God's Son. Shepherds in the nearby fields saw angels and came to visit the new King. What would the life of this child look like? How would Mary and Joseph handle the responsibility of parenting Him? If this life was beginning with such fanfare, what miracles would come in the next few years? Mary kept these things in her heart. She treasured them and pondered them constantly. She held the work and words of God with a sacred wonder. She modeled how we are to respond when the divine agenda intersects our lives in a miraculous way.

Lord, sometimes I'm amazed at what You're doing in my life. I don't take Your words for granted. I won't assume the ordinary in my relationship with You. I choose to walk with wonder in every step You lead me to take.

DECEMBER 26

I long for the Lord more than sentries long for the dawn, yes, more than sentries long for the dawn.
PSALM 130:6

Sometimes we have to encounter God. We just have to. The situation is desperate, the need is overwhelming, the next step is too urgent, yet unclear. We need to feel God's touch, hear the sound of His voice, receive His answer to prayer. The crises of life drive us to Him, pleading for Him to intervene or even to whisper His will. In those moments, our souls long for Him more than sentries who wait for the dawn. Like watchmen on the walls, we scan the horizon for any hint of the rising sun. We wait for the morning. And wait some more.

During those times of waiting and watching, we need to remember one thing: The sun always rises. The sentries on the wall don't wonder whether the darkness will give way to the dawn; they only wonder exactly when. They don't have to fear that perhaps this time the sun won't rise, that maybe they will be stuck in some deep night's perpetual shroud. The dawn will come. It always does. It may seem slow, like the watched pot that seems never to boil or a long-anticipated vacation that seems like it may never arrive. Eventually, the darkness breaks and the light shines. The day of favor comes.

Waiting for God can be a lot like that, and if we're watching the clock, the wait can be awfully frustrating. But He does come. He breaks through like the rising sun, dispelling the darkness of our desperation and bringing warmth to the cold places of our lives. He responds faithfully to whatever prayers we've prayed with persistent faith. He speaks to ears that remain open. Like the watchmen who wait for the morning, we will see the sunrise.

Lord, You have seen my seasons of desperation. You know how I've watched for You more than the sentries long for the dawn. Reward my wait—my persistent, hopeful wait—with the sight tired eyes need to see: You. I look to You as the light that interrupts all the darkness in my life.

DECEMBER 27

No matter how many promises God has made, they are "Yes" in Christ. And so through him the "Amen" is spoken by us to the glory of God.
2 CORINTHIANS 1:20, NIV

If a survey of Christians asked, (1) "Do you have a strong desire to hear God's voice?" and (2) "How much time and effort do you spend listening to Him?" the majority would probably answer "yes" to the first and "not much" to the second. Why? Because if we're really honest with ourselves, we would have to admit that there are certain things we want to hear from God, and we have significant fears that He won't say them. In other words, we want to hear "yes" but suspect we'll hear "no." We listen with negative expectations. And few people want to invest much time and energy in that.

God gives us full permission to listen for His "yes." That doesn't mean He endorses everything we desire or promises to fulfill every whim. But He is kindly predisposed toward us and is far more willing to give than we think He is. We tend to assume "no" as His default answer with an occasional "yes" thrown in, but it's really the other way around. We don't have to listen pessimistically.

God fulfills His promises in and through Jesus, and because of our life in Him, we receive all the answers to those promises by hearing them and adding our own "amen." What could possibly be discouraging about that? As Paul writes in another letter, "Since he did not spare even his own Son but gave him up for us all, won't he also give us everything else?" (Romans 8:32). God has given us no reason to fear His voice. He has already said yes to our biggest questions. The lesser yeses are even easier for Him.

That means we never need to listen pessimistically and can invest our time in hearing Him without fear of wasting it. He rewards those who seek Him with faith and high expectations.

Lord, I will not shy away from Your voice; Your perfect love overcomes all my fear. I run toward Your "yes" with an "amen" in my heart. Fulfill Your promise in me.

The glory of the LORD rises to shine on you. Darkness as black as night covers all the nations of the earth, but the glory of the LORD rises and appears over you. All nations will come to your light; mighty kings will come to see your radiance.

ISAIAH 60:1-3

God speaks to His people about His glorious future for us. He sees the end of our stories and knows how good they are. When we're in the middle of the story, with all its formidable obstacles and grim plot twists—you've probably noticed that all good stories have them, including yours—God encourages us with glimpses of the last page. He wants us to know that everything ends well.

When God gave the future exiles of Jerusalem a glorious picture of their return from captivity, He was also giving us a prophetic picture of His promises to us. We reflect the glory of God, not only one day in heaven, but now, while the world lies in darkness. All nations will come to our light, and mighty kings will see our radiance. How is this possible? God shines on us. He speaks to us. He identifies us as His sons and daughters. As we see Him, listen to Him, draw close to Him, and bathe in His love, His favor on us becomes clear. We take on His nature. We become noticeable.

Reflecting God's glory is a by-product of hearing His voice. When we learn to hear Him well, we no longer blend in with the spiritual landscape. People start coming to us for counsel, listening to our God-given ideas, and recognizing our wisdom, which we happen to know really isn't ours at all. Jesus is the desire of all nations, according to the prophets, though the nations hardly admit their desire goes by that name. Yet when people see God in us, many will be drawn to His light. And we will be able to express His words to them.

Glory? Light? Radiance? These hardly seem to describe me, Lord. Yet if this is Your description of me—now or in the future—I want to grow into it daily. Let me hear—and reflect—Your glory.

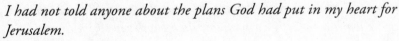

I had not told anyone about the plans God had put in my heart for Jerusalem.
NEHEMIAH 2:12

The woman had been noticing a trend, and her heart was burdened by it. Single parents from an economically challenged neighborhood would drop their children off at church on Sunday mornings and leave. Some in the congregation were offended—"The church isn't a babysitting service," they would say—but she saw it as an opportunity. The kids needed God, and by investing attention in them in Sunday school, the church would also have an avenue into the lives of the parents. This was not an intrusion; it was an open invitation from God.

So the woman told the pastor and asked if the church could expand their Sunday school to meet the specific needs of the children and their families. Wisely, he deferred action back to the one who had the vision for it. "Sure, we can help them. Why don't you develop a plan for it?" At first intimidated, then inspired, she grabbed hold of the vision and ran with it. God had put the burden in her heart for a reason. She was the one He was calling to intervene.

As Nehemiah affirmed before moving to Jerusalem, God puts His purposes into the hearts of His people. He gives a sense of mission and calling to those who can take the lead in meeting the needs around them. We may think our burdens are for others to fulfill, and others may certainly be involved. But our burdens are usually the prompting of the Holy Spirit—not for someone else to do something about the problem, but for us to address it ourselves. Where there's a strong vision to fulfill a Kingdom-oriented purpose, the Spirit has been speaking. And no matter how intimidated we may feel, we're to begin walking in that direction and follow as the Spirit leads.

Holy Spirit, help me sort out the burdens in my heart. Are they all Yours? Which ones should I follow? Lead me to fulfill the purposes You have placed within me. Clarify my vision and secure my steps. Lead me through open doors to accomplish Your Kingdom mission wherever I can.

DECEMBER 30

[Jesus said,] "It is best for you that I go away, because if I don't, the Advocate won't come. If I do go away, then I will send him to you."
JOHN 16:7

FROM THE HEART OF GOD

"Very few of My people believe that it was best for them for Me to go away. Many long for the experience of the disciples who sat around Me listening to My words. It's hard for many to see their relationship with My Spirit as 'better,' because for most, it isn't. They have forgotten how real and tangible that relationship is supposed to be.

"The Father and I are seated in heaven. The Spirit is your essential relationship with God. Yes, I promised I would always be with you, and I am—in the Spirit. He and the Father and I are one, just as you are in Me and I am in you. But as you practically connect with Me, as you pray to the Father, as you listen for My voice, as you read My Word—as you relate to God in every way—remember that, in this age, it is all through the Spirit. Don't neglect Him.

"In a relationship between the humble and the proud, the humble defers to the proud. Remember that God is humble. Refuse to be prideful, or you will rarely experience His presence.

"The Spirit doesn't advertise Himself, so you will have to look for Him. He lives in you, but you won't be aware of that unless you choose to be. He is available to guide you, but only when you ask. He is available to empower you, but only when you depend on Him to do so. He is available to speak to you, but only when you engage in conversation and remember to listen at least as much as you talk. He is, in truth, everything you need Him to be, but in practice only what you allow Him to be in you."

Holy Spirit, make me more aware of You. Help me depend on Your enormous power and emulate Your enormous humility. I submit to Your leadership. I listen in silence as I invite You to speak as freely and loudly as You want to.

DECEMBER 31

Today when you hear his voice, don't harden your hearts.
HEBREWS 3:7-8, 15; 4:7

The people of Israel had hardened their hearts in the wilderness, complaining against God and rebelling against His ways. They had heard His voice, but they didn't believe it or cling to it for long. This hard-heartedness became a theme for prophetic voices and psalmists centuries later, and the writer of Hebrews brings it up again. God's people were once again tempted to reject what He was saying because His ways seemed too difficult. They were contending against the direction God was leading.

This is a lesson for all of God's people throughout all generations. The most important rule—and the one perhaps most neglected—is that those who hear Him must listen with a soft heart. That's always the right response to God. A soft heart will yield to His words without complaint, without resistance, without suspicion, and without demanding to know why He says what He says. A soft heart will say yes to whatever God wants because it trusts His goodness implicitly. A soft heart complies with God—not one day, not tomorrow, but today.

That's always the right time to respond to God, just as surely as a soft heart is always the right response. When He speaks—and as we've seen, He certainly does when we persevere in listening—there is no reason to delay our acceptance of what He has said. He may give us future direction, but He wants present faith—an immediate embrace of His voice. When you hear His voice, do not harden your heart. Soften it and respond to what He says. Today.

Lord, today is always the day to hear. My ears are always open. Every day, I'm listening, hungering for the sound of Your voice and attentive to Your words. My heart is Yours. And my ears are ready for anything You want to say.

SCRIPTURE INDEX

ABOUT THE AUTHOR

CHRIS TIEGREEN is the author of more than forty books, including *The One Year Walk with God Devotional*, *The One Year At His Feet Devotional*, *365 Pocket Devotions*, *90 Days Thru the Bible*, and *Unburdened*. In addition, he has been a collaborative writer on more than a dozen book projects. He has also written hundreds of magazine and newspaper articles, ranging from cultural commentary to inspirational devotionals to features on ministry and international missions.

Chris is a seasoned photojournalist, a student of languages, a dabbler in art, an occasional pianist, a rabid-yet-reasonable college football fan, and a zealous traveler. He especially loves beaches and third-world adventures. In addition to writing and doing photography for periodicals and books, he has been a pastor, a missionary, and a university instructor on global issues. He currently works at Walk Thru the Bible and serves at Daystar Atlanta church. He and his family live in Atlanta. To learn more, visit www.chris-tiegreen.com.